Some of Freud's Views
on Sex and Love

"Whenever we find a sexual aberration in adults—perversion, fetishism, inversion . . . investigation will reveal some experience in the nature of a fixation in childhood."

"The Oedipus-complex is the actual nucleus of neuroses. . . . What remains of the complex in the unconscious represents the disposition to the later development of neuroses in the adult."

"The poets are right who are so fond of portraying people in love without knowing it, or uncertain whether they do love. It would seem that the knowledge received by our consciousness of what is happening to our love-instincts is especially liable to be incomplete, full of gaps, or falsified."

"To ensure a fully normal attitude in love, two currents of feeling have to unite . . . the tender, affectionate feelings and the sensual feelings."

"Whoever is to be really free and happy in love must have overcome his deference for women and come to terms with the idea of incest with mother or sister."

"It is easy to show that the value the mind sets on erotic needs instantly sinks as soon as satisfaction becomes readily obtainable."

"A husband is, so to speak, never anything but a proxy, never the right man; the first claim upon the feeling of love in a woman belongs to someone else, in typical cases to her father; the husband is at best a second. Now whether the husband is rejected depends upon the strength of this fixation."

SEXUALITY
AND THE
PSYCHOLOGY OF LOVE

SIGMUND FREUD

WITH AN INTRODUCTION BY THE EDITOR,
PHILIP RIEFF

A TOUCHSTONE BOOK
Published by Simon & Schuster Inc.

TOUCHSTONE
Rockefeller Center
1230 Avenue of the Americas
New York, NY 10020

First Touchstone Edition 1997

This Touchstone edition is published by arrangement
with Basic Books, Inc.

TOUCHSTONE and colophon are registered
trademarks of Simon & Schuster Inc.

3   5   7   9   10   8   6   4   2

Manufactured in the United States of America

Library of Congress Catolog Card Number: 63-14965

ISBN   0-684-83824-9

CONTENTS

INTRODUCTION

I have collected below, in approximate order of their first appearance, Freud's papers on sexuality. Though he hoped, as the first paper indicates, for some remission in the repressive controls over sexuality in Western culture, Freud was no naïve advocate of the body's pleasures nor a romantic critic of our culture. On the contrary, Freud was on the side of culture against the instincts, and of the "reality principle" against the "pleasure principle." It must be remembered that Freud is writing in the context of cases in which the emotional cost had been excessive and the cultural income too low. Where that uneconomic relation does not exist, Freud's culture criticism is irrelevant.

Again, readers with a prurient interest in literature having to do with sexuality will find nothing satisfying in Freud's writings. He is neither a pansexualist nor an antisexualist. Freud succeeds at once in deflating the sexual fact while championing its freer expression. After the first essay announces the general theme, there follows one of Freud's great polemical essays " 'Civilized' Sexual Morality and Modern Nervousness." Here Freud did assert what is now the popular "frustration" theory of culture and neurosis. But a misunderstanding of the implications of the psychoanalytic connection between culture and neurosis has led many into the game of seeking sensuality without affection. Success at this game is, from the psychoanalytic point of view, more sick than the achievement of affection without sensuality. The normal attitude in love was, Freud believed, a fusion of tenderness with sensuality.

In the paper on "Types of Neurotic Nosogenesis," the "frustration" theory is carried forward decisively, making it the parallel term to repression, and thus the sociological counterpart to the psychodynamics of neurosis. But it must be noted that the later Freud had a much more complicated notion of the genesis of neurosis than appears in these early papers.

Again, in the "Contributions to the Psychology of Love," the great theme is the tension between culture and the natural man. Frigidity in women, impotence in men—these essays carry an exquisite detailed analysis of the many ways in which humans pay what Freud considered too high a price for their civil capacities. An implicit theme throughout is the way in which the psychopathology of love is linked to patterns of parental domination during the early years of childhood.

"The Predisposition to Obsessional Neurosis" is included in this volume of papers on sexuality and the psychology of love as representative of Freud's shorter writing on the phases through which the sexual instinct passes on its uncertain way to genitality. This paper treats the "anal-sadistic" stage (in fact, each stage has a synec-dochical relation to a body zone), indicating various points at which sexual development can get "stuck," or "fixed," to use a word closer to the psychoanalytic vocabulary.

Much of what Freud wrote on homosexuality is scattered through many essays. His general thesis, on the relation between paranoia and homosexuality, is elaborated in "A Case of Paranoia Running Counter to the Psychoanalytic Theory of the Disease." There follows "The Psychogenesis of a Case of Homosexuality in a Woman," which ought to be read with the one mentioned immediately above; I have separated the two only to keep some semblance of chronological order. But it is not really possible to group Freud's papers thematically while respecting the chronology. The themes simply will not behave; they do not stay in one essay or another, but go their own discursive ways. Freud did not write for the convenience of the anthologist, or in the boring and externally ordered academic manner. These two papers contribute some fundamental insights to the analysis of sexuality in women. This case of homosexuality is the first history of a woman Freud wrote after the memorable experience with Dora. The important point to keep in mind in reading this case of homosexuality in a young and beautiful girl is Freud's elaboration of the universal bisexuality of human beings; any simple account of the dynamics of homosexuality is futile and downright wrongheaded. "In all of us," Freud writes, "throughout life, the libido normally oscillates between male and female objects; the bachelor gives up his men friends when he marries, and returns to clublife when married life has lost its savor." In a homosexual, the swing over to an object of his or her own sex contains some special additional factor that must be determined for each case. And yet, there is a principle upon which such inverse swings occur: the inversion is not only the result of rejecting the opposite sex, but also of a correlative overstrong identification with it, as a way out of some forbidden love—as, in this case, the girl's love for her father. But the case is complicated beyond the scope of summary. The excursus on "lying dreams" is particularly brilliant. There is a further discussion of homosexuality in "Some Neurotic Mechanisms in Jealousy, Paranoia, and Homosexuality."

I have intruded "A Child Is Being Beaten" between these two expeditions into the psychology of women mainly because chronological criteria demand it. Moreover, this essay contains some essential comparative material on the erotic development of male and female, with special emphasis on masochism that will further illuminate the general subject of this volume. Here, too, is Freud's finest elaboration of the psychoanalytic "view that the motive forces of repression must not be sexualized." It is infantile sexuality which, held under repression, "acts as the chief motive force in the formation of symptoms." Thus, Freud is saying that until man learns to cope with his own genetic past, he cannot hope to live well in the present. Finally, under such conditions, the archaic will always return, the future parody the past, in cruel repetitions.

"The Infantile Genital Organization of the Libido" is, of course, an amplification of Freud's three essays on the subject of infantile sexuality. The present essay has other internal intellectual connections as well with the materials in this volume, in particular with that of "The Disposition to Obsessional Neurosis," mainly on the problems of pregenital sexual organization.

The next papers—"The Passing of the Oedipus-Complex" and

"Some Psychological Consequences of the Anatomical Distinction between the Sexes"—ought to be read as a pair, containing as they do excellent and brief explanations of comparative sexual development. It is commonly supposed that Freud did not really understand women, thinking them a "mystery." But the essay on "Female Sexuality" indicates a rather profound insight into the mystery. In the final three papers, Freud returns to problems in the psychopathology of love and sexuality. Other major questions, of theoretical import, are introduced, but this is characteristic of Freud as a writer, and I have had to make a decision about the general shape of the volume with the chief contents of the paper as a determining factor.

PHILIP RIEFF
University of Pennsylvania
1962

I

My Views on the Part Played by Sexuality in the Aetiology of the Neuroses[1] (1905)

I am of opinion that the best idea of my theory concerning the aetiological significance of the sexual factor in neurosis is obtained by examining its evolution. For I have no sort of wish to deny that this theory has passed through a process of development and has undergone a transformation during this process. My colleagues could regard this admission as evidence that the doctrine is nothing but the result of continued and constantly extended experience; for anything that arises from speculation may very easily appear once for all complete in form and then remain unalterable.

The theory originally applied merely to the morbid states embraced under the term neurasthenia; among these, I noticed two which occasionally appeared in a pure form and which I have named "neurasthenia proper" and "anxiety-neurosis." It was indeed always a matter of general knowledge that sexual factors may play a part in the causation of these forms of disease, but neither were these factors found to be regularly active nor was there any thought of allotting them a preferential position among other aetiological influences. I was surprised to begin with at the frequency of grave disturbances in the *vita sexualis* of nervous invalids; the more I enquired into such disturbances (bearing in mind that all men conceal the truth in these matters) and the more adept I became at persisting in my interrogations in spite of denials at the

---

[1] First published in Löwenfeld's *Sexualleben und Nervenleiden*, IVte Auflage, 1906. [Translated by J. Bernays.]

beginning, the more regularly did pathogenic factors from sexual life disclose themselves, until there seemed to me little to prevent an assumption of their general occurrence. Nevertheless, it was necessary to be prepared at the outset for a frequent incidence of sexual irregularities such as this, in view of the pressure of present-day social conditions, and one might still be doubtful what degree of deviation from normal sexual functioning was to be regarded as pathogenic. I therefore could attribute less importance to the regular, demonstrable appearance of sexual noxiae than to another observed phenomenon which seemed to me less ambiguous in character. It appeared that each type of ailment, whether neurasthenia or anxiety-neurosis, showed a constant relation to the type of sexual noxia. In typical cases of neurasthenia evidence of masturbation or frequent pollutions would come to light; in anxiety-neurosis, factors such as coitus interruptus and "frustrated excitation" could be shown which appeared to contain one common element, namely, an unsatisfying discharge of the libido aroused. Only after this recognition, which was easily observed and could at will be frequently confirmed, had I the courage to accord a preferential position to sexual influences in the aetiology of the neuroses. In addition, a combination of the aetiologies ascribed to these manifestations was discoverable in the cases of combined neurasthenia and anxiety-neurosis which often occur; and it appeared that such a dualism in the manifestations of neurosis accorded well with the polar character of sexuality, male and female.

At the time that I attributed to sexuality this part in the creation of simple neuroses[2] I still adhered as regards the psychoneuroses (hysteria and obsessions) to a purely psychological doctrine in which sexual factors had no more significance than other sources of emotion. In conjunction with J. Breuer, and based upon observations made by him at least a decade before on an hysterical patient, I had studied, by means of awakening memories in hypnotic states, the mechanism of the origin of hysterical symptoms. We had reached inferences which helped to bridge the gap between

---

[2]See "The Justification for Detaching from Neurasthenia a Particular Syndrome: The Anxiety-Neurosis," *Early Psychoanalytic Writings*, Collier Books edition BS 188V.

Charcot's traumatic hysteria and the common, non-traumatic hysteria.[3] We had arrived at the conception that the symptoms of hysteria were lasting effects of psychic traumas, whose sum of affect had by peculiar circumstances been prevented from being worked off in consciousness and had therefore forced an abnormal outlet into bodily innervation. The terms "strangulated affect," "conversion" and "abreaction" embrace the distinctive points of this conception.

In view of the close relation of the psychoneuroses to the simple neuroses, which can go so far that an unpractised physician often finds it difficult to make a diagnostic distinction, it became inevitable that the knowledge acquired in one field would throw light as well on the other. Moreover, quite apart from such a correlation, closer examination of the psychical mechanism of hysterical symptoms led to the same result. For, as the psychical traumas which were the starting-point of the hysterical symptoms were followed— by means of the cathartic method initiated by Breuer and myself— further and further back into the patient's past, experiences were finally reached which belonged to his infancy and concerned his sexual life; and this was so even where an ordinary emotion, not of a sexual kind, had led to the outbreak of the disease. Without taking into account these sexual traumas of childhood it was impossible to explain the symptoms, comprehend their determination, or prevent their return. After this, the unique significance of sexual experiences in the aetiology of the psychoneuroses seemed incontestably established; and this fact remains to-day one of the cornerstones of the theory.

When this theory is described in the statement that the cause of a life-long hysterical neurosis lies in sexual experiences of infancy, usually common-place in themselves, it may indeed sound strange enough. Yet if allowance is made for the historical development of the theory, if its main content be summarised in the thesis that hysteria is the expression of a peculiar behaviour of the sexual function in the person concerned and that this behaviour is already decisively determined by the first impressive influences and experiences during infancy, we shall indeed be the poorer by a paradox,

---

[3]See *Studien über Hysterie*, 1895.

yet the richer by a motive for directing our attention to these most significant after-effects of infantile impressions which have hitherto been so grossly neglected.

Reserving for a later, more detailed discussion the question whether the aetiology of hysteria and the obsessional neurosis is to be regarded as contained in the sexual experiences of childhood, I will return to the form the theory assumed in some short preliminary papers published in the years 1895 and 1896.[4] By emphasizing the aetiological factors already inferred, it was possible at that time to contrast the common neuroses, which had a current aetiology, with the psychoneuroses, the aetiology of which lay particularly in sexual experiences of the remote past. The doctrine culminated in the sentence: No neurosis is possible with a normal *vita sexualis*.

Although even to-day I do not regard these statements as incorrect, it is surely not surprising that during ten years of constant work towards elucidation of these problems I should have travelled some distance beyond my previous point of view and now believe that further more extensive experience has placed me in a position to correct the incompleteness, the displacements and the misconceptions under which the theory then laboured. It happened by chance that my earlier, not very plentiful material contained a disproportionately large number of cases in whose infantile history seduction by adults or other older children had played the chief part. I overestimated the frequency of these occurrences, which are otherwise quite authentic, and all the more so since I was not at this period able to discriminate between the deceptive memories of hysterics concerning their childhood and the memory-traces of actual happenings. I have since learned to unravel many a phantasy of seduction and found it to be an attempt at defence against the memory of sexual activities practised by the child himself (masturbation of children). This explanation deprived the "traumatic" element in the sexual experiences of childhood of their importance,

---

and there remained a recognition that the form of the infantile sexual activity (whether spontaneous or provoked) determines the direction taken by later sexual life after maturity. This same explanation, by which I was able to correct the most momentous of my early errors, necessitated a change in the conception of the mechanism of hysterical symptoms. These now no longer appeared as direct derivations of repressed memories of sexual experiences in childhood; but, on the contrary, it appeared that between the symptoms and the infantile impressions were interpolated the patient's phantasies (memory-romances), created mostly during the years of adolescence and relating on one side to the infantile memories on which they were founded, and on the other side to the symptoms into which they were directly transformed. Only after the factor of the hysterical phantasies had been introduced did the structure of the neurosis and its relation to the patient's life become perspicuous; at the same time a really surprising analogy came to light between these unconscious phantasies of hysterics and the romances which become conscious as delusions in paranoia.

After this correction, the "infantile sexual traumas" were in a sense supplanted by the "infantilism" of the sexuality in these cases. It was not a far step to a second modification of the original theory. When the frequency of seduction in childhood was no longer assumed, there vanished also the over-emphasis on the "accidental," external influencing of the sexuality to which I had attributed the chief part in the causation of the disease, without, however, denying the existence of constitutional and hereditary elements. In connection with the details of the various sexual experiences of childhood, I had even hoped to solve the problem of the "choice of neurosis," that is, to ascertain what form of psychoneurosis would develop from each type of experience; I believed at that time, though with some reservations, that passivity in such experiences produced a specific predisposition to hysteria, and activity to obsessional neurosis. These views I was later compelled to abandon entirely, although many actual facts seem to suggest that the supposed correlation between passivity and hysteria and activity and the obsessional neurosis should be retained in some form or other. With the decline in importance of the influences experienced accidentally the constitutional and hereditary elements again won the upper hand; with this difference, however, from prevailing opinion, that in my conception the "sexual constitution" took the place of a general neuropathic disposition. In my recently published *Drei Abhandlungen zur Sexualtheorie* (1905) I have attempted to describe the many aspects and varieties of this sexual constitution, as well as the composite nature of the sexual instinct as a whole and its origin from various contributory sources in the organism.

While still maintaining the modifications imposed by the altered conception of the "infantile sexual traumas," the theory now advanced in a direction which had already been indicated in the publications of the years 1894–96. Already at that time, and even before sexuality had been accorded its proper position in the aetiology, I had put it forward as a condition of the pathogenic effectiveness of a given experience that it must seem to the ego intolerable and must evoke an effort towards defence.[5] To this defence I had referred the mental dissociation—or as it was then called, the dissociation of consciousness—of hysteria. If the defence succeeded, then the unbearable experience and its affective consequences were banished from consciousness and from the memory of the ego; but under certain conditions the banished material—now become unconscious—became operative and returned into consciousness by way of the symptoms and the affects attached to them, so that the outbreak of the disease represented a failure of the defence. This conception had the merit of taking into account the interplay of the mental forces, thereby bringing the mental processes of hysteria nearer to the normal, instead of reducing the characteristic of the neurosis to a mysterious disturbance incapable of further analysis.

Investigation into the mental life of normal persons then yielded the unexpected discovery that their infantile history in regard to sexual matters was not necessarily different in essentials from that of the neurotic, and that seduction particularly had played the same part in it; the result was that the accidental influences receded still further into the background in favour of the influence of "repres-

---

[5]See *op. cit.*, "The Defence Neuro-Psychoses."

sion," as I had begun to call what I had formerly termed "defence." The important thing, therefore, was evidently not the sexual stimulation that the person had experienced during childhood; what mattered was, above all, how he had reacted to these experiences, whether he had responded to them with "repression" or not. With regard to spontaneous sexual activity it became evident that in the course of development it was often broken off by an act of repression. Thus the sexually mature neurotic regularly carried within him a fragment of "sexual repression" from his childhood days, which came to expression under the stress imposed upon him by real life. And psychoanalysis of hysterics showed that their illness was the result of a conflict between the libido and the sexual repression, their symptoms being equivalent to compromises in the conflict between these two mental currents.

I could not expound this part of my theory further without a detailed discussion of my views on the subject of repression. It must suffice to bring the reader's notice at this point to my *Drei Abhandlungen zur Sexualtheorie,* in which I have attempted to throw some light, even if only a meagre ray, on the somatic processes in which the essence of sexuality lies. I have there described how the constitutional disposition of the child is by far more variegated than we might have expected, how it deserves to be called "polymorphously perverse" and how what is called the normal sexual function develops from this disposition through certain components of it becoming repressed. The infantile characteristics of sexuality provided a clue which enabled me to establish a simple correlation between health, perversion, and neurosis. It appeared that normality developed as the result of repression of certain component-instincts and components of the infantile disposition, and of a subordination of the remainder under the primacy of the genital zone in the service of the reproductive function; perversions represented disturbances in this process of coalescence caused by an excessive (obsessive, as it were) development of certain of the component-instincts; and neurosis could be traced back to unduly severe repression of libidinal tendencies. Since almost all the perverse impulses comprising the infantile disposition demonstrably constitute the symptom-forming forces of neurosis, though in the latter they are in a state of repression, I was able to designate neurosis as the "negative" of perversion.

I consider it worth emphasis that, in spite of all changes in them, my views concerning the aetiology of the psychoneuroses have never yet caused me to disavow or abandon two points of view: namely, the importance of sexuality and of infantilism. In other respects, constitutional factors have supplanted accidental influences; "sexual repression" has taken the place of the concept of "defence" which was intended purely psychologically. Now if anyone should enquire where he is to look for an incontestable proof of the aetiological importance of sexual factors in the psychoneuroses—since these maladies are observed to ensue after the most commonplace emotional, or even somatic disturbances, and since a specific aetiology in the form of particular infantile experiences is not forthcoming—then I would indicate psychoanalytic investigation of neurotics as the source from which the disputed conviction springs. When this irreplaceable method of investigation is used one learns that the *symptoms represent the patient's sexual activity*, either the whole of it or a part of it, and are rooted in the normal or the perverse component-instincts of sexuality. Not only does a considerable portion of hysterical symptomatology spring directly from the manifestations of sexual excitement; not only does a series of erotogenic zones assume the importance of genital organs in the neurosis by intensification of their infantile qualities; but even the most complicated symptoms reveal themselves as "converted" representations of phantasies which have a sexual situation as their content. Whoever knows how to interpret the language of hysteria can perceive that the neurosis deals only with the patient's repressed sexuality. Only one must conceive of the sexual function in its true range, as circumscribed by the infantile disposition. Wherever a commonplace emotion must be included among the causative factors of the illness, analysis will regularly show that the pathogenic effect has been exercised by the ever-present sexual element in the traumatic occurrence.

This has led us imperceptibly away from the question of the causation of the psychoneuroses to the problem of their nature. On the basis of the knowledge acquired by means of psychoanalysis one can only say that the nature of these maladies lies in disturbances of the sexual processes, of those organic processes which determine the development and form of expression of the sexual craving. One can scarcely avoid, in the last analysis, picturing those processes as chemical, so that we might recognize the so-called actual neuroses as the somatic effects of disturbances in sexual metabolism, and the psychoneuroses as, in addition, the psychical effects of these disturbances. The similarity of the neuroses to the phenomena of intoxication and abstinence following upon certain alkaloids, as well as to Graves' and to Addison's diseases, is readily apparent on the clinical side; and, just as we can no longer describe as "nervous diseases" the two maladies mentioned, so the "actual neuroses" also, despite their name, will probably soon have to be removed from this category.

Thus, whatever has a harmful effect on the processes serving the sexual function belongs to the aetiology of the neuroses. In the first place, accordingly, there are the noxiae affecting the sexual function itself, in so far as they are felt to be harmful by the sexual constitution, which varies with social culture and education. In the next place, there are all the other noxiae and traumas which are capable of injuring the sexual processes secondarily through general injury to the whole organism. It should not, however, be forgotten that the aetiological problem presented by the neuroses is at least as complicated as the causative factors of any other disease. A single pathogenic influence is scarcely ever adequate to cause disease; most often a number of aetiological factors supporting one another are necessary and these are consequently not to be opposed to one another. This is the reason why a condition of neurotic invalidism is not sharply distinguished from that of normal health. The malady results from a summation of causes, and the measure of the aetiological conditions may be filled from various accessory sources. To seek the aetiology of the neuroses exclusively in heredity or in the constitution would be no less one-sided than to attempt to find this aetiology only in the accidental modifications undergone by sexuality during life, although investigations show that the nature of these disorders consists only of a disturbance of the sexual processes within the organism.

II

"Civilized" Sexual Morality and Modern Nervousness[1] (1908)

In his recently published book on sexual ethics, von Ehrenfels dwells on the difference between "natural" and "civilized" (cultural) sexual morality. By "natural" sexual morality he understands that system of control which enables a race to preserve its health and efficiency; by "civilized," that system which when followed spurs man to more intensive and productive cultural activity. According to him this contrast is best elucidated by comparing the innate character of a people with its cultural attainments. While referring to von Ehrenfels' paper[2] for the better appreciation of this significant line of thought, I shall take from it only so much as I need to establish the connection with my own contribution to the subject.

It is natural to suppose that under the domination of a "civilized" morality the health and efficiency in life of the individuals may be impaired, and that ultimately this injury to the individual, caused by the sacrifices imposed upon him, may reach such a pitch that the "civilized" aim and end will itself be indirectly endangered. Indeed, von Ehrenfels points to a series of injurious effects, responsibility for which he attributes to the code of sexual morality at present prevailing in our Western society; and although he fully acknowledges its high value for the furtherance of civilization, he

---

[1] First published in *Sexualprobleme*, new issue of the periodical *Mutterschutz*, Bd. IV., 1908; reprinted in *Sammlung*, Zweite Folge. [Translated by E. B. Herford and E. Colburn Mayne.]

[2] *Sexualethik*, Grenzfragen des Nerven- und Seelenlebens.

10

concludes by judging it to be in need of reform. Characteristic of present-day sexual morality is the extension of the demands made upon women on to the sexual life of the male, and the taboo on all sexual intercourse except in monogamous marriage. Even so, consideration of the natural difference in the sexes necessitates less condemnation of lapses in the male, and so in effect admission of a double code of morality for him. But a society which accepts this double code cannot attain to "love of truth, honesty and humanity" except to a certain narrowly limited degree, and must incline its members to concealment of the truth, to euphemism, to self-deception, and to the deception of others. Civilized sexual morality does worse, indeed, than this, for by glorifying monogamy it cripples virile selection—the sole influence by which an improvement of the race can be attained, for among civilized peoples vital selection is reduced to a minimum by humane and hygienic considerations.[3]

Among the injurious effects attributed to sexual morality the physician misses precisely the one whose significance we are now to consider. I refer to the way in which it promotes modern nervousness, which under our present social conditions is rapidly spreading. Occasionally a nervous patient will himself draw the physician's attention to the part played in the causation of his sufferings by the opposition between his constitution and the demands of civilization, and will remark: "We in our family have all become nervous because we wanted to be something better than what with our origin we were capable of being." The physician is also frequently given matter for thought by observing that neurosis attacks precisely those whose forefathers, after living in simple, healthy, country conditions, offshoots of rude but vigorous stocks, came to the great cities where they were successful and were able in a short space of time to raise their children to a high level of cultural attainment. But, most cogent of all, neurologists themselves have loudly proclaimed the connection between the "increasing nervousness" of the present day and modern civilized

---

[3] [The preceding paragraph is clearly an abstract of v. Ehrenfels' views, and does not necessarily represent Freud's own.]

life. A few extracts from the opinions of eminent observers will show clearly upon what they base this connection.

W. Erb:[4] "The original question may now be summarized thus: Are those causes of nervousness which have been put before you so markedly on the increase under modern conditions of life as to declare those conditions responsible? This question can be answered without hesitation in the affirmative, as a cursory glance at our modern life and its character will show.

"This is already clearly evidenced by an array of general facts: the extraordinary achievements of modern times, the discoveries and inventions in every field, the maintenance of progress in the face of increasing competition, have been gained and can be held only by great mental effort. The demands on the ability of the individual in the struggle for existence have enormously increased, and he can meet them only by putting forth all his mental powers; at the same time the needs of the individual, and the demand for enjoyment, have increased in all circles; unprecedented luxury is displayed by classes hitherto wholly unaccustomed to any such thing; irreligion, discontent, and covetousness are spreading widely through every degree of society. The illimitable expansion of communication brought about by means of the network of telegraphs and telephones encircling the world has completely altered the conditions of business and travel. All is hurry and agitation: night is used for travel, day for business; even "holiday trips" keep the nervous system on the rack; important political, industrial, financial crises carry excitement into far wider circles than formerly; participation in political life has become quite general: political, religious, and social struggles, party-interests, electioneering, endless associations of every kind heat the imagination and force the mind to ever greater effort, encroaching on the hours for recreation, sleep and rest; life in large cities is constantly becoming more elaborate and more restless. The exhausted nerves seek recuperation in increased stimulation, in highly-seasoned pleasures, only thereby to become more exhausted than before; modern literature is concerned predominantly with the most questionable prob-

---

[4]*Über die wachsende Nervosität unserer Zeit*, 1893.

lems, those which stir all the passions—sensuality and the craving for pleasure, contempt of every fundamental ethical principle and every ideal demand; it brings pathological types, together with sexual psychopathic, revolutionary and other problems, before the mind of the reader. Our ears are excited and overstimulated by large doses of insistent and noisy music. The theatres captivate all the senses with their exciting modes of presentation; the creative arts turn also by preference to the repellent, ugly and suggestive, and do not hesitate to set before us in revolting realism the ugliest aspect offered by actuality.

"This merely general picture suffices to show a series of dangers in our modern cultural evolution, the details of which may be filled in by a few strokes!"

Binswanger:[5] "Neurasthenia especially has been described as essentially a modern disorder, and Beard, to whom we are first indebted for a general description of it, believed that he had discovered a new nervous disease which had developed specifically in America. This assumption was of course erroneous; nevertheless the fact that an *American* physician was the first to perceive and maintain—as the fruit of great experience—the particular symptoms of this disorder cannot fail to point to a close connection between them and the modern way of life—the unbridled lust and haste for gold and possessions, those immense advances in technical spheres which have reduced to insignificance all limitations of time and space where communication is concerned."

Von Krafft-Ebing:[6] "The mode of life of innumerable civilized peoples shows at the present time an abundance of anti-hygienic factors which make it easy to understand the deplorable increase of nervousness, for these harmful factors take effect first and foremost on the brain. Changes have taken place in the political and social, and particularly in the mercantile, industrial and agricultural conditions of civilized peoples, in the course of no more than the last decade, which have abruptly transformed professional life, citizenship and property at the direct cost of the nervous system;

---

[5]*Die Pathologie und Therapie der Neurasthenie*, 1896.

[6]*Nervosität und neurasthenische Zustände*, 1895, p. 11.

this is then called upon to meet the increased social and domestic demands by a greater expenditure of energy, unredressed by any satisfactory forms of recuperation.''

Of these and many other similarly-worded opinions I have to observe, not that they are erroneous, but that they show themselves insufficient to explain in detail the manifestations of nervous disturbance, and that they leave out of account the most important aetiological factor. If one passes over the less definite forms of "nervousness" and considers the actual forms of nervous disease, the injurious influence of culture reduces itself in all essentials to the undue suppression of the sexual life in civilized peoples (or classes) as a result of the "civilized" sexual morality which prevails among them.

The proof of this statement I have attempted to establish in a series of technical papers.[7] It cannot be repeated here; still I will at this point put forward the most important arguments arising from my researches.

Close clinical observation empowers us to distinguish two groups of nervous disorder, the true neuroses, and the psychoneuroses. In the former, the disturbances (symptoms), whether bodily or mental, appear to be of a toxic character. The phenomena are essentially the same as those due to excess or deficiency of certain nerve-poisons. These neuroses, usually designated collectively as "neurasthenia," can be induced by certain injurious influences in the sexual life, without any hereditary taint being necessarily present; indeed, the form taken by the disease corresponds with the nature of these noxiae, so that not seldom the clinical picture can be directly employed as a key to the particular sexual aetiology. Any such regular correspondence between the form of nervous disorder present and the other injurious influences of civilization to which the writers quoted above attribute so much is, however, entirely absent. It may, therefore, be maintained that the sexual factor is the essential one in the causation of the true neuroses.

With the psychoneuroses, hereditary influence is more marked,

[7]See *supra*, essay I; also "Sexuality in the Aetiology of the Neuroses," *Early Psychoanalytic Writings*, Collier Books edition BS 188V.

and the causation less transparent. A peculiar method of investigation known as psychoanalysis has, however, enabled us to recognize that the symptoms of these disorders (hysteria, obsessional neurosis, etc.) are psychogenic, and depend upon the operation of unconscious (repressed) ideational complexes. This same method has taught us what these unconscious complexes are, and has shown us that, speaking quite generally, they have a sexual content. They originate in the sexual needs of unsatisfied people, and represent a kind of substitute for gratification of them. So that we must regard all factors which operate injuriously upon the sexual life and suppress its activity or distort its aims as likewise pathological factors in the psychoneuroses.

The value of the theoretical distinction between the toxic and the psychogenic neuroses is, of course, in no way lessened by the fact that disturbances arising in both sources are to be observed in most nervous people.

Anyone who is prepared to look with me for the aetiology of nervousness pre-eminently in influences which cripple the sexual life, will willingly give his attention to some further considerations, to be appended here, which are intended to review the question of increasing nervousness in a broader application.

Our civilization is, generally speaking, founded on the suppression of instincts. Each individual has contributed some renunciation—of his sense of dominating power, of the aggressive and vindictive tendencies of his personality. From these sources the common stock of the material and ideal wealth of civilization has been accumulated. Over and above the struggle for existence, it is chiefly family feeling, with its erotic roots, which has induced the individuals to make this renunciation. This renunciation has been a progressive one in the evolution of civilization; the single steps in it were sanctioned by religion. The modicum of instinctual satisfaction from which each one had abstained was offered to the divinity as a sacrifice; and the communal benefit thus won was declared "holy." The man who in consequence of his unyielding nature cannot comply with the required suppression of his instincts, becomes a criminal, an outlaw, unless his social position or striking abilities enable him to hold his own as a great man, a "hero."

The sexual instinct—or, more correctly, the sexual instincts, since analytic investigation teaches us that the sexual instinct consists of many single component impulses—is probably more strongly developed in man than in most of the higher animals; it is certainly more constant, since it has almost entirely overcome the periodicity belonging to it in animals. It places an extraordinary amount of energy at the disposal of "cultural" activities; and this because of a particularly marked characteristic that it possesses, namely, the ability to displace its aim without materially losing in intensity. This ability to exchange the originally sexual aim for another which is no longer sexual but is psychically related, is called the capacity for sublimation. In contrast with this ability for displacement in which lies its value for civilization, the sexual instinct may also show a particularly obstinate tendency to fixation, which prevents it from being turned to account in this way, and occasionally leads to its degenerating into the so-called abnormalities. The original strength of the sexual instinct probably differs in each individual; certainly the capacity for sublimation is variable. We imagine that the original constitution pre-eminently decides how large a part of the sexual impulse of each individual can be sublimated and made use of. In addition to this, the forces of environment and of intellectual influence on the mental apparatus succeed in disposing of a further portion of it by sublimation. To extend this process of displacement illimitably is, however, certainly no more possible than with the transmutation of heat into mechanical power in the case of machines. A certain degree of direct sexual satisfaction appears to be absolutely necessary for by far the greater number of natures, and frustration of this variable individual need is avenged by manifestations which, on account of their injurious effect on functional activity and of their subjectively painful character, we must regard as illness.

Further aspects are opened up when we take into consideration the fact that the sexual instinct in man does not originally serve the purposes of procreation, but has as its aim the gain of particular kinds of pleasure.[8] It manifests itself thus in infancy, when it

---

[8] Cf. my *Drei Abhandlungen zur Sexualtheorie*.

attains its aim of pleasurable gratification not only in connection with the genitalia, but also in other parts of the body (erotogenic zones), and hence is in a position to disregard any other than these easily accessible objects. We call this stage that of auto-erotism, and assign to the child's training the task of circumscribing it, because its protracted continuance would render the sexual instinct later uncontrollable and unserviceable. In its development the sexual instinct passes on from auto-erotism to object-love and from the autonomy of the erotogenic zones to the subordination of these under the primacy of the genitals, which come into the service of procreation. During this development a part of the self-obtained sexual excitation is checked, as being useless for the reproductive functions, and in favourable cases is diverted to sublimation. The energies available for "cultural" development are thus in great part won through suppression of the so-called perverse elements of sexual excitation.

It would be possible to distinguish three stages in cultural development corresponding with this development in the sexual instinct: first, the stage in which the sexual impulse may be freely exercised in regard to aims which do not lead to procreation; a second stage, in which the whole of the sexual impulse is suppressed except that portion which subserves procreation; and a third stage, in which only *legitimate* procreation is allowed as a sexual aim. This third stage represents our current "civilized" sexual morality.

If we regard the second of these stages as our standard, we must acknowledge that a number of people, on account of their constitution, are not equal to its demands. With whole classes of individuals, the development of the sexual impulse referred to above, from auto-erotism to object-love, with its aim of union of the genitalia, has not been correctly and sufficiently completed. As a result of this disturbance of development there arise two kinds of harmful deviation from normal or "civilized" sexuality; and these are related to one another almost as positive to negative. They are, first (disregarding altogether those persons with an over-powerful and uncontrollable sexual instinct in general), the different varieties of perverts, in whom an infantile fixation on a preliminary sexual aim has impeded the establishing of the primacy of the reproductive function; secondly, the homosexuals or inverts, in whom, in a way not yet quite understood, the sexual aim has been deflected from the opposite sex. If the injurious results of these two forms of disturbance in development are less than might have been expected, this can be directly ascribed to the complicated co-ordination within the sexual instinct, which makes it possible for the sexual life to express itself finally in some form or other, even if one or more components of the instinct have been excluded from development. The constitution of those suffering from inversion—the homosexuals—is indeed often distinguished by the sexual impulse lending itself to "cultural" sublimation in a special degree.

Stronger developments of the perversions and of homosexuality, especially if exclusive, do indeed make those who harbour them socially unadaptable and unhappy, so that even the cultural demands of the second stage must be recognized as a source of suffering for a certain proportion of human beings. The fate of those persons who differ constitutionally in this way from their fellows depends on whether they are endowed with comparatively stronger or weaker sexual impulses in an absolute sense. In the latter case, that of an impulse which is on the whole weaker, perverts succeed in completely suppressing those tendencies which bring them in conflict with the moral demands of their level of civilization. But this, from the ideal point of view, remains also their only achievement, because for this repression of their sexual instinct they make use of all those energies which otherwise they would employ in cultural activity. They are at once inwardly stunted, and outwardly crippled. What we shall presently say about the state of abstinence (of men and women) demanded by the third state of culture applies to these also.

Where the sexual instinct is very strong but yet perverted, there are two possible outcomes. In the first, which it is not necessary to consider further, the afflicted person remains perverted, and has to bear the consequences of his deviation from the prevailing level of culture. The second way is much more interesting. Here, under the pressure of education and social demands, a suppression of the perverse impulse is indeed attained, but it is of such a kind as not to be a true one, and can be better described as a miscarriage of suppression. The inhibited sexual impulses are not expressed as such—and to that extent the inhibition is successful—but they are expressed in other ways which are quite as injurious to the person concerned, and make him quite as useless to society as satisfaction of these suppressed impulses in their original form would have done; and in this lies the failure of the process, which in the long run far outweighs the success of the suppression. The substitute-manifestations which thus present themselves in consequence of suppression of the impulses constitute what we describe as neurosis, in particular the psychoneuroses. Neurotics are that class of people, naturally rebellious, with whom the pressure of cultural demands succeeds only in an apparent suppression of their instincts, one which becomes ever less and less effective. Consequently their co-operation in civilized life is maintained only by means of a great expenditure of energy, combined with inner impoverishment, and at times it has to be suspended altogether during periods of illness. I have, however, described the neuroses as the "negative" of the perversions, because in the neuroses the perverse tendencies come to expression from the unconscious part of the mind, after the repression, and because they contain the same tendencies in a state of repression that manifest perverts exhibit.

Experience teaches that for most people there is a limit beyond which their constitution cannot comply with the demands of civilization. All who wish to reach a higher standard than their constitution will allow, fall victims to neurosis. It would have been better for them if they could have remained less "perfect." The realization that perversion and neurosis stand to one another as positive and negative is often unambiguously confirmed by observations made on members of the same family. Quite often in one family the brother will be sexually perverted, while the sister, who as a woman is endowed with a weaker sexual instinct, becomes a neurotic—one whose symptoms, however, express the same tendencies as the perversion of the brother who has a more active sexual impulse. Accordingly in many families the men are healthy, but from the social point of view undesirably immoral: while the women are high-principled and over-refined, but highly neurotic.

It is one of the obvious injustices of social life that the standard of culture should demand the same behaviour in sexual life from everyone—a course of conduct which, thanks to his nature, one person can attain without effort, whereas it imposes on another the severest mental sacrifices; though, indeed, the injustice is ordinarily nullified by disregard of the commands of morality.

These considerations have been confined so far to what applies to the second stage of cultural development, postulated as interdicting every "perverse" sexual activity, so-called, but allowing the free practice of "normal" sexual intercourse. We have found that even when the line between sexual freedom and restriction is drawn at this point, a number of persons have to be ruled out as perverse, while others who endeavour not to be perverse, and yet constitutionally should be so, are forced into neurosis. It is now easy to predict the result which will ensue if sexual freedom is still further circumscribed, and the standard demanded by civilization is raised to the level of the third stage, which taboos every sexual activity other than that in legitimate matrimony. Under these conditions the number of strong natures who openly rebel will be immensely increased: and likewise the number of weaker natures who take refuge in neurosis owing to their conflict between the double pressure from the influences of civilization and from their own rebellious constitutions.

We propose to answer three questions which now arise:

1. What is the task that is laid upon the individual as a result of the demands of the third cultural stage?

2. Whether the legitimate sexual satisfaction allowed may be said to offer reasonable compensation for the abstention in other directions?

3. In what relation the possible injurious effects of this abstention stand to the benefit accruing to culture?

The answer to the first question touches a problem which has often been discussed and cannot here be treated exhaustively, i.e., that of sexual abstinence. The third stage of our civilization demands from both sexes abstinence until marriage, and lifelong abstinence for all who do not enter into legal matrimony. The position sanctioned by every authority, that sexual abstinence is not harmful and not difficult to maintain, has also obtained a good deal of support from physicians. It may be said that the task of mastering such a mighty impulse as the sexual instinct is one which may well absorb all the energies of a human being. Mastery through sublimation, diverting the sexual energy away from its sexual goal to higher cultural aims, succeeds with a minority, and with them only intermittently; while the period of passionate youth is precisely that in which it is most difficult to achieve. Of the others, most become neurotic or otherwise come to grief. Experience shows that the majority of those who compose our society are constitutionally unfit for the task of abstinence. Those who would have fallen ill even under moderate sexual restrictions succumb to illness all the earlier and more severely under the demands of our present civilized sexual morality; for we know no better security against the menace to normal sexual life caused by defective predisposition and disturbances in development than sexual satisfaction itself. The greater the disposition to neurosis, the less can abstinence be tolerated. For in proportion as the component-impulses have been excluded from development (as described above) they become precisely thereby less controllable. But even those who would have retained their health while complying with the demands of the second stage of civilization will in many cases succumb to neurosis in the third stage; for the psychical value of sexual satisfaction increases under privation. The frustrated libido is now put in the position of spying out one or other of the weaker spots which are seldom wanting in the structure of the sexual life, so that it may break through at that point as a neurotic substitute-gratification in the form of a morbid symptom. Anyone who understands how to penetrate to the factors conditioning nervous illness will soon be convinced that its increase in our society originates in the greater stringency of sexual restraint.

We thus come closer to the question whether sexual intercourse in legitimate marriage can offer full compensation for the restraint before marriage. The abundance of the material supporting a reply in the negative is so overwhelming that we are obliged to make only the briefest summary of it. We must above all keep in mind that our civilized sexual morality also restricts sexual intercourse even in marriage itself, for it compels the married couple to be satisfied, as a rule, with a very small number of acts leading to conception. As a consequence of this, satisfying sexual intercourse occurs in marriage only over a period of a few years, allowing also, of course, for intervals of abstention on hygienic grounds required by the woman's state of health. After these three, four or five years, marriage ceases to furnish the satisfaction of the sexual needs that it promised, since all the contraceptives available hitherto impair sexual enjoyment, disturb the finer susceptibles of both partners, or even act as a direct cause of illness. Anxiety for the consequences of sexual intercourse first dissipates the physical tenderness of the married couple for each other, and usually, as a more remote result, also the mental affection between them which was destined to succeed the originally tempestuous passion. Under the spiritual disappointment and physical deprivation which thus become the fate of most marriages, both partners find themselves reduced again to their pre-conjugal condition, but poorer by the loss of an illusion, and are once more driven back to their determination to restrain and "side-track" their sexual instinct. We will not inquire how far a man in mature years succeeds in this task; experience seems to show that he very frequently makes use of that amount of freedom which is allowed him even by the strictest sexual code, though but reluctantly and furtively. The "double" code of morality conceded to the male in our society is the plainest possible admission that society itself does not believe in the possibility of adherence to those precepts which it has enjoined on its members. But experience also shows that women, as the true guardians of the sexual interests of the race, are endowed with the power of sublimation only in a limited degree; as a substitute for the sexual object the suckling child may suffice, but not the growing child, and under the disappointments of matrimony women succumb to severe, lifelong neurosis affecting the whole course of their lives. Marriage under the present cultural standard has long ceased to be a panacea for the nervous sufferings of women; even if we physicians in such cases still advise matrimony, we are nevertheless aware that a girl must be very healthy to "stand" marriage, and we earnestly counsel our male inquirers not to marry a girl who has been neurotic. Marital unfaithfulness would, on the other hand, be a much more probable cure for the neurosis resulting from marriage; the more strictly a wife has been brought up, the more earnestly she has submitted to the demands of civilization, the more does she fear this way of escape, and in conflict between her desires and her sense of duty she again will seek refuge in a neurosis. Nothing protects her virtue so securely as illness. The conjugal state, which is held out to the youthful among civilized people as a refuge for the sexual instinct, thus proves inadequate even to the demands of the later period which it covers; beyond all question, it fails to compensate for the earlier abstention.

To our third question, even he who admits the injurious results thus attributable to civilized sexual morality may reply that the cultural gain derived from the sexual restraint so generally practised probably more than balances these evils, which after all, in their more striking manifestations, affect only a minority. I own myself unable to balance gain and loss precisely: nevertheless I could advance a good many considerations as regards the loss. Returning to the theme of abstinence, already touched on, I must insist that yet other injurious effects besides the neuroses result therefrom, and that the neuroses themselves are not usually appraised at their full significance.

The retardation of sexual development and sexual activity at which our education and culture aim is certainly not injurious to begin with; it is seen to be a necessity, when one reflects at what a late age young people of the educated classes attain independence and begin to earn a living. Incidentally, one is reminded here of the intimate relations existing between all our civilized institutions, and of the difficulty of altering any part of them irrespective of the whole. But the benefit, for a young man, of abstinence continued much beyond his twentieth year, cannot any longer be taken for granted; it may lead to other injuries even when it does not lead to neurosis. It is indeed said that the struggle with such powerful instincts and the consequent strengthening of all ethical and aesthetic tendencies "steels" the character; and this, for some specially constituted natures, is true. The view may also be accepted that the differentiation of individual character, now so much in evidence, only becomes possible with sexual restraint. But in the great majority of cases the fight against sexuality absorbs the available energy of the character, and this at the very time when the young man is in need of all his powers to gain his share of worldly goods and his position in the community. The relation between possible sublimation and indispensable sexual activity naturally varies very much in different persons, and indeed with the various kinds of occupation. An abstinent artist is scarcely conceivable: an abstinent young intellectual is by no means a rarity. The young intellectual can by abstinence enhance his powers of concentration, whereas the production of the artist is probably powerfully stimulated by his sexual experience. On the whole I have not gained the impression that sexual abstinence helps to shape energetic, self-reliant men of action, nor original thinkers, bold pioneers and reformers; for more often it produces "good" weaklings who later become lost in the crowd that tends to follow painfully the initiative of strong characters.

In the results produced by efforts towards abstinence the stubbornness and insubordination characteristic of the sexual instinct also come to expression. Civilized education attempts, in a sense, only a temporary suppression of it up to the period of matrimony, intending then to give it free rein in order to make use of it. Extreme measures, however, are more successful in effecting repression of the instinct than are moderate ones; but then suppression very often goes too far, with the unwished-for result that when the sexual instinct is set free it shows itself permanently impaired. For this reason complete abstinence during youth is often not the best preparation for marriage in a young man. Women dimly recognize this, and among their suitors prefer those who have already proved themselves men with other women. The injurious results which the strict demand for abstinence before marriage produces are quite particularly apparent where women are concerned. Clearly, education does not look lightly on the task of suppressing the sensuality of the girl until marriage, for it employs the most drastic measures. It not only forbids sexual intercourse and sets a high premium upon the preservation of sexual chastity, but it also protects the developing young woman from temptation by keeping her in ignorance of all the facts concerning the part she is ordained to play, and tolerates in her no love-impulse which cannot lead to marriage. The result is that when the girl is suddenly allowed by parental authority to fall in love, she cannot accomplish this mental operation and enters the state of marriage uncertain of her own feelings. As a result, the artificial retardation in the development of the love-function provides nothing but disappointments for the husband, who has treasured up all his desires for her. Psychically she is still attached to her parents, whose authority has brought about the suppression of the sexual feeling; and physically she shows herself frigid, which prevents her husband finding any great enjoyment in relations with her. I do not know whether the anaesthetic type of woman is also found outside the range of civilized education, but I consider it probable. In any case this type is directly cultivated by education, and these women who conceive without pleasure show later little willingness to endure frequent childbirths, accompanied as they are by pain: so that the training that precedes marriage directly frustrates the very aim of marriage. When later the retarded development of the wife becomes rectified, and during the climax of her womanly life the full power to love awakens in her, her relation to her husband has been long undermined. As a reward for her previous submission, there remains for her only the choice between unappeased desire, infidelity, or neurosis.

The behaviour of a human being in sexual matters is often a prototype for the whole of his other modes of reaction to life. A man who has shown determination in possessing himself of his love-object has our confidence in his success in regard to other aims as well. On the other hand, a man who abstains, for whatever reasons, from satisfying his strong sexual instinct, will also assume a conciliatory and resigned attitude in other paths of life, rather than a powerfully active one. A particular application of the general statement that the course of the sexual life is typical for the way in which other functions are exercised is easily demonstrable in the entire female sex. Their training excludes them from occupying themselves intellectually with sexual problems, in regard to which naturally they have the greatest thirst for knowledge, and terrifies them with the pronouncement that such curiosity is unwomanly and a sign of immoral tendencies. And thus they are thoroughly intimidated from all mental effort, and knowledge in general is depreciated in their eyes. The prohibition of thought extends beyond the sexual sphere, partly through unavoidable associations, partly automatically, acting precisely in the same way as the prohibition of religious speculation among men, and the taboo of any thought out of harmony with loyalty in faithful subjects. I do not support Moebius in the view he has put forward, which has met with so much opposition, that the biological contrast between intellectual work and sexual activity explains the "physiological mental weakness" of women. On the contrary, I think that the undoubted fact of the intellectual inferiority of so many women can be traced to that inhibition of thought necessitated by sexual suppression.

In considering the question of abstinence, far too little distinction is made between two forms of it, namely, abstention from any kind of sexual activity at all, and abstention from heterosexual intercourse. Many who are proud of maintaining abstinence successfully have only been able to achieve it with the help of masturbation and other similar means of satisfaction, which are connected with the auto-erotic sexual activities of early childhood. But this very connection makes these substitutive measures of sexual satisfaction by no means harmless; they predispose to the numerous forms of neurosis and psychosis, which are conditional on a regression of the sexual life to its infantile form. Nor does masturbation at all correspond to the ideal demands of civilized sexual morality, and it therefore drives young people into the same conflicts with the ideals of education which they design to escape by abstinence. Further, the character is undermined in more ways than one by this indulgence; first, because it shows the way to attain important aims in an otiose manner, instead of by energetic effort, in line with the view that the attitude to sex is the prototype of the attitude to life; and secondly, because in the phantasies accompanying this gratification the sexual object is exalted to a degree which is seldom to be reproduced in reality. A witty writer, K. Kraus in the

Vienna *Fackel*, has, as it were, expressed this truth paradoxically in the cynical saying: "Coitus is merely an unsatisfactory substitute for onanism!"

The severe standard demanded by civilization and the arduous task of abstinence have combined to make avoidance of the genital union of the sexes the main point of abstinence, whilst favouring other forms of sexual activity—two results which may be said to betoken obedience by halves. The so-called perverse forms of intercourse between the sexes, in which other parts of the body assume the rôle of the genitalia, have undoubtedly become of greater social significance since normal intercourse has been so remorselessly tabooed in the name of morality—and also on grounds of hygiene because of the possibility of infection. These activities, however, cannot be regarded as so harmless as irregularities of a similar kind interwoven with a normal love-intercourse: ethically they are reprehensible, for they degrade the love-relationship of two human beings from being a serious matter to an otiose diversion, attended neither by risk nor by spiritual participation. The spread of the homosexual means of gratification must be regarded as a further consequence of the difficulties placed in the way of normal sexual life; and in addition to those who are constitutionally homosexual, or who become so in childhood, must be reckoned the great number of those in whom, by reason of the check on the main stream of the libido, the lateral channel of homosexuality is forced open in maturer life.

All these unavoidable and unintended consequences of the insistence upon abstinence unite in one general result: they strike at the roots of the condition of preparation for marriage, which according to the intentions of civilized sexual morality should after all be the sole heir of all sexual tendencies. All those men whose libido, as the result of masturbatory or perverse sexual practices, has become habituated to situations and conditions of satisfaction other than the normal develop in marriage a diminished potency. And all those women who could preserve their virginity only by similar means show themselves anaesthetic to normal intercourse in marriage. A marriage begun with impaired capacity to love on both sides succumbs to the process of dissolution even more quickly than otherwise. As a result of the diminished potency of the man, the woman will not be satisfied and will remain anaesthetic, whereas a powerful sexual experience might have been the means of overcoming the disposition to frigidity that results from her education. The prevention of conception is also more difficult to such a couple than to a healthy pair, because the weakened potency of the man tolerates the use of contraceptives badly. In such perplexity, sexual intercourse comes to be regarded as the source of all difficulties and is soon abandoned, and with it the fundamental condition of married life.

I call upon all who have studied these matters to aver that I am not exaggerating, but am describing conditions glaringly evident to any observant eye. The uninitiated can hardly believe how rarely normal potency is to be found in the men, and how often frigidity in the women, among those married couples living under the sway of our civilized sexual morality; what a degree of renunciation, often for both partners, is associated with marriage, and of how little the marriage comes to consist, instead of bringing the happiness that was so ardently desired. I have already shown that neurosis is the most obvious way of escape from these conditions. I would, however, further point out how such a marriage will increasingly affect the only child—or the limited number of children—which spring from it. On appearance it looks as if we then had an inherited condition to deal with, but closer inspection shows the effect of powerful infantile impressions. As a mother, the neurotic woman who is unsatisfied by her husband is over-tender and over-anxious in regard to the child, to whom she transfers her need for love, thus awakening in it sexual precocity. The bad relations between the parents then stimulate the emotional life of the child, and cause it to experience intensities of love, hate and jealousy while yet in its infancy. The strict training which tolerates no sort of expression of this precocious sexual state lends support to the forces of suppression, and the conflict at this age contains all the elements needed to cause lifelong neurosis.

I return now to my earlier assertion that, in appraising the neuroses, their full significance is seldom reckoned with. I do not mean by this the insufficient appreciation of these states exhibited in the frivolous dismissal of them on the part of relatives, or in the magniloquent assurances on the part of physicians that a few weeks of cold-water cure or a few months of rest and convalescence will cure the condition—these are merely the opinions of ignorant physicians and laymen, and mostly nothing but forms of speech designed to afford the sufferer a short-lived consolation. Rather, it is established that a chronic neurosis, even if it does not completely paralyse existence, represents for the person concerned a heavy handicap in life, much the same as tuberculosis or a cardiac affection. We might in a measure compound with this if neurotic illness merely excluded from communal activity a number of individuals in any case infirm, and permitted the remainder to take their share at the cost of merely subjective disabilities; but I would rather draw attention to the point of view that the neuroses, as far as they extend and in whomever they occur, always succeed in frustrating the social purpose, and thereby actually do the work of the socially inimical mental forces which have been suppressed. So that in paying for compliance with its own exorbitant prescriptions by increased neurosis, society cannot claim an advantage purchased by sacrifice—cannot indeed claim any advantage whatever. Let us examine, for example, the frequent case of a woman who does not love her husband, because, owing to the conditions of the consummation of her marriage and the experience of her married life, she has no cause to love him; but who ardently wishes to do so, because this alone corresponds to the ideal of marriage in which she has been brought up. She will then suppress in herself all impulses which seek to bring her true feelings to expression and contradict her ideal endeavours, and will take particular pains to play the part of a loving, tender and obedient wife. The result of this self-suppression will be a neurotic illness, and this neurosis will in a short time have taken revenge upon the unloved husband and have caused him precisely as much dissatisfaction and trouble as would have arisen merely from an acknowledgement of the true state of affairs. This example is literally typical of what neurosis can do. A similar miscarriage of compensation can be observed after suppression of other socially inimical impulses not directly sexual. A man, for example, who has become excessively "kind-hearted'' as the result of powerful suppression of a constitutional tendency to harshness and cruelty, often loses by so doing so much energy that he does not achieve the full measure of his compensatory impulses, and on the whole does rather less good than he would have done without suppression.

Let us add that together with the restrictions on sexual activity in any nation there always goes an increase of anxiety concerning life and of fear of death, which interfere with each individual's capacity for enjoyment, and do away with his willingness to incur risk of death in whatever cause—showing itself in a diminished inclination to beget offspring, thus excluding any people or group of such a type from participation in the future. We may thus well raise the question whether our "civilized" sexual morality is worth the sacrifice which it imposes upon us, the more so if we are still so insufficiently purged of hedonism as to include a certain degree of individual happiness among the aims of our cultural development. It is certainly not the physician's business to come forward with proposals for reform, but it seemed to me that, by pointing out what significance the injurious results of our sexual morality, enumerated by von Ehrenfels, have in connection with the increase in modern nervousness, I could supplement the account he gives of them, and could thus support the urgency of such reform.

III

Types of Neurotic Nosogenesis[1] (1912)

In the ensuing remarks, which are based on impressions obtained empirically, it is proposed to describe those changes of conditions which operate to bring about the onset of neurotic illness in a person predisposed to it. We are concerned, that is, with the exciting cause of illness; scarcely at all with the form of it. The following view is distinguishable from other formulations concerning the exciting causes of illness in that it connects the changes to be described entirely with the libido of the person concerned. Psychoanalysis has shown us that the course taken by the libido is decisive for nervous health or ill-health. The concept of predisposition needs no discussion in this connection; for psychoanalytic research has made it possible for us to trace back the predisposition to neurosis to its source in the developmental history of the libido, and to reveal the factors operative in this predisposition as inborn varieties of the sexual constitution and the effects of external experiences in early childhood.

(*a*) The most immediate, most easily discerned, and most comprehensible exciting cause of the onset of neurotic illness lies in that external factor which may generally be described as *frustration*. The person was healthy as long as his erotic need was satisfied by an actual object in the outer world; he becomes neurotic as soon as he is deprived of this object and no substitute is forthcoming. Happiness here coincides with health, unhappiness with neurosis. By providing a substitute for the lost source of gratification, fate can effect a cure more easily than the physician.

---

[1] First published in *Zentralblatt*, Bd. II., 1912; reprinted in *Sammlung*, Dritte Folge. [Translated by E. Colburn Mayne.]

31

For this type, which may be said to include the majority of mankind, the possibility of an outbreak of illness begins only with abstinence—which may give us some indication of the significance for the causation of neuroses of cultural restrictions in facilities for satisfaction. Frustration operates pathogenically in that it dams up the libido, and thus puts to the test both the person's power of tolerating the increase of mental tension, and his manner of taking steps to release himself from it. There are only two possible methods of retaining health in a continuous state of actual frustration of satisfaction: first, that of transposing the mental tension into active energy which remains directed towards the outer world and finally wrests from that world an actual satisfaction for the libido; and secondly, that of renouncing the libidinal satisfaction, sublimating the stored-up libido and making use of it to ends which are no longer erotic and thus elude the frustration. Both possibilities can be realized in the destinies of mankind, which shows that unhappiness does not necessarily coincide with neurosis, and frustration is not alone decisive for the health or ill-health of the person concerned. The effect of frustration lies principally in its bringing into action dispositional factors which have hitherto remained inoperative.

When these are present in sufficient strength there arises the danger of the libido becoming *introverted*.[2] It turns away from reality, which on account of the unrelenting frustration experienced has lost all its value for the person concerned, and takes refuge in the life of phantasy where it creates new wish-formations and re-animates the vestiges of earlier, forgotten ones. In consequence of the intimate connection between phantasy-activity and the infantile, repressed, and now unconscious material existing in every individual, and thanks to that attribute of the life of phantasy which exempts it from the "testing of reality,"[3] the libido may now begin to flow backward, may seek out infantile paths in the course of its regression, and may strive after corresponding aims. When

---

[2] A term introduced by C. G. Jung.

[3] Cf. Freud, "Formulations Regarding the Two Principles in Mental Functioning" *General Psychological Theory*, Collier Books edition AS 582V.

such strivings, which are incompatible with the person's state of mind in real life, have become sufficiently intensified, there must ensue a conflict between them and the other part of the personality which has remained in relation with reality. This conflict issues in symptom-formations and ends in manifest illness. That the whole process originates in the actual frustration may be clearly perceived from the circumstance that the symptoms by means of which the sphere of reality is regained represent substitutive gratifications.

(*b*) The second type of occasion for the outbreak of illness is by no means so obvious as the first, and could not indeed be discerned before the searching analytic studies stimulated by the complex-theory of the Zürich School.[4] In these cases the person falls ill not as a result of some alteration in the outer world which has replaced gratification by frustration, but as a result of an inner effort to seize a gratification which reality offers to him. He falls ill of the attempt to adapt himself to reality and to fulfil the *requisitions of reality*, for in doing so he is confronted with insurmountable inward obstacles.

It will be convenient to set these two types of falling ill in sharp antithesis to one another—sharper, indeed, than observation for the most part warrants. In the first type an alteration in the external world is prominent; in the second, the accent falls upon an internal change. In the first type, the person falls ill from an event; in the second, from a developmental process. In the first case the task is one of renouncing a gratification, and the person falls ill because of his lack of resistance; in the second case the task is that of exchanging one kind of gratification for another, and the person is wrecked by his rigidity. In the second case the conflict between the endeavour to keep as he is and the other endeavour to alter himself in accordance with new aims and new demands in reality already exists in him; in the first case, the conflict does not begin until the dammed-up libido has chosen other and incompatible possibilities of gratification. The part played by the conflict and the previous fixation of the libido is in the second type incomparably more striking than in the first, for in the first it may well be

---

[4] Cf. Jung. *Die Bedeutung des Vaters für das Schicksal des Einzelnen*, 1909.

that undesirable fixations of this kind only re-establish themselves in consequence of the external frustration.

The young man who has hitherto gratified his libido by phantasies issuing in masturbation and now desires to exchange this state of affairs, so closely related to auto-erotism, for actual object-choice; the girl who has given all her affection to her father or brother and now would fain exchange the hitherto unconscious incestuous libido-wishes for the conscious wish towards the man who is wooing her; the wife who would be glad to abandon her polygamous inclinations and phantasies of prostitution so as to be a faithful companion to her husband and a blameless mother to her child—all these fall ill in consequence of most laudable endeavours if the earlier fixations of their libido are powerful enough to oppose themselves to the displacement; for this again the factors of predisposition, constitutional basis and infantile experiences prove to be of decisive significance. They all, as it were, undergo the fate of the little tree in Grimm's fairy-tale which wanted to have different foliage. From the hygienic standpoint, which is certainly not the only one to be considered, one could but desire for them that they might have remained to the end as undeveloped, as inferior, and as good-for-nothing as they were before they fell ill. The change for which such patients strive, but which they achieve only imperfectly or not at all, is regularly equivalent to a step forward for them in real life. It is otherwise if we reckon by ethical standards; we as often see people fall ill when they divest themselves of an ideal as when they strive to attain it.

Despite the very evident distinctions between the two types of falling ill here described, they have essential points in common, and it is not hard to find a formula which will apply to both. Falling ill of a deprivation (frustration) likewise comes under the head of incapacity for adaptation to reality, only that the incapacity is confined to occasions when reality denies gratification to the libido. Falling ill under the conditions belonging to the second type points merely to a necessary peculiarity in the frustration. What is denied is not every form of gratification in reality, but merely just the one which the person declares to be the one and only form for him; further, the frustration does not derive directly from the outer world but primarily from certain trends within the ego. Yet the factor of frustration remains common to both, and the most significant one for both. As a result of the conflict which forthwith ensues in the second type, both kinds of gratification, the customary as well as the desired, become equally inhibited; damming-up of the libido and its attendant results follow as they did in the first case. The mental processes involved in the course of symptom-formation are in the second type more easily discoverable than in the first, since the pathogenic fixations of the libido had not first to be re-established but had been potentially active during the healthy period. A certain degree of introversion of the libido was mostly already existent; some degree of the regression to the infantile is spared because the development had never traversed its entire course.

(c) The next type seems an exaggeration of the second type, that of succumbing before the requisitions of reality; I shall describe it as outbreak of illness through *inhibition of development*. There would be no theoretical reason for distinguishing this from the rest, but there is a practical need to do so; since here we have to deal with those persons who fall ill as soon as they pass beyond the irresponsible age of childhood, and thus never attain a phase of health—that of unrestricted capacity in general for production and enjoyment. The essential part played by the dispositional processes is in these cases quite apparent. The libido has never forsaken its infantile fixations; the demands of reality do not suddenly confront an individuality which is wholly or partially matured, but arise out of the bare fact of its having grown older, and are of course continually changing with the age of the person concerned. The conflict is subordinate in importance to the incapacity; but if we take into account the other results of our researches, we must postulate a striving to overcome the infantile fixations, for otherwise the outcome of the process would never be neurosis but only stationary infantilism.

(d) Just as the third type shows us the dispositional condition in an almost isolated form, so the now following fourth one directs our attention to another factor, the operation of which has to be reckoned with in all cases, and for that very reason might easily be overlooked in a theoretical discussion. That is to say, we see people fall ill who have hitherto been healthy, to whom no new experience has presented itself, whose relation to the outer world has undergone no change, so that their falling ill makes an inevitable impression of spontaneity. Closer scrutiny of such cases shows us, nevertheless, that a change *has* taken place in them which we cannot but regard as highly significant in the causation of the illness. As a result of reaching a certain period of life, and in accordance with regular biological processes, the *quantity* of libido in their mental economy has increased to an extent which by itself suffices to upset the balance of health and establish the conditions for neurosis. As is well known, such rather sudden intensifications in libido are regularly connected with puberty and the menopause, with the reaching of a certain age in women; in many people they may in addition manifest themselves in periodicities as yet unrecognized. The damming-up of the libido is here the primary factor; it becomes pathogenic as a result of the *relative* frustration coming from the outer world, which would have afforded sufficient gratification to a lesser need in the libido. The dissatisfied and dammed-up libido may now open up the path to regression and excite the same conflicts as those found in cases of absolute external frustration. This warns us never to leave the quantitative factor out of consideration when we are dealing with the outbreak of illness. All the other factors—frustration, fixation, inhibition in development—remain inoperative as long as they do not involve a certain amount of libido and produce a definite degree of damming-up. We cannot, it is true, measure the amount of libido essential to produce pathological effects; we can only postulate it after the effects of the illness have evinced themselves. In only one direction can we define it more closely; we may assume that it is not a question of an absolute quantity, but of the relation of this effective amount of libido to that quantity of libido which the particular ego in question can control, that is, can hold in suspension, sublimate, or make direct use of. Therefore a relative increase in the quantity of libido may have the same effects as one that is absolute. An enfeeblement of the ego through organic illness or an unusual demand upon its energy will be capable of producing neuroses which would otherwise have remained latent in spite of all dispositional tendencies.

The significance which we must attribute to the quantity of libido in the causation of illness is in satisfactory accord with two axioms of the new theory of neurosis which have emerged from psychoanalysis: first, with the axiom that the neuroses have their source in a conflict between the ego and the libido; secondly, with the view that no qualitative distinction exists between the conditions of health and those of neurosis, but rather that the healthy have to contend with the same difficulties in controlling the libido—only they succeed better in doing so.

There still remain a few words to be said about the relation of these "types" to clinical experience. When I review the number of patients with whose analysis I am at this moment occupied, I must admit that none of them represents any of the four types in its pure form. Instead, I find in each an element of frustration operating along with a certain degree of incapacity for adaptation to reality; the standpoint of inhibition in development, which of course coincides with a tenacity of fixations, is to be reckoned with in all of them; and the significance of the quantity of libido we can never, as was set forth above, afford to overlook. Indeed, it is my experience that in several of these patients the illness has been manifested in accesses, between which there were intervals of health, and that every one of these accesses was to be traced to a different type of exciting cause. The formulation of these four types has therefore no great theoretical value: they are merely different paths by which a definite pathogenic constellation in the mental economy may be achieved—I refer to a damming-up of the libido which the ego is not able to master with the means at its disposal without some damage. The situation itself, however, becomes pathogenic only as a result of a quantitative factor; it is in no way a novelty in the mental economy, nor is it created by the advent of a so-called "cause of illness."

A certain practical importance may readily be granted to these types of falling ill. Indeed, in individual cases they may be observed in a pure form: we should not have been made aware of the third and fourth types if they did not comprise the sole exciting causes of onset in some persons. The first type reveals to us the extraordinarily powerful influence of the outer world; the second that, no less significant, of the peculiarities of the individual who opposes himself to that influence. Pathology could never master the problem of the outbreak of illness in the neurotic so long as it was occupied merely with deciding whether these affections were of an endogenous or an exogenous nature. To all the experience which points to the significance of abstinence (in the broadest sense) as an exciting cause, pathology then necessarily objected that other persons suffered a similar fate without falling ill. But if it elected to lay emphasis upon individual peculiarities as essential in sickness or health, it was obliged to bow to the objection that persons with such peculiarities could permanently retain their health provided only that they could preserve their peculiarity. Psychoanalysis warns us to abandon the unfruitful antithesis of external and internal factors, of fate and constitution, and has taught us regularly to discover the cause of an outbreak of neurosis in a definite mental situation, which can be brought into being in different ways.

IV

Contributions to the Psychology
of Love

1. A Special Type of Object Choice Made by Men[1] (1910)

Hitherto we have left it to poets and imaginative writers to depict
for us the "conditions of love" under which men and women make
their choice of an object, and the way in which they reconcile the
demands expressed in their phantasy with the exigencies of real
life. Writers indeed have certain qualities which fit them for such
a task; more especially, a sensitiveness of perception in regard to
the hidden feelings of others, and the courage to give voice to
their own unconscious minds. But from the point of view of
knowledge one circumstance lessens the value of what they tell
us. Writers are bound to certain conditions; they have to evoke
intellectual and aesthetic pleasure as well as certain effects on the
emotions. For this reason they cannot reproduce reality unchanged;
they have to isolate portions of it, detach them from their connection with disturbing elements, fill up gaps and soften the whole.
This is the privilege of what is called "poetic licence." They can
display no great interest, moreover, in the origin and growth of
those conditions of mind which they portray in being. It is inevitable, therefore, that science should lay hands on the stuff which
poets have fashioned so as to give pleasure to mankind for thou-
sands of years, although its touch must be clumsier and the result
in pleasure less. These considerations may serve to vindicate our

---

[1]First published in *Jahrbuch*, Bd. II., 1910; reprinted in *Sammlung*, Vierte Folge.
[Translated by Joan Riviere.]

handling of the loves of men and women as well as other things in a strictly scientific way. For science betokens the most complete renunciation of the pleasure-principle of which our minds are capable.

During psychoanalytic treatment one has plenty of opportunity for collecting impressions about the erotic life of neurotics, and when this happens one also recalls having noticed or heard of similar behaviour on the part of ordinary healthy persons or even in people of exceptional qualities. When by a lucky chance any such impressions are multiplied in the material that comes under observation, distinct types clearly emerge. I shall first describe one type of this kind relating to a choice of object effected by men, because it is characterized by a series of "conditions of love" the juxtaposition of which is unintelligible or indeed disconcerting, and because it admits of a simple psychoanalytic explanation.

1. The first of these conditions of love must be described as quite specific; wherever one discovers it one may look out for the presence of the other features belonging to the type. It may be termed the "need for an injured third party"; its effect is that the person in question never chooses as an object of love a woman who is unattached, that is, a girl or an independent woman, but only one in regard to whom another man has some right of possession, whether as husband, betrothed, or near friend. In some cases this condition is so peremptory that a given woman can be ignored or even treated with contempt so long as she belongs to no other man, but instantly becomes the object of feelings of love as soon as she comes into a relationship of the kind described with another man.

2. The second condition is perhaps a less constant one, but it is no less remarkable. The type I am speaking of is only built up by the two conditions in combination; the first condition seems also to occur very frequently by itself. The second condition is thus constituted: a virtuous and reputable woman never possesses the charm required to exalt her to an object of love; this attraction is exercised only by one who is more or less sexually discredited, whose fidelity and loyalty admit of some doubt. This last element may vary within the limits of a significant series, from the faint

breath of scandal attaching to a married woman who is not averse to flirtation up to the openly polygamous way of life of a prostitute, or of a *grande amoureuse*—but the man who belongs to the type in question will never dispense with something of the kind. By a rough characterization this condition could be called that of "love for a harlot."

While the first condition provides an opportunity for gratification of the feelings of enmity against the man from whom the loved woman is wrested, the second, that of the woman's infidelity, is connected with feelings of jealousy, which seem to be a necessity to lovers of this type. Not until they have some occasion for jealousy does their passion reach its height and the woman acquire her full value to them, and they never fail to seize upon some incident by which this intensity of feeling may thus be called out. Strange to say, it is not the lawful possessor of the loved one against whom this jealousy is directed, but new acquaintances or strangers in regard to whom she may be brought under suspicion. In pronounced cases the lover shows no desire to possess her for himself alone and seems altogether contented with the triangular situation. One of my patients, who had suffered torments from his lady's escapades, had no objection to her marrying, doing all he could to bring it about; and after, throughout several years, he never showed a trace of jealousy against the husband. Another typical case had, it is true, in his first love-affair been very jealous of the husband and had insisted on the lady ceasing marital relations; but in his numerous later relationships he behaved like the others and no longer regarded the lawful husband as any disturbance.

So much for the conditions required in the loved object; the following points relate to the lover's behaviour towards the object of his choice.

3. In normal love between the sexes the value of the woman is measured according to her sexual integrity and sinks with any approach to the character of a "light woman." It seems to be a striking departure from the normal, therefore, that men of this type should set the *highest value* upon women of this character as their love-objects. Their love-relationships with such women absorb the

whole of their mental energy, to the exclusion of all other interests; such women are "the only ones it is possible to love" and the ideal of the lover's own fidelity is invariably set up again, however often it may be shattered in reality. A high degree of compulsion, which indeed in some measure characterizes every case of passionate love, is clearly discernible in these features of the love-relationships described. But the sincerity and intensity of the attachment in these cases is no indication that any one such relationship makes up the whole erotic life of the person concerned or happens only once in it. On the contrary, passionate attachments of this kind are repeated many times over with all the same peculiarities—each an exact replica of the others—in the lives of those belonging to this type; indeed, in consequence of external conditions, such as changes of residence and environment, the loved objects may be so often replaced by others that it comes in the end to a long chain of such experiences being formed.

4. The trait in this type of lover that is most astonishing to the observer is the desire they express to "rescue" the beloved. The man is convinced that the loved woman has need of him, that without him she would lose all hold on respectability and rapidly sink to a deplorable level. He saves her from this fate, therefore, by not letting her go. The impulse to rescue the woman is occasionally justified by her untrustworthy temperament sexually and by the danger to her social position; it is no less plainly marked, however, where any such real occasion for it is absent. One of the men belonging to the type, who knew how to win his ladies by the subtlety of his methods of seduction and his skill in argument, spent endless pains during the course of each of these love-relationships in composing tracts to induce the loved one to keep in the path of "virtue."

When we review the various features of the picture presented here—the condition that the woman should belong to another man, her "light" nature, the high value set on this last, the thirst for jealousy, the fidelity which is in spite of all compatible with the long chain of repetitions, and the longing to "save"—any hope of tracing them all back to a single source will seem very remote. And yet penetrating psychoanalytic study of the lives of those concerned yields this quite easily. The choice of an object comply-ing with these peculiar conditions and this strange way of loving her have the same source as the normal attitude in love; they are derived from a fixation of the infantile feelings of tenderness for the mother and represent one of the forms in which this fixation expresses itself. In the normal attitude there remain only a few traces unmistakably betraying the maternal prototype behind the chosen object, for instance, the preference young men show for mature women; the detachment of the libido from the mother is accomplished comparatively swiftly. In our type, on the contrary, the libido has dwelt so long in its attachment to the mother, even after puberty, that the maternal characteristics remain stamped on the love-objects chosen later—so long that they all become easily recognizable mother-surrogates. The comparison with the way in which the skull of a new-born child is shaped comes irresistibly to one's mind; after a protracted labour it always bears the form of a cast of the maternal pelvis.

It is now obligatory on us to show some probable grounds for the statement that the characteristic features of this type, both as to conditions of love and behaviour in love, actually derive from the group of feelings relating to the mother. This is most easily accomplished in reference to the first condition, that the woman should belong to another man, the "need for an injured third party." One sees at once that the fact of the mother belonging to the father would come to be an inseparable part of the mother's nature to the child growing up in the family circle, also that the "injured third party" is none other than the father himself. The feature of overestimation by which the loved one becomes the unique, the irreplaceable one, fits just as readily into the infantile set of ideas, for no one possesses more than one mother, and the relation to her rests on an experience which is assured beyond all doubt and can never be repeated again.

If the love-objects chosen by our type are above everything mother-surrogates, then the formation of a long series of them, which seems so directly to contradict the condition of fidelity to the woman, becomes comprehensible as well. We learn through other examples which psychoanalysis has brought to light that the pressing desire in the unconscious for some irreplaceable thing often resolves itself into an endless series in actuality—endless for the very reason that the satisfaction longed for is in spite of all never found in any surrogate. The insatiable questioning which children are given to at a certain age is explicable in this way—they have one single question to ask, the words of which they cannot bring their lips to form; and in the same way, too, the garrulity of many neurotically crippled persons may be explained—what makes them talk is the burden of a secret pressing for disclosure, which in spite of all temptation they never reveal.

The second condition of love, that of the "loose" character of the object chosen, seems on the other hand to stand in sharp opposition to a derivation from the mother-complex. The grown man's conscious mind likes to regard the mother as a personification of impeccable moral purity, and few suggestions from without are so insulting, or from within so painful, as those which cast doubt on the mother's character in this respect. This very relation, however, of sharpest possible contrast between the "mother" and the "harlot" would prompt us to study the developmental history of the two complexes and unconscious relation between them, since we long ago discovered that a thing which in consciousness makes its appearance as two contraries is often in the unconscious a united whole. Investigation then leads us back to the period in the boy's life at which he first obtained more or less detailed knowledge of the sexual relations between adults, somewhere in the years before puberty. The secret of sexual life is revealed to him then in coarse language, undisguisedly derogatory and hostile in intent, and the effect is to destroy the authority of adults, which is irreconcilable with these revelations about their sexual activities. The greatest impression on the child who is being initiated is made by the relation the information bears to his own parents, which is often instantly repudiated in some such words as these: "It may be true that your father and mother and other people do such things, but it is quite impossible that mine do."

Along with this piece of "sexual enlightenment" there seldom fails to go, as a corollary, a further one about the existence of certain women who practise sexual intercourse as a means of livelihood and are universally despised in consequence. To the boy himself this contempt is necessarily quite foreign; as soon as he realizes that he too can be initiated by these unfortunates into that sexual life which he has hitherto regarded as the exclusive prerogative of "grown-ups," his feeling for them is only a mixture of longing and shuddering. Then, when he cannot any longer maintain the doubt that claims exception for his own parents from the ugly sexual behaviour of the rest of the world, he says to himself with cynical logic that the difference between his mother and a whore is after all not so very great, since at bottom they both do the same thing. What he has been told has in fact revived the memory-traces of his early infantile impressions and desires, and thus re-activated certain feelings in his mind. In the light of this new knowledge he begins to desire the mother herself and to hate the father anew for standing in his way; he comes, as we say, under the sway of the Oedipus complex. He does not forget that the mother has given the privilege of sexual intercourse with her to the father instead of to him, and he regards it as an act of infidelity on her part. If these feelings do not rapidly pass, there is only one way in which they can find an outlet—the way of phantasies, in which the mother is represented in sexual situations of the most manifold kind, and in which also the accompanying excitement leads particularly readily to culmination in an onanistic act. In consequence of the constant simultaneous pressure of the two currents of feeling, desire for the mother and revenge against the father, phantasies of the mother's infidelity are by far the most favoured; the lover with whom the mother commits the act of unfaithfulness almost invariably bears the features of the boy himself, or, to be more correct, of the idealized image he forms of himself as brought to equality with his father by growing to manhood. What I have elsewhere[2] described as the "family-romance" comprises the manifold elaborations of this work of phantasy, which is interwoven with various egoistic interests active at this period of life. Now, however, that we have had a glimpse into this phase of mental development we can no longer regard it as

---

[2] In Otto Rank's *Der Mythus von der Geburt des Helden*, p. 64.

contradictory or extraordinary that the condition of a "loose" character in the woman should derive directly from the mother-complex. The type of erotic life in men which we are considering bears the marks of this historical development, and is easily to be understood as a fixation on the phantasies formed by the boy during puberty which have after all found their way to realization later in life. There is no difficulty in assuming that the ardent masturbation practised in the years of puberty contributed to the fixation of these phantasies.

The impulse to "rescue" the beloved appears to stand merely in a loose and superficial relation, founded entirely on conscious grounds, to these phantasies that have gained control of the love-experiences of real life. Her propensity to fickleness and infidelity brings the loved woman into dangerous situations, so it is natural that the lover should do all he can to protect her by watching over her virtue and opposing her evil ways. Study of the screen-memories, phantasies and nocturnal dreams of men and women shows, however, that an exceptionally felicitous "rationalization" of an unconscious motive is present here, comparable to a very successful secondary elaboration of a dream. The idea of "rescue" actually has a significance and history of its own and is an independent derivative of the mother-complex, or, more correctly, of the parental complex. When a child hears that he owes his life to his parents, that his mother gave him life, the feelings of tenderness in him mingle with the longing to be big and independent himself, so that he forms the wish to repay the parents for this gift and requite it by one of a like value. It is as though the boy said in his defiance: "I want nothing from father; I shall repay him all I have cost him." He then weaves a phantasy of saving his father's life on some dangerous occasion by which he becomes quits with him, and this phantasy is commonly enough displaced on to the Emperor, the King, or any other great man, after which it can enter consciousness and is even made use of by poets. So far as it applies to the father, the attitude of defiance in the "saving" phantasy far out-weighs the tender feeling in it, the latter being usually directed towards the mother. The mother gave the child his life and it is not easy to replace this unique gift with anything of equal value. By a slight change of meaning, which is easily effected in the unconscious—comparable to the way in which shades of meaning merge into one another in conscious conceptions—rescuing the mother acquires the significance of giving her a child or making one for her—one like himself, of course. The departure from the original meaning of the idea of "saving life" is not too great, the change in sense is no arbitrary one. The mother gave him his own life and he gives her back another life, that of a child as like himself as possible. The son shows his gratitude by wishing to have a son by his mother that shall be like himself; in the rescue phantasy, that is, he identifies himself completely with the father. All the instincts, the loving, the grateful, the sensual, the defiant, the self-assertive and independent—all are gratified in the wish to be *the father of himself*. Even the element of danger is not lost in the change of meaning; the experience of birth itself is the danger from which he was saved by the mother's efforts. Birth is in fact the first of all dangers to life, as well as the prototype of all the later ones we fear; and this experience has probably left its mark behind it on that expression of emotion which we call anxiety. Thus it was that Macduff of the Scottish legend, who was not born of his mother but "ripp'd from her womb," knew no fear.

The ancient dream-interpreter Artemidorus was undoubtedly right in his opinion that dreams have different meanings according to the person of the dreamer. Under the laws governing the expression of unconscious thoughts, the meaning of "saving life" can vary according to whether the phantasy is framed by a man or a woman. It can mean either: making a child, bringing it to life (in a man); or giving birth to a child (in a woman).

These various significations of "saving" in dreams and phantasies are especially clearly recognizable when they occur in some connection with water. When in a dream a man rescues a woman from the water, it means that he makes her a mother, which in view of the considerations discussed above means that he makes her his own mother. When a woman rescues someone else (a child) out of the water, she represents herself as the mother who bore him, like Pharaoh's daughter in the Moses legend.[3]

---

[3] Rank, *loc. cit.*

The phantasy of rescuing the father will also occasionally have a tender meaning. It then expresses the wish to have the father for a son, that is, to have a son like the father. On account of all these connections between the idea of "saving" and the parental complex, the desire to rescue the loved woman forms an essential feature of the type under discussion.

I do not consider it necessary to advance any justification for my method of working out my observations; here, as also in the matter of anal erotism, the aim of it is first of all to single out extreme types in sharp outline. In both these fields there is a far greater number of persons in whom only one or two of the typical features, and even these but indistinctly traced, are recognizable; it is evident, therefore, that it will not be possible to appreciate them correctly until the whole range of ideas to which these elements belong has been explored.

2. The Most Prevalent Form of Degradation in Erotic Life[1] (1912)

I

If a practising psychoanalyst asks himself what disorder he is most often called upon to remedy, he is obliged to reply—apart from anxiety in all its many forms—psychical impotence. This strange disorder affects men of a strongly libidinous nature, and is manifested by a refusal on the part of the sexual organs to execute the sexual act, although both before and after the attempt they can show themselves intact and competent to do so, and although a strong mental inclination to carry out the act is present. The man gets his first inkling in the direction of understanding his condition by discovering that he fails in this way only with certain women, whereas it never happens with others. He knows then that the inhibition of his masculine potency is due to some quality in the

---

[1]First published in *Jahrbuch*, Bd. IV., 1912; reprinted in *Sammlung*, Vierte Folge. [Translated by Joan Riviere.]

sexual object, and sometimes he describes having had a sensation of holding back, of having perceived some check within him which interfered successfully with his conscious intention. What this inner opposition is, however, he cannot guess, or what quality in the sexual object makes it active. If the failure has been repeated several times he probably concludes, by the familiar erroneous line of argument, that a recollection of the first occasion acted as a disturbance by causing anxiety and brought about the subsequent failures; the first occasion itself he refers to some ''accidental'' occurrence.

Psychoanalytic studies of psychical impotence have already been carried out and published by various writers.[2] Every analyst can, from his own experience, confirm the explanations adduced in them. The disorder is in fact due to the inhibiting influence of certain complexes in the mind that are withdrawn from the knowledge of the person in question. As the most universal feature of this pathogenic material an incestuous fixation on mother and sister which has not been surmounted stands out. In addition to this, the influence of accidental impressions of a painful kind connected with infantile sexuality comes into consideration, together with those factors which in general reduce the amount of libido available for the female sexual object.[3]

When cases of severe psychical impotence are subjected to exhaustive study by means of psychoanalysis, the following psychosexual processes are found to be operative. Here again—as very probably in all neurotic disorders—the root of the trouble lies in an arrest occurring during the course of development of the libido to that ultimate form which may be called normal. To ensure a fully normal attitude in love, two currents of feeling have to unite—we may describe them as the tender, affectionate feelings and the sensual feelings—and this confluence of the two currents has in these cases not been achieved.

---

[2]M. Steiner, *Die funktionelle Impotenz des Mannes und ihre Behandlung*; W. Stekel, in *Nervöse Angstzustände und ihre Behandlung*; Ferenczi, ''Analytic Interpretation and Treatment of Psychosexual Impotence.''

[3]W. Stekel, *loc. cit.* p. 191 *et seq.*

Of these two currents affection is the older. It springs from the very earliest years of childhood, and was formed on the foundation provided by the interests of the self-preservative instinct; it is directed towards the members of the family and those who have care of the child. From the very beginning elements from the sexual instincts are taken up into it—component-parts of the erotic interest—which are more or less clearly visible in childhood and are invariably discovered in the neurotic by psychoanalysis in later years. This tender feeling represents the earliest childish choice of object. From this we see that the sexual instincts find their first *objects* along the paths laid down by the ego-instincts and in accordance with the value set by the latter on their objects, in just the same way that the first sexual *satisfactions* are experienced, *i.e.* in connection with the bodily functions necessary for self-preservation. The "affection" shown to the child by its parents and attendants which seldom fails to betray its erotic character ("a child is an erotic plaything") does a great deal to increase the erotic contributions to the cathexes that are put forth by the ego-instincts in the child, and to raise them to a level which is bound to leave its mark on future development, especially when certain other circumstances leading to the same result are present.

These fixations of the child's feelings of affection are maintained through childhood, continually absorbing erotic elements, which are thus deflected from their sexual aims. Then, when the age of puberty is reached, there supervenes upon this state of things a powerful current of "sensual" feeling the aims of which can no longer be disguised. It never fails, apparently, to pursue the earlier paths and to invest the objects of the primary infantile choice with currents of libido that are now far stronger. But in relation to these objects it is confronted by the obstacle of the incest-barrier that has in the meanwhile been erected; consequently it seeks as soon as possible to pass on from these objects unsuited for real satisfaction to others in the world outside, with whom a real sexual life may be carried on. These new objects are still chosen after the pattern (imago) of the infantile ones; in time, however, they attract to themselves the tender feeling that had been anchored to those others. A man shall leave father and mother—according to the Biblical precept—and cleave to his wife;

then are tenderness and sensuality united. The greatest intensity of sensual passion will bring with it the highest mental estimation of the object (the normal overestimation of the sexual object characteristic of men).

Two factors will determine whether this advance in the development of the libido is accomplished successfully or otherwise. First, there is the degree of frustration in reality which is opposed to the new object-choice and reduces its value for the person concerned. For there is no sense in entering upon a choice of object if one is not to be allowed to choose at all or has no prospect of being able to choose one fit for the part. The second factor is the degree of attraction that may be exercised by the infantile objects which should be relinquished, and this is proportionate to the erotic cathexis already attaching to them in childhood. If these two factors are sufficiently powerful, the general mechanism leading to the formation of neurosis will come into operation. The libido turns away from reality, and is absorbed into the creation of phantasy (introversion), strengthens the images of the first sexual objects, and becomes fixated to them. The incest-barrier, however, necessarily has the effect that the libido attaching to these objects should remain in the unconscious. The sensual current of feeling is now attached to unconscious ideas of objects, and discharge of it in onanistic acts contributes to a strengthening of this fixation. It constitutes no change in this state of affairs if the step forward to extraneous objects which miscarried in reality is now made in phantasy, if in the phantasied situations leading up to onanistic gratification the extraneous objects are but replacements of the original ones. The phantasies become capable of entering consciousness by this replacement, but in the direction of applying the libido externally in the real world no advance has been made.

In this way it may happen that the whole current of sensual feeling in a young man may remain attached in the unconscious to incestuous objects, or, to put it in another way, may be fixated to incestuous phantasies. The result of this is then total impotence, which is perhaps even reinforced by an actual weakening, developing concurrently, of the organs destined to execute the sexual act.

Less severe conditions will suffice to bring about what is usually called psychical impotence. It is not necessary that the whole amount of sensual feeling should be fated to conceal itself behind the tender feelings; it may remain sufficiently strong and unchecked to secure some outlet for itself in reality. The sexual activity of such people shows unmistakable signs, however, that it has not behind it the whole mental energy belonging to the instinct. It is capricious, easily upset, often clumsily carried out, and not very pleasurable. Above all, however, it avoids all association with feelings of tenderness. A restriction has thus been laid upon the object-choice. The sensual feeling that has remained active seeks only objects evoking no reminder of the incestuous persons forbidden to it; the impression made by someone who seems deserving of high estimation leads, not to a sensual excitation, but to feelings of tenderness which remain erotically ineffectual. The erotic life of such people remains dissociated, divided between two channels, the same two that are personified in art as heavenly and earthly (or animal) love. Where such men love they have no desire and where they desire they cannot love. In order to keep their sensuality out of contact with the objects they love, they seek out objects whom they need not love; and, in accordance with the laws of the "sensitivity of complexes" and the "return of the repressed," the strange refusal implied in psychical impotence is made whenever the objects selected in order to avoid incest possess some trait, often quite inconspicuous, reminiscent of the objects that must be avoided.

The principal means of protection used by men against this complaint consists in *lowering* the sexual object in their own estimation, while reserving for the incestuous object and for those who represent it the overestimation normally felt for the sexual object. As soon as the sexual object fulfils the condition of being degraded, sensual feeling can have free play, considerable sexual capacity and a high degree of pleasure can be developed. Another factor also contributes to this result. There is usually little refinement in the ways of obtaining erotic pleasure habitual to people in whom the tender and the sensual currents of feeling are not properly merged; they have remained addicted to perverse sexual aims which they feel it a considerable deprivation not to gratify, yet to such men this seems possible only with a sexual object who in their estimate is degraded and worth little.

The motives behind the phantasies mentioned in the preceding paper,[4] by which boys degrade the mother to the level of a prostitute, now become intelligible. They represent efforts to bridge the gulf between the two currents of erotic feeling, at least in phantasy: by degrading her, to win the mother as an object for sensual desires.

II

So far we have pursued our inquiry into psychical impotence from a medico-psychological angle which is not justified by the title of this paper. It will prove however, that this introduction was necessary in order to provide an approach to our actual theme.

We have reduced psychical impotence to a disunion between the tender and sensual currents of erotic feeling, and have explained this inhibition in development itself as an effect of strong fixations in childhood and of frustration in reality later, after the incest-barrier has intervened. There is one principal objection to raise against this doctrine: it does too much, it explains why certain persons suffer from psychical impotence, but it makes it seem puzzling that others can escape the affliction. Since all the factors that appear to be involved, the strong fixation in childhood, the incest-barrier, and the frustration in the years of development after puberty, are demonstrably present in practically all civilized persons, one would be justified in expecting that psychical impotence was universally prevalent in civilized countries and not a disease of particular individuals.

It would not be difficult to escape from this conclusion by pointing to the quantitative element in the causation of disease, that greater or lesser amount of each single factor which determines whether or not recognizable disease results. But although this argument is in my opinion sound, I do not myself intend to employ it in refuting the objection advanced above. I shall, on the contrary,

---

[4]Cf. p. 44

put forward the proposition that psychical impotence is far more widespread than is generally supposed, and that some degree of this condition does in fact characterize the erotic life of civilized peoples.

If one enlarges the meaning of the term psychical impotence, and ceases to limit it to failure to perform the act of coitus, although an intention to derive pleasure from it is present and the genital apparatus is intact, it would comprise, to begin with, all those men who are described as psychoanaesthetic, *i.e.* who never fail in the act but who perform it without special pleasure—a state of things which is commoner than one might think. Psychoanalytic study of such cases has discovered the same aetiological factors in them as those found in psychical impotence, when employed in the narrower sense, without at first discovering any explanation of the symptomatic difference between the two. By an analogy which is easy to justify, one is led on from these anaesthetic men to consider the enormous number of frigid women, whose attitude to love can in fact not be described or understood better than by equating it with psychical impotence in men, although the latter is more conspicuous. [5]

If, however, instead of attributing a wide significance to the term psychical impotence, we look about for instances of its peculiar symptomatology in less marked forms, we shall not be able to deny that the behaviour in love of the men of present-day civilization bears in general the character of the psychically impotent type. In only very few people of culture are the two strains of tenderness and sensuality duly fused into one; the man almost always feels his sexual activity hampered by his respect for the woman and only develops full sexual potency when he finds himself in the presence of a lower type of sexual object; and this again is partly conditioned by the circumstance that his sexual aims include those of perverse sexual components, which he does not like to gratify with a woman he respects. Full sexual satisfaction only comes when he can give himself up wholeheartedly to enjoy-

---

[5] At the same time I willingly admit that the frigidity of women is a complicated subject which can be approached from another angle.

ment, which with his well-brought-up wife, for instance, he does not venture to do. Hence comes his need for a less exalted sexual object, a woman ethically inferior, to whom he need ascribe no aesthetic misgivings, and who does not know the rest of his life and cannot criticize him. It is to such a woman that he prefers to devote his sexual potency, even when all the tenderness in him belongs to one of a higher type. It is possible, too, that the tendency so often observed in men of the highest rank in society to take a woman of a low class as a permanent mistress, or even as a wife, is nothing but a consequence of the need for a lower type of sexual object on which, psychologically, the possibility of complete gratification depends.

I do not hesitate to lay the responsibility also for this very common condition in the erotic life of civilized men on the two factors operative in absolute psychical impotence, namely, the very strong incestuous fixation of childhood and the frustration by reality suffered during adolescence. It has an ugly sound and a paradoxical as well, but nevertheless it must be said that whoever is to be really free and happy in love must have overcome his deference for women and come to terms with the idea of incest with mother or sister. Anyone who in the face of this test subjects himself to serious self-examination will indubitably find that at the bottom of his heart he too regards the sexual act as something degrading, which soils and contaminates not only the body. And he will only be able to look for the origin of this attitude, which he will certainly not willingly acknowledge, in that period of his youth in which his sexual passions were already strongly developed but in which gratification of them with an object outside the family was almost as completely prohibited as with an incestuous one.

The women of our civilized world are similarly affected by their up-bringing and further, too, by the reaction upon them of this attitude in men. Naturally the effect upon a woman is just as unfavourable if the man comes to her without his full potency as if, after overestimating her in the early stages of falling in love, he then, having successfully possessed himself of her, sets her at naught. Women show little need to degrade the sexual object; no doubt this has some connection with the circumstance that as a rule they develop little of the sexual overestimation natural to men. The long abstinence from sexuality to which they are forced and the lingering of their sensuality in phantasy have in them, however, another important consequence. It is often not possible for them later on to undo the connection thus formed in their minds between sensual activities and something forbidden, and they turn out to be psychically impotent, *i.e.* frigid, when at last such activities do become permissible. This is the source of the desire in so many women to keep even legitimate relations secret for a time; and of the appearance of the capacity for normal sensation in others as soon as the condition of prohibition is restored by a secret intrigue—untrue to the husband, they can keep a second order of faith with the lover.

In my opinion the necessary condition of forbiddenness in the erotic life of women holds the same place as the man's need to lower his sexual object. Both are the consequence of the long period of delay between sexual maturity and sexual activity which is demanded by education for social reasons. The aim of both is to overcome the psychical impotence resulting from the lack of union between tenderness and sensuality. That the effect of the same causes differs so greatly in men and in women is perhaps due to another difference in the behaviour of the two sexes. Women belonging to the higher levels of civilization do not usually transgress the prohibition against sexual activities during the period of waiting, and thus they acquire this close association between the forbidden and the sexual. Men usually overstep the prohibition under the condition of lowering the standard of object they require, and so carry this condition on into their subsequent erotic life.

In view of the strenuous efforts being made in the civilized world at the present day to reform sexual life, it is not superfluous to remind the reader that psychoanalytic investigations have no more bias in any direction than has any other scientific research. In tracing back to its concealed sources what is manifest, psychoanalysis has no aim but that of disclosing connections. It can but be satisfied if what it has brought to light is of use in effecting reforms by substituting more advantageous for injurious conditions. It cannot, however, predict whether other, perhaps even greater, sacrifices may not result from other institutions.

III

The fact that the restrictions imposed by cultural education upon erotic life involve a general lowering of the sexual object may prompt us to turn our eyes from the object to the instincts themselves. The injurious results of the deprivation of sexual enjoyment at the beginning manifest themselves in lack of full satisfaction when sexual desire is later given free rein in marriage. But, on the other hand, unrestrained sexual liberty from the beginning leads to no better result. It is easy to show that the value the mind sets on erotic needs instantly sinks as soon as satisfaction becomes readily obtainable. Some obstacle is necessary to swell the tide of the libido to its height; and at all periods of history, wherever natural barriers in the way of satisfaction have not sufficed, mankind has erected conventional ones in order to be able to enjoy love. This is true both of individuals and of nations. In times during which no obstacles to sexual satisfaction existed, such as, may be, during the decline of the civilizations of antiquity, love became worthless, life became empty, and strong reaction-formations were necessary before the indispensable emotional value of love could be recovered. In this context it may be stated that the ascetic tendency of Christianity had the effect of raising the psychical value of love in a way that heathen antiquity could never achieve; it developed greatest significance in the lives of the ascetic monks, which were almost entirely occupied with struggles against libidinous temptation.

One's first inclination undoubtedly is to see in this difficulty a universal characteristic of our organic instincts. It is certainly true in a general way that the importance of an instinctual desire is mentally increased by frustration of it. Suppose one made the experiment of exposing a number of utterly different human beings to hunger under the same conditions. As the imperative need for food rose in them all their individual differences would be effaced and instead the uniform manifestations of one unsatisfied instinct would appear. But is it also true, conversely, that the mental value of an instinct invariably sinks with gratification of it? One thinks, for instance, of the relation of the wine-drinker to wine. Is it not a fact that wine always affords the drinker the same toxic satisfaction—one that in poetry has so often been likened to the erotic and that science as well may regard as comparable? Has one ever heard of a drinker being forced constantly to change his wine because he soon gets tired of always drinking the same? On the contrary, habit binds a man more and more to the particular kind of wine he drinks. Do we ever find a drinker impelled to go to another country where the wine is dearer or where alcohol is prohibited, in order to stimulate his dwindling pleasure in it by these obstacles? Nothing of the sort. If we listen to what our great lovers of alcohol say about their attitude to wine, for instance, B. Böcklin,[6] it sounds like the most perfect harmony, a model of a happy marriage. Why is the relation of the lover to his sexual object so very different?

However strange it may sound, I think the possibility must be considered that something in the nature of the sexual instinct itself is unfavourable to the achievement of absolute gratification. When we think of the long and difficult evolution the instinct goes through, two factors to which this difficulty might be ascribed at once emerge. First, in consequence of the two "thrusts" of sexual development impelling towards choice of an object, together with the intervention of the incest-barrier between the two, the ultimate object selected is never the original one but only a surrogate for it. Psychoanalysis has shown us, however, that when the original object of an instinctual desire becomes lost in consequence of repression, it is often replaced by an endless series of substitute-objects, none of which ever give full satisfaction. This may explain the lack of stability in object-choice, the "craving for stimulus," which is so often a feature of the love of adults.

Secondly, we know that at its beginning the sexual instinct is divided into a large number of components—or, rather, it develops from them—not all of which can be carried on into its final form; some have to be suppressed or turned to other uses before the final form results. Above all, the coprophilic elements in the instinct have proved incompatible with our aesthetic ideas, probably since the time when man developed an upright posture and so removed his organ of smell from the ground; further, a considerable propor-

---

[6]G. Floerke, *Zehn Jahre mit Böcklin*, 2 Aufl., 1902, p. 16.

tion of the sadistic elements belonging to the erotic instinct have to be abandoned. All such developmental processes, however, relate only to the upper layers of the complicated structure. The fundamental processes which promote erotic excitation remain always the same. Excremental things are all too intimately and inseparably bound up with sexual things; the position of the genital organs—*inter urinas et faeces*—remains the decisive and unchangeable factor. One might say, modifying a well-known saying of the great Napoleon's, "Anatomy is destiny." The genitals themselves have not undergone the development of the rest of the human form in the direction of beauty; they have retained their animal cast; and so even to-day love, too, is in essence as animal as it ever was. The erotic instincts are hard to mould; training of them achieves now too much, now too little. What culture tries to make out of them seems attainable only at the cost of a sensible loss of pleasure; the persistence of the impulses that are not enrolled in adult sexual activity makes itself felt in an absence of satisfaction.

So perhaps we must make up our minds to the idea that altogether it is not possible for the claims of the sexual instinct to be reconciled with the demands of culture, that in consequence of his cultural development renunciation and suffering, as well as the danger of his extinction at some far future time, are not to be eluded by the race of man. This gloomy prognosis rests, it is true, on the single conjecture that the lack of satisfaction accompanying culture is the necessary consequence of certain peculiarities developed by the sexual instinct under the pressure of culture. This very incapacity in the sexual instinct to yield full satisfaction as soon as it submits to the first demands of culture becomes the source, however, of the grandest cultural achievements, which are brought to birth by ever greater sublimation of the components of the sexual instinct. For what motive would induce man to put his sexual energy to other uses if by any disposal of it he could obtain fully satisfying pleasure? He would never let go of this pleasure and would make no further progress. It seems, therefore, that the irreconcilable antagonism between the demands of the two instincts—the sexual and the egoistic—have made man capable of ever greater achievements, though, it is true, under the continual menace of danger, such as that of the neuroses to which at the present time the weaker are succumbing.

The purpose of science is neither to alarm nor to reassure. But I myself freely admit that such far-reaching conclusions as those drawn here should be built up on a broader foundation, and that perhaps developments in other directions will enable mankind to remedy the effects of these, which we have here been considering in isolation.

3. The Taboo of Virginity[1] (1918)

There are few details of the sexual life of primitive races which seem so strange to our feeling as their attitude towards virginity, the condition in a woman of being sexually untouched. The high value set upon her virginity by a man wooing a woman seems to us so deeply planted and self-evident that we become almost perplexed if called upon to give reasons for it. The demand that the girl shall bring with her into marriage with one man no memory of sexual relations with another is after all nothing but a logical consequence of the exclusive right of possession over a woman which is the essence of monogamy—it is but an extension of this monopoly on to the past.

From this it is not difficult to go on and justify what at first appeared to be a prejudice by referring to our ideas concerning the character of the erotic life in women. The maiden whose desire for love has for so long and with such difficulty been held in check, in whom the influences of environment and education have formed resistances, will take the man who gratifies her longing, and thereby overcomes her resistances, into a close and lasting relationship which will never again be available to any other man. This experience brings about a state of "thraldom" in the woman that assures the man lasting and undisturbed possession of her and

---

[1] First published in *Sammlung*, Vierte Folge, 1918. [Translated by Joan Riviere.]

makes her able to withstand new impressions and temptations from without.

The expression "sexual thraldom"[2] was adopted by von Krafft-Ebing in 1892 to denote the fact that one person may develop an unusually high degree of dependence and helplessness towards another with whom he has a sexual relationship. This "thraldom" can at times go to great lengths, even to the total loss of independent will and the heaviest sacrifices of personal interests; the author has not failed to observe, however, that a certain degree of this dependence is "absolutely necessary if the relationship is to have any permanence." Some measure of sexual thraldom is indeed indispensable in maintaining civilized marriage and restraining the polygamous tendencies that threaten to undermine it, and in our social communities this factor is regularly taken into account.

Krafft-Ebing derives the origin of sexual thraldom from the conjunction of "an unusual degree of development of love and of weakness of character" in the one partner with unbounded egoism in the other. Analytic experience, however, makes it impossible for us to be content with this simple explanation. On the contrary, one can clearly see that the decisive factor is the strength of the sexual resistances that are surmounted, together with the extent to which this conquest is concentrated in one single act and carried out once and for all. For this reason sexual thraldom is incomparably more frequent and more intense in women than in men, though it is nowadays much commoner in the latter than it was in antiquity. Where we have been able to study sexual thraldom in men it has proved to be the result of a victory over psychical impotence in respect of one particular woman, to whom the man in question thenceforward remained bound. Many a surprising marriage and many a tragic fate—even some of far-reaching consequences—seem to find their explanation in this course of events.

The attitude of primitive races which I shall now discuss would be incorrectly described by saying that they set no value on virginity and by seeking to prove this from the circumstance that the

---

[2]Von Krafft-Ebing, "Bemerkungen über 'geschlechtliche Hörigkeit' und Masochismus."

defloration of girls is performed apart from marriage and before the first act of marital intercourse. On the contrary, it appears that the act of defloration has great significance for them also, but it has become the subject of a taboo, of what may be called a religious prohibition. Instead of reserving it for the bridegroom and future husband of the girl, custom demands that he should abstain from the performance of it.[3]

It is not my intention to reproduce in full the evidence in the literature concerning the existence of this prohibition, to follow out its geographical distribution or to enumerate the various forms in which it is expressed. I shall content myself with the statement that the custom of rupturing the hymen in this way apart from subsequent marriage is a very widespread one among primitive races. Thus Crawley says:[4] "This marriage ceremony consists in perforation of the hymen by some appointed person other than the husband; it is most common in the lowest stages of culture, especially in Australia."

If, however, defloration is not to be effected through the first act of marital intercourse, it must, in some way or other and by some person or other, be performed beforehand. I shall quote some passages from Crawley's *Mystic Rose* which give some information on this point, but also give ground for some critical remarks.

P. 191. "Thus in the Dieri and neighbouring tribes (in Australia) it is the universal custom when a girl reaches puberty to rupture the hymen" (*Journal of the Royal Anthropological Institute*, xxiv. 169). In the Portland and Glenelg tribes this is done to the bride by an old woman; and sometimes white men are asked for this reason to deflower maidens (Brough Smith, *op. cit.* ii. 319).

P. 307. "The artificial rupture of the hymen sometimes takes place in infancy, but generally at puberty. . . . It is often combined, as in Australia, with a ceremonial act of intercourse."

P. 348. (In communications made by Spencer and Gillen about

---

[3]Crawley, *The Mystic Rose: a Study of Primitive Marriage*, 1902; Ploss-Bartels, *Das Weib in der Natur- und Völkerkunde*, 1891; various passages in Frazer's *Taboo and the Perils of the Soul*; and Havelock Ellis, *Studies in the Psychology of Sex*.

[4]*Loc. cit.* p. 347.

Australian tribes in which the well-known exogamic restrictions in regard to marriage are customary.) "The hymen is artificially perforated, and then the men who are assisting have access (ceremonial, be it observed) to the girl in a stated order. . . . The act is in two parts, perforation and intercourse."

P. 349. "An important preliminary of marriage amongst the Masai (in Equatorial Africa) is the performance of this operation on the girl (J. Thomson, *op. cit.* ii. 258). This defloration is performed by the father of the bride amongst the Sakais (Malay), Battas (Sumatra), and Alfoers of Celebes (Ploss and Bartels, *op. cit.* ii. 490). In the Philippines these were certain men whose profession it was to deflower brides, in case the hymen had not been ruptured in childhood by an old woman who was sometimes employed for this (Featherman, *op. cit.* ii. 474). The defloration of the bride was amongst some Eskimo tribes entrusted to the *angekok*, or priest (*id.* iii. 406)."

The critical remarks to which I alluded refer to two points. First, it is unfortunate that in these accounts a closer distinction is not drawn between mere rupture of the hymen without coitus and coitus for the purpose of rupturing the hymen. Only in one place is it expressly stated that the process was divided into two actions, *i.e.* defloration (by manual or instrumental means) followed by an act of intercourse. The material collected by Ploss-Bartels, which is in other respects most fruitful, is almost useless for our purpose, because in their account the psychological significance of the act of defloration is entirely displaced by interest in its anatomical result. Secondly, one would like to hear more about the difference between the "ceremonial" (purely formal, ritual, official) coitus performed on these occasions and ordinary sexual intercourse. The writers of such works as I could obtain were either too much ashamed to mention such things or else they again underestimated the psychological importance of these sexual details. It is to be hoped that the firsthand reports of travellers and missionaries may be fuller and less equivocal, but in view of the inaccessibility at the present time of publications of this nature,[5] which are mostly

---

[5][Owing to the European War.—Trans.]

foreign, I cannot speak with any certainty upon the matter. In any event one is entitled to pass over the doubt arising on the second point, in view of the consideration that a ceremonial mock-coitus would only be a substitute for the complete act and perhaps a commutation of the act itself performed in earlier times.[6]

Various factors, which I shall now briefly discuss, can be adduced in explanation of this taboo of virginity. Defloration of a maiden usually causes a flow of blood; the first attempt at explanation refers therefore to the dread of shedding blood among primitive races who regard blood as the seat of life. This blood-taboo is expressed in many different regulations which have nothing to do with sexuality; it is clearly connected with the prohibition against murder and represents a defensive measure against the primordial bloodthirstiness, primitive man's lust to kill. This conception of it brings the taboo of virginity into relation with the taboo of menstruation that is almost universally observed. The primitive cannot help connecting the mysterious phenomenon of the monthly flow of blood with sadistic ideas. Thus he interprets menstruation, especially at its onset, as the bite of a spirit-animal, or possibly as the token of sexual intercourse with this spirit. Occasionally the reports reveal this spirit as one of an ancestor and then from other knowledge we have gained[7] we understand that it is in virtue of her being the property of this spirit-ancestor that the menstruating girl is taboo.

Other considerations, however, warn us not to exaggerate the influence of a factor such as the horror of blood. After all, the latter does not suffice to suppress customs like the circumcision of boys and the still more cruel extirpation of the clitoris and labia minora in girls, which are practised to some extent by the same races, nor to abolish the prevalence of other ceremonies at which blood is shed. It would not have been surprising, therefore, if this taboo had been relaxed in favour of the husband on the occasion of the first cohabitation.

---

[6]There can be no doubt that in a large number of other forms of wedding-ceremony other persons beside the bridegroom, *i.e.* his friends and companions (the "best man" of our custom), were accorded full sexual access to the bride.

[7]Cf. Freud, *Totem und Tabu.*

The second explanation is also unconnected with sexuality; it is even more general, however, and less specific than the first. It suggests that primitive man is a prey to a perpetual "anxious expectation," to a lurking sense of apprehension, just like those suffering from the anxiety-neurosis classified by us in the psychoanalytical theory of the neuroses. This "anxious expectation" shows itself most intensely on all occasions that depart from what is usual, in regard to anything that involves something novel, unexpected, unexplained, uncanny. It is also the origin of the ritual, so widely adopted in later religions, that is observed in connection with beginning any new undertaking, with the commencement of each new period of time, or with the first-fruits of human, animal and plant life. The dangers which in his imagination menace the fearful are never expected to be more terrible than at the beginning of a perilous enterprise, and it is consequently only at that point that protective measures can avail him. The first act of intercourse in marriage certainly has sufficient importance to justify its being preceded by precautionary measures of this kind. These two attempts at explanation, by reference to the horror of blood and the dread of what is novel, do not gainsay each other; on the contrary, they reinforce each other. The first act of intercourse is certainly a critical matter and all the more if it causes blood to flow.

A third explanation—it is that preferred by Crawley—points out that the taboo of virginity belongs to a range of ideas that includes the whole of sexual life. Not only is the first act of coitus with any woman taboo, but sexual intercourse in general; it might almost be said that woman is altogether taboo. Not merely is woman taboo in special situations connected with her sexual life, such as during menstruation, pregnancy, child-birth and lying-in; but quite apart from these occasions intercourse with a woman is subject to such heavy and numerous restrictions that we have every reason to question the apparent sexual liberty of savages. It is true that on special occasions the sexuality of primitive man sets all these restraints at naught; ordinarily, however, it seems to be more strictly circumscribed than it is in higher levels of civilization. As soon as a man sets about any special undertaking, such as an expedition, a hunt, a campaign, he must avoid women, and especially abstain from sexual intercourse with them; otherwise his strength will be paralysed and the result of the enterprise disaster. Also in the customs relating to daily life there exists an unmistakable tendency to keep the sexes apart. Women live with women and men with men; family life as we know it is said to be hardly known in many primitive tribes. At times the separation goes so far that one sex may not speak the names of the other sex, and the women develop a special vocabulary. These dividing barriers may be broken through from time to time by sexual need, but in many tribes even intercourse between married couples must take place outside the house in secret.

Wherever primitive man institutes a taboo, there he fears a danger; and it cannot be disputed that the general principle underlying all these regulations and avoidances is a dread of woman. Perhaps this fear is founded on the difference of woman from man, on her eternally inexplicable, mysterious and strange nature, which thus seems hostile. Man fears that his strength will be taken from him by woman, dreads becoming infected with her femininity and then proving himself a weakling. The effect of coitus in discharging tensions and inducing flaccidity may be a prototype of what these fears represent; and realization of the influence gained by the woman over a man as a result of sexual relations, and the favours she extorts by this means, may all conduce to justify the growth of these fears. There is nothing in all this which is extinct, which is not still alive in the heart of man to-day.

Many observers of primitive races existing at the present time have formed the opinion that the erotic instinct in them is comparatively weak and never reaches the intensity usually found in civilized man. Others again contradict this statement; but in any event the taboos described are evidence of the existence of a force which, by rejecting woman as strange and hostile, sets itself against love.

Crawley, in terms that are hardly distinguishable from those employed by psychoanalysis, sets forth how each individual is separated from the others by a "taboo of personal isolation" and that it is precisely the little dissimilarities in persons who are otherwise alike that arouse feelings of strangeness and enmity between them. It would be tempting to follow up this idea and trace back to this "narcissism of small differences" the antagonism which in all human relations we see successfully combating feelings of fellowship and the commandment of love towards all men. Psycho-analysis believes that, in pointing out the castration complex and its influence on the estimation in which women are held, it has discovered one of the chief factors underlying the narcissistic rejection of women by men that is so liberally mingled with disdain.

We perceive, however, that these later considerations go far beyond the subject under discussion. The universal taboo of women throws no light on special regulations for the first sexual act with a virgin. As regards this, we have got no further than the two first explanations relating to the dread of blood and the dread of what is novel, and even these, we must object, do not touch the core of the taboo-ordinance in question. The purpose underlying the latter is quite clearly that of denying to the future husband in particular, or of relieving him from, something inseparably connected with the first sexual act; although, according to the statements with which this paper opened, this very relation would give rise to a specially close attachment in the woman to this one man.

Our present task is not that of examining the origin and ultimate significance of taboo-ordinances in general. In my book *Totem und Tabu* I have done so, and have gone into the question of an innate ambivalence inherent in taboo and argued the genesis of taboo from prehistoric conditions and events leading up to the foundation of the human family. This earlier significance pertaining to taboo is no longer recognizable in the ceremonies of those primitive men we can observe to-day. Any such expectation shows how easily we forget that the conditions of life under which even the most primitive peoples live are a complicated development far removed from the primeval state and just as old as our own, representing a later, if different, stage of development just as our own civilization does.

We find the taboos of primitive races to-day already elaborated into intricate systems, just like those constructed by our neurotics in their phobias; the original motives in them are replaced by newer ones which harmonize with the others. Leaving these genetic problems on one side, however, we will return to the point of view that where primitive man fears a danger there he institutes a taboo.

This danger that he fears is, taken altogether, a psychical one, for the primitive is not constrained to make the distinctions which to us seem so necessary. He does not separate physical danger from psychical, nor real from imaginary danger. In his animistic view of life, logically worked out as it is, every danger proceeds from a hostile impulse on the part of some being with a soul like his own, just as much if the menace comes from some force of nature as from other human beings or animals. On the other hand, however, he has the habit of projecting his own inner feelings of hostility on to the outside world, that is, of ascribing them to whatever objects he dislikes or even is merely unfamiliar with. Now woman is also looked upon as a source of such dangers and the first sexual act with a woman stands out as a specially perilous one.

I think now we shall obtain some light on the question of what this specially intense danger consists in, and why it menaces the future husband in particular, by examining the behaviour of present-day civilized women in the same circumstances. I will anticipate the result of such an examination by saying that a danger of the kind does really exist, so that with his taboo primitive man is protecting himself from a danger—a psychical one, it is true—which his intuition had quite correctly divined.

We regard it as the normal reaction to coitus for a woman to hold the man closely in her arms and press him to her at the climax of gratification, and this seems to us an expression of her gratitude and an assurance of lasting thraldom to him. We know, however, that the first act of intercourse is by no means always followed by this behaviour; very often the experience merely signifies a disappointment to the woman, who remains cold and unsatisfied; usually it takes some time and frequent repetition of the sexual act before satisfaction in it for her too sets in. From these cases of merely initial and quite temporary frigidity there proceeds a gradation up to the unsatisfactory extreme case of permanent and unremitting frigidity, which not the utmost tenderness and eagerness on the part of the husband is able to overcome. In my opinion this frigidity in women is not yet sufficiently understood; wherever the insufficient potency of the husband is not to blame, it demands explanation, which must be sought, if necessary, in other phenomena of a similar nature.

I shall not here consider the frequent attempts of women to escape the first sexual act, because they can have more than one meaning, and in the main, if not entirely, are to be construed as expressions of the general female tendency to ward off sexuality. I believe, on the other hand, that certain pathological cases throw a light on the riddle of female frigidity; these are women who after the first act of intercourse—and, indeed, after every renewed act—openly express their enmity against the man by reviling him, threatening to strike him or even actually striking him. In one very pronounced case of this kind, which I was able to subject to thorough analysis, this animosity displayed itself although the woman loved the man deeply, used to demand intercourse and unquestionably obtained great satisfaction in it. I believe this strangely self-contradictory reaction is due to the very feelings that generally attain to expression only in the form of frigidity, *i.e.* that are then capable of preventing the tender reaction though unable to break through to expression themselves. That which in the far more common type of frigid woman unites to form an inhibition in the pathological case fell into its two components; just as happens in what are called the "two-movement" symptoms of the obsessional neurosis which were long ago recognized. The danger which is thus aroused through defloration of a woman would consist in drawing down upon oneself this animosity, and the future husband would be the very man with most reason to avoid so doing.

Now analysis enables us easily to discover what those impulses in women are that bring about this paradoxical behaviour, and which, as I expect, explain frigidity. The first act of coitus stirs up a number of impulses which can find no place in the womanly attitude proper to the situation, some of which, moreover, do not necessarily arise during subsequent intercourse. First of all one thinks of the pain inflicted on a virgin at defloration; indeed, one might be inclined to regard this factor as the decisive one and give up looking for any others. But so much importance cannot well be attributed to pain; we must set in its place the narcissistic wound which follows the destruction of an organ, and which even finds rationalized expression in the realization of a diminished sexual value after virginity is lost. The marriage-ceremonies of primitives warn us, however, not to overestimate this. We have seen that often the rite consists of two parts; after the rupture of the hymen has been carried out (with the hand or some instrument) there follows an official act of intercourse, or a mock-coitus, with certain persons who take the husband's place; this is evidence that the purpose of the taboo-ordinance is not fully achieved by avoidance of the anatomical defloration and that the husband is to be spared something else besides the woman's reaction to the painful injury.

A further ground for disappointrnent on experiencing the first sexual act is found to lie in its failure to fulfil expectations, at least so far as civilized women are concerned. Until this moment sexual intercourse has been closely associated with a heavy prohibition; lawful and permissible intercourse is apprehended consequently as a quite different thing. How fundamental this association can be is illustrated in an almost comic manner by the behaviour of so many young women about to be married, who try to keep the new experience of a love-relationship secret from anyone, including even their parents, where there is no sort of need to do so and no objection is anticipated. Girls openly declare that love loses its value to them if others know about it. This feeling can sometimes outweigh all others and totally prevent any development of the capacity to love in marriage. The woman then recovers her feelings of tenderness only in an illicit relationship which must be kept secret, and in which she feels certain of being actuated by her own will alone.

Not even this motive goes deep enough, however; it is bound up, moreover, with civilized conditions and lacks sufficient connection with primitive states of culture. The next factor, therefore, which depends on the evolution of the libido, is all the more important. Analytic researches have discovered how universal and how powerful the first attachments of the libido are. It is a question of sexual wishes active in childhood and never relinquished—in women generally a fixation of the libido upon the father, or upon a brother taking his place—wishes that often enough were directed to things other than coitus, or that included it among others only as a vaguely conceived aim. A husband is, so to speak, never anything but a proxy, never the right man; the first claim upon the feeling of love in a woman belongs to someone else, in typical cases to her father; the husband is at best a second. Now whether the husband is rejected as unsatisfying depends upon the strength of this fixation and the tenacity with which it is upheld. The same conditioning factors thus lead to the development of frigidity as to neurosis. The more powerful the mental element in a woman's sexual life, the more her libido-distribution will resist the shock involved in the first sexual act and the less overwhelming will be the effect of a man taking bodily possession of her. Frigidity may establish itself thenceforth as a neurotic inhibition or become the soil from which other neuroses can spring, and even a quite moderate diminution of potency in the man contributes appreciably to this.

Primitive custom appears to accord some recognition to the existence of the early sexual wish by assigning the duty of defloration to an elder, a priest, or a holy man, that is, to a father-substitute (*vide supra*). This seems to lead directly to the much-contested *jus primae noctis* of mediaeval feudal lords. A. J. Storfer[8] has expressed the same view of this matter, and, further, has construed the widespread custom of the "Tobias nights" (the custom of continence during the first three nights) to be an acknowledgement of the prerogative of the patriarch, as C. G. Jung had done before him.[9] It is only in accord with our expectations, therefore, to find divine figures, too, among the father-surrogates to whom defloration is entrusted. In many districts in India the bride was obliged to sacrifice the hymen as an offering to the wooden lingam; and according to St. Augustine the same custom obtained in Roman marriage-ceremonies (of his time?), though toned down to the extent that the young wife had only to seat herself upon the gigantic stone phallus of Priapus.[10]

There is another motive reaching down into yet deeper strata,

---

[8]*Zur Sonderstellung des Vatermordes.*

[9]"Die Bedeutung des Vaters für das Schicksal des Einzelnen."

[10]Ploss und Bartels, *Das Weib*, I., XIL., and Dulaure, *Des Divinités génératrices*, p. 142 *et seq.*

on which can be seen to rest the chief blame for the paradoxical reaction towards the man, and the influence of which in my opinion is still at work in female frigidity. The first coitus stirs yet other, older impulses in the woman besides those described—impulses which in their whole tendency oppose the female function and the female part.

From the analyses of many neurotic women we have learnt that women go through an early phase in which they envy their brothers the token of maleness and feel themselves handicapped and ill-treated on account of the lack of it (really, on account of its diminutive form). In our view this "penis-envy" forms part of the castration complex. If "masculine" is to include the connotation of "wishing to be masculine," the term "masculine protest" fits this attitude; this term was coined by Alfred Adler for the purpose of proclaiming this factor as the foundation of all neurosis in general. During this early phase little girls often make no secret of their envy of the favoured brother, and the animosity it gives rise to against him; they even try to urinate standing upright like the brother, thus asserting the equality with him that they claim. In the case mentioned of unbridled aggressiveness after coitus against the man who was otherwise greatly loved, I was able to establish that this phase had existed before object-choice had set in. Only later did the libido of the little girl turn towards the father and then her desire was, instead of the penis—a child.[11]

I should not wonder if in other cases this sequence were found to be reversed, this element of the castration complex becoming operative only after object-choice had been effected. But the masculine phase in woman during which she envies the boy his penis is at all events developmentally the earlier and more closely allied to primal narcissism than to object-love.

Not long ago chance gave me an opportunity of obtaining insight into a dream of a newly married woman, which revealed itself as a reaction to the loss of her virginity. It betrayed unmistakably the wish to castrate the young husband and keep his penis for herself. There was room, to be sure, for the more harmless

---

[11]Cf. "On the Transformation of Instincts with Special Reference to Anal Erotism," *Character and Culture*, Collier Books edition BS 193.

interpretation that it was prolongation and repetition of the act that she wanted; unfortunately, however, some details of the dream overstepped this possibility, and both the character and subsequent behaviour of the dreamer were evidence for the graver view of it. Now, upon this penis-envy follows that hostile embitterment displayed by women against men, never entirely absent in the relations between the sexes, the clearest indications of which are to be found in the writings and ambitions of "emancipated" women. Ferenczi, in a palaeo-biological speculation, traces this enmity in women back to the era when differentiation between the sexes took place—I do not know whether the priority for it is his. First of all, he believes, copulation was effected between two single organisms of the same kind, one of which, however, developed until it was stronger and then forced the weaker to submit to sexual union; and the embitterment on account of this subjection is still an active predisposition in women to-day. I see no harm in such speculations, so long as one does not overestimate their value.

After this enumeration of the motives underlying the paradoxical reaction of women to defloration and traceable in frigidity, one may sum up and say that it is the immature sexuality of the woman which discharges itself upon the man who first introduces her to sexual intercourse. With this, the taboo of virginity becomes intelligible enough, and we understand a regulation which enjoins avoidance of these dangers on the very man who is entering upon life in company with this woman. In higher levels of culture the importance attaching to this danger has given way before the promise of the woman's thraldom, and certainly too for other reasons and inducements; the virginity of the woman is looked upon as an asset which the man should not resign. Analysis of the causes of unhappy marriage, however, shows that the motives impelling the woman to revenge herself for her defloration are not entirely extinguished even in the minds of civilized women. The surprisingly large number of women who remain anaesthetic and unhappy throughout their first marriage and then, after this is dissolved, become a loving wife, able to make another man happy, must, I think, strike any observer. The archaic reaction has exhausted itself, so to speak, on the first object.

But elsewhere too in our civilized life the taboo of virginity is not extinct. The soul of the people knows it, and poets have at times made use of this material. In one of Anzengruber's comedies, a simple peasant youth refuses to marry his intended bride, because she is "a girl who'll cost her first his life." He agrees to her marrying another man, and then when she is a widow and no longer dangerous he will have her. The title of the piece, *Das Jungferngift* (The Virgin's Poison), reminds one of the practice of snake-charmers who first make the snake bite a rag so that they can afterwards handle it safely.[12]

The taboo of virginity and some part of its motivation has been portrayed most powerfully of all in the well-known figure of Judith in Hebbel's tragedy, *Judith und Holofernes*. Judith is one of those women whose virginity is protected by a taboo. Her first husband was paralysed on the wedding-night by an inexplicable fear and never again dared to touch her. "My beauty is like deadly nightshade," she says, "enjoyment of it brings madness and death." When the Assyrian general is besieging the city, she conceives the plan of enticing him with her beauty and destroying him, thus using a patriotic motive to mask a sexual one. After being deflowered by the masterful man who makes a boast of his might and his ruthlessness, she in her fury finds strength to strike off his head and so becomes the saviour of her people. Decapitation is to us a well-known symbolic substitute for castration; so Judith is a woman who castrates the man by whom she was deflowered, just as the newly married woman wished to do in the dream I mentioned. Hebbel deliberately sexualized the patriotic narrative in the Apocrypha, for there Judith boasts after her return to the city of not having been polluted, nor is there any mention in the Biblical text of her uncanny nuptials. But with the sensitive intuition of a

---

[12]A masterly short story of Arthur Schnitzler's (*Das Schicksal des Freiherrn von Leisenbogh*) deserves to be mentioned in this connection, in spite of a departure in it from the situation under discussion. The lover of an actress who had had great experience in love is dying as the result of an accident; and he creates a new virginity for her, as it were, by uttering a curse of death upon the next man to possess her after him. For a time the woman who is thus placed under a taboo does not venture to have intercourse with anyone. Then she falls in love with a singer, and resorts to the plan of first granting a night with her to Freiherr von Leisenbogh, who has for years tried in vain to win her. And the curse fulfils itself on him; he dies of a stroke on hearing the reason of his unexpected good fortune.

poet Hebbel probably divined the primordial theme that had been lost in the tendentious story, and only gave back to the content its earlier currency.

Sadger has worked out in an excellent analysis the way in which Hebbel's choice of material was determined by his own parental complex, and how it was that in a struggle between the sexes he invariably took the part of woman and knew intuitively the most hidden feeling of her soul.[13] He quotes also the reasons the poet himself gave for his alterations of the material, and rightly finds them factitious and apparently designed superficially to justify the poet's own unconscious to himself, but ultimately to conceal it. I will not touch Sadger's explanation of why the widowed Judith of the Bible had to become a virgin widow. He adduces the motive in the infantile phantasy of denying the sexual intercourse of the parents, so that the mother becomes an untouched virgin. But I will continue: after the poet has duly established his heroine's virginity, his phantasy probes into and dwells upon the resentful reaction let loose after maidenhood has been violated.

In conclusion, then, we may say that the act of defloration has not merely the socially useful result of binding the woman closely to the man; it also liberates an archaic reaction of enmity towards the man, which may assume pathological forms, and often enough expresses itself by inhibitions in the erotic life of the pair, and to which one may ascribe the fact that second marriages so often turn out better than first. The strange taboo of virginity—the fear which among primitive peoples induces the husband to avoid the performance of defloration—finds its full justification in this hostile turn of feeling.

It is interesting now to find that psychoanalysts come across women in whom the two contrary attitudes—thraldom and enmity—both come to expression and remain in close association. There are women who appear to be utterly alienated from their husbands and who can yet make only vain attempts to separate from them. As often as they try to turn their love to some other man, the image of the first, who is nevertheless not loved, comes

---

[13]Sadger, "Von der Pathographie zur Psychographie."

as a barrier between. Analysis then shows that these women still cling to their first husbands, in thraldom, truly, but no longer from affection. They cannot free themselves from him because their revenge upon him is not yet complete; and, indeed, in extreme cases they have never even let the vengeful impulse reach their conscious minds.

V

The Predisposition to Obsessional Neurosis[1] (1913)

A Contribution to the Problem of the Option of Neurosis

The problem of why and how a person may fall ill of a neurosis
assuredly belongs to those which psychoanalysis is called upon to
solve. It is, however, probable that the solution will be found by
way of the answer to another and more specific problem—that of
why any particular person is bound to succumb to one particular
neurosis, and no other. This is the problem of the option of
neurosis.

What do we know so far about this problem? Strictly speaking,
only one general principle has been established. We divide the
causes of neurotic disease into those which the individual himself
brings with him into life, and those which life brings to him—that
is to say, into constitutional and accidental. It is the interaction of
these that as a rule first gives rise to illness. Now the general
principle just referred to implies that the basic factors which determine the option of neurosis are entirely of the former kind, that
is, are of the nature of dispositions, and are independent of experiences that operate pathogenically.

Where are we to look for the origin of these dispositions? We
have come to realize that the mental functions concerned—above
all, the sexual function, but also various important ego-functions—

---

[1] Paper read before the International Psycho-Analytical Congress at Munich in 1913;
reprinted in *Sammlung*, Vierte Folge. [Translated by Edward Glover and E. Colburn
Mayne.]

have to go through a long and complicated process of development before they reach the state characteristic of a normal adult. We must further assume that these developments are not always carried out without a hitch, so that the function as a whole is not always subjected to progressive modification. Should any component of it remain arrested at an earlier phase there results what is known as a "fixation-point," to which the function can regress if external hardships give rise to illness.

Our predispositions to various neuroses are thus seen to be inhibitions in development. The analogy with the facts of the general pathology of other diseases strengthens this view. The question of what factors can induce such disturbances in development does not lie within the boundaries of psychoanalytic investigations; we must leave it to biological research.[2]

With the help of such hypotheses, we were emboldened some years ago to attack the problem of the option of neurosis. The line taken by our method of investigation, which consists in tracing out normal conditions from a study of their disturbances, led us to choose a very singular and unexpected point of attack. The order in which the principal forms of neurosis are customarily ranked—namely, hysteria, obsessional neurosis, paranoia, dementia praecox—corresponds (if not quite exactly) to the order of incidence of these diseases from childhood onward. Hysterical manifestations may be observed already in early childhood; the first symptoms of obsessional neurosis usually declare themselves in the second period of childhood (from six to eight years of age); whilst the two other psychoneuroses, which I have coupled under the joint designation paraphrenia, first appear after puberty and during adult life. Although last in order of incidence, these two conditions were the first to yield results from investigations regarding the predispositions determining the option of neurosis. The peculiar characteristics of them both, *i.e.* megalomania, turning from objective reality and difficulty in effecting transference, have forced us to the conclusion that the predisposing fixation is to be

---

[2]Since the work of W. Fliess has revealed the biological importance of periodicity, it has become conceivable that developmental disturbances may be ascribed to modifications in the duration of the various stages.

sought in a stage of libido-development prior to the establishment of object-choice, that is to say, in the stage of auto-erotism and narcissism.[3] Paranoia and dementia praecox then, although manifesting themselves so late in life, derive from very early inhibitions and fixations.

As a result of this, it seemed reasonable to suppose that the disposition to hysteria and obsessional neurosis, the two transference-neuroses proper, both of which show early symptom-formation, would be found at still earlier stages of libido-development. But where could an arrest in development be found before this, and above all, where could lie that difference between two phases of development which would give rise in one case to an obsessional disposition and in another to that of hysteria? For a long time no light could be obtained on these points, and earlier surmises of my own about the nature of these dispositions—*e.g.* the idea that hysteria and the obsessional neurosis were conditioned respectively by passivity and activity in infantile experiences—had soon to be discarded as erroneous.

I will now return to individual clinical study, and will consider the case of a woman patient who was under observation for a considerable period, and whose neurosis underwent an unusual transformation. The case was at first one of pure anxiety-hysteria, following on a traumatic experience, and it preserved that character for some years. One day, however, it suddenly changed into an exceedingly severe obsessional neurosis. A case of this kind must be significant from more than one point of view. On the one hand, it might turn out to have the value of a bilingual document, and show how the two neuroses would express an identical content in different languages. On the other hand, it threatened wholly to overthrow our theory of disposition as a result of arrest in development; unless we were prepared to assume that an individual could have more than one weak spot in his libido-development. I told myself that one had no right to reject the latter possibility, but I was nevertheless very eager to arrive at an understanding of the case.

As this came to me in the course of the analysis, it became

---

[3]Cf. Notes Upon an Autobiographical "Account of a Case of Paranoia" (Dementia Paranoides), *Three Case Histories*, Collier Books edition BS 191V.

evident that the state of affairs was quite otherwise than I had imagined it. The obsessional neurosis was not a further reaction to the same trauma which had originally called forth the anxiety-hysteria: it was a reaction to a second experience which had entirely eclipsed the first—it was therefore an exception, although, to be sure, a still debatable one, to our proposition that the option of neurosis does not depend upon experience.

Unfortunately I cannot—for the usual reasons—go into the case-history as fully as I could wish, but must confine myself to the following details. Before she fell ill the patient had been a happy and almost entirely contented married woman. She wished to have children, a wish itself determined by infantile fixation, and fell ill when she realized that her husband, to whom she was entirely devoted, could not satisfy this longing. The anxiety-hysteria with which she reacted to this frustration corresponded to a rejection of seduction-phantasies in which she achieved her enduring wish for a child. She was not long in coming to realize this herself, and did her utmost to prevent her husband guessing that her illness was due to a privation for which he was responsible. It is not without good reason, however, that I have maintained that every man possesses in his unconscious an instrument by which he can interpret the expressions of the unconscious of another; the husband understood, without any confession or explanation, what his wife's anxiety signified, was deeply hurt by the discovery, though he made no sign, and then began to react neurotically himself by becoming for the first time impotent during sexual intercourse. Immediately after he went on a journey, and his wife, believing him to be permanently impotent, produced her first obsessional symptom on the day before his expected return.

The content of her obsessional neurosis consisted in a tormenting obsession about washing and cleanliness and in exceedingly vigorous protective measures against wicked injuries which others might have to fear from her; that is to say, it consisted of reaction-formations against anal-erotic and sadistic impulses. In such forms her sexual need was driven to find expression, as a result of the entire bankruptcy of her genital life brought about by the impotence of her husband, who was the only man to whom she could look for satisfaction.

At this point I was able to fit in a fragment of a new theory which had recently been shaping in my mind. Although seemingly based on the present isolated observation, it is, as a matter of fact, the result of numerous earlier impressions, the significance of which first became clear at this stage of the case under discussion. I told myself that my original sketch of the development of the libidinal function required another amplification. Formerly I had simply distinguished a phase of auto-erotism, in which the various component-impulses, each for itself, seek independent gratification on the body itself, from a phase when in the interests of reproduction they unite under the primacy of the genital system to effect object-choice. As is already known, the analysis of paraphrenics had obliged us to interpolate a stage of narcissism during which object-choice is already effected but in which the object is still the ego itself. Now we are faced with the necessity of reckoning with yet another stage before the ultimate condition, one in which, although the component-impulses have been co-ordinated for purposes of object-choice, and although the object does present itself as one outside the self, nevertheless *the primacy of the genital zone has not yet been established*. The component-impulses which govern this *pregenital* organization of the sexual life are, moreover, the anal-erotic and sadistic impulses.

I know that general statements of this kind appear very startling at first hearing. We become reconciled to them only after correlation with our previous knowledge, and it often happens that in the long run they come to be accepted as an insignificant innovation which had already been long suspected. We may proceed therefore to consider this "pregenital sexual organization" with somewhat similar anticipations.

(*a*) The all-important part played by hate impulses and anal erotism in the symptomatology of the obsessional neurosis has impressed many observers, and recently Ernest Jones has called attention to it in a particularly penetrating study.[4] This observation would be established as an immediate corollary to our own views should it prove that the component-impulses referred to, which

---

[4] Ernest Jones, *Hate and Anal Erotism in the Obsessional Neurosis*, 1913.

precede the genital impulses in the process of development, can act for the latter in this neurosis.

At this point we may appropriately refer to a detail in the patient's history which has not so far been mentioned. The patient's sexual life began with sadistic beating-phantasies in her earliest childhood. Following on their suppression an unusually long latency period set in, in the course of which the girl achieved a far-reaching moral development without awakening to the womanly sexual sensations. With her early marriage began a period of normal sexual activity as a happy wife, which lasted for a number of years, until the first great privation brought on the hysterical neurosis. With the ensuing destitution of her genital life, her sexual activity, as has been said, relapsed to the infantile stage of sadism.

It is not difficult to define the characteristic distinguishing this case of obsessional neurosis from those many others which begin in early years and follow a chronic course with more or less notable exacerbations. In these latter, when once the stage of sexual organization which contains the predisposition to obsessional neurosis is established, it is never really overcome; in our case this organization is, to begin with, superseded by a higher stage of development, then subsequently reactivated by regression from that higher stage.

(b) When we attempt to correlate our views with biological considerations, we must bear in mind that the antithesis of masculine and feminine which is set up by the reproductive function cannot be present at the stage of pregenital object-choice. Instead we find an antithesis of trends with active and passive aims which ultimately resolves into the antithesis of sex (male and female). The active trend is supplied by that general instinct of mastery which when we find it serving the sexual function we call sadism; in the fully developed normal sexual life it has also important accessory services to render. The passive trend is fed from anal erotism, the erotogenic zone of which corresponds with the old, undifferentiated cloaca. Accentuation of anal erotism at the stage of pregenital organization gives rise in a man to a marked predisposition to homosexuality, when the next stage of the sexual function, that of genital primacy, is reached. The building up of this last phase on the foundation of the previous phases, and the subsequent transformation of the libidinal cathexes, provides us with some of the most interesting openings for psychoanalytic research.

It may be thought that all such difficulties and complications could be avoided by denying the pregenital organization of sexual life and adopting the view that sexual life coincides with the genital and reproductive function, making its appearance at the same time as this. If this course were followed and use were made of such psychoanalytic findings as are beyond dispute, the theory might be advanced that as a result of sexual repression the neuroses are compelled to express sexual strivings by means of other non-sexual instincts, *i.e.* by compensatory sexualization of the latter. Anyone so doing, however, would find himself in complete retreat from the position taken up by psychoanalysis. He would stand where he was before the advent of psychoanalysis and must abandon all the comprehension it affords of the inter-connection between health, perversion and neurosis. Psychoanalysis stands or falls by the recognition of the sexual component-impulses, of the erotogenic zones, and by the consequent expansion of the idea of the "sexual function" as opposed to the narrower one of a "genital function." Moreover, observation of the normal development of the child is in itself sufficient to obviate any such temptation.

(c) In the sphere of character-development we again meet with the same instinctual forces whose workings we have already discovered in the neuroses. A sharp theoretical distinction between the two becomes, however, necessary from the single circumstance that in character-formation one feature is absent which is peculiar to the mechanism of neurosis—namely, miscarriage of repression and the return of the repressed. In the formation of character either repression is not at work at all or it easily attains its aim, which is to replace the repressed impulses by reaction-formations and sublimations. The processes of character-formation are therefore less transparent and less accessible to analysis than those of neurosis.

In this very sphere of character-formation, however, we do come upon a good analogy to the case of illness described, one which confirms the existence of the pregenital sadistic-anal-erotic sexual organization. It is well known, and has been a matter for much complaint, that women often alter strangely in character after they have abandoned their genital functions. They become quarrelsome, peevish and argumentative, petty and miserly; in fact, they display sadistic and anal-erotic traits which were not theirs in the era of womanliness. Writers of comedy and satirists have in all ages launched their invectives against the "old termagant" into which the sweet maiden, the loving woman, the tender mother, has deteriorated. This metamorphosis corresponds, as can be seen, with a regression of sexual life to the pregenital anal-sadistic level, the one in which we have found the predisposition to obsessional neurosis. It would thus be not only the precursor of the genital phase, but often enough its successor and resolvent as well, after the genital function has been fulfilled.

The comparison of this alteration of character with the obsessional neurosis is very impressive. Both are the result of regression, but in the first the regression is complete and follows a process of repression (or suppression) which has been accomplished smoothly; in neurosis we find conflict, followed by efforts to prevent regression, reaction-formations against it and symptom-constructions representing compromises between the opposing tendencies, also a cleavage of the mental processes into those which are capable of reaching consciousness and those which are unconscious.

(d) Our formulation of the pregenital sexual organization is incomplete in two directions. First it takes no account of the behaviour of other component-impulses and is content to single out the very definite primacy of sadism and anal erotism. There are many points concerning the other component-impulses which would repay careful investigation and collation; the desire for knowledge, in particular, often gives one the impression that it can actually take the place of sadism in the mechanism of the obsessional neurosis. After all, it is at bottom an off-shoot, sublimated and raised to the intellectual sphere, of the possessive instinct and its rejection in the form of doubt bulks largely in the picture of obsessional neurosis.

The other defect in our formulation is much more important.

We know that a full understanding of any neurotic predisposition from the developmental point of view is never complete without taking into account not merely the stage of libido-development at which fixation occurs but also the stage of ego-development. Our concern has been confined to libido-development, however, and consequently does not afford all the information we are entitled to expect. At the present time little is known of the developmental stages of the ego-instincts; I know only of one highly promising attempt by Ferenczi[5] to approach this problem. I do not know if it will seem too daring if I assume from the clues at our disposal that a premature advance of the ego-development ahead of the libido-development contributes to the obsessional disposition. Precocious development of this kind on the part of the ego-instincts would necessitate the formation of object-choice before the sexual function had reached its final configuration and would thus leave a legacy of fixation at the pregenital stage of sexual organization. When we take into consideration that, in order to protect object-love from the hostility which lurks behind it, the obsessional neurotic is compelled to build up an overconscientious system of ultra-morality, one feels inclined to go a step further and regard a certain degree of precocious ego-development as characteristic of human nature in general and to trace the capacity for morality to the circumstance that, developmentally, hate is the forerunner of love. Perhaps this is the meaning of a statement made by W. Stekel, which seemed incomprehensible to me at the time, that hate, not love, is the primary state of feeling between human beings.[6]

(e) The above considerations have some bearing on the subject of hysteria; they bring out the intimate relation between this condition and the last phase of libido-development characterized by genital primacy and the introduction of the reproductive function. These newly acquired activities undergo repression in hysteria, but no regression to the pregenital phase takes place. The inadequacy of this description of an hysterical disposition, due to our incom-

---

[5]Ferenczi, *Stages in the Development of the Sense of Reality.*

[6]W. Stekel, *Die Sprache des Traumes*, 1911, S. 536.

plete understanding of ego-development, makes itself felt more than in the case of the obsessional neurosis.

Nevertheless it is not difficult to see that a different regression to an earlier level occurs in hysteria too. As we know, the sexuality of a female child is governed by an organ that is essentially male (the clitoris) and the manifestations of this sexuality are in many ways similar to those occurring in boys. A final thrust of development at the period of puberty must eliminate this masculine sexuality and promote the vagina, a derivative of the cloaca, to the position of leading erotogenic zone. Hence it is very usual in women suffering from hysteria for a reactivation of this repressed masculine sexuality to take place, against which defensive measures are directed by the ego-syntonic instincts. It seems to me, however, a little premature to discuss the problems of hysterical predisposition at this point.

A Case of Paranoia Running Counter to the Psychoanalytical Theory of the Disease[1]
(1915)

Some years ago a well-known lawyer consulted me about a case which had raised some doubts in his mind. A young woman had asked him to protect her from the molestations of a man who had drawn her into a love-affair. She declared that this man had abused her confidence by getting invisible witnesses to photograph them in the act of love-making, and that by exhibiting these pictures he could bring shame upon her and force her to resign her position. Her legal adviser was experienced enough to recognize the pathological stamp of this accusation; he remarked, however, that, as what appears to be incredible often actually happens, he would appreciate the opinion of a psychiatrist in this matter. He promised to call on me again, accompanied by the plaintiff.

Before I continue the account, I will say that I have altered the *milieu* of this case in order to preserve the incognito of those concerned, but that I have altered nothing else. I consider it an undesirable practice, however excellent the motive may be, to alter any detail in the presentation of a case. One can never tell which aspect of a case may be picked out by a reader of independent judgement, and one runs the risk of giving the latter a false impression.

Shortly afterwards I met the patient in person. She was thirty years old, a singularly attractive and handsome girl, who looked

---

[1] First published in *Zeitschrift*, Bd. III., 1915; reprinted in *Sammlung*, Vierte Folge. [Translated by Edward Glover.]

much younger than her age and was of a distinctly feminine type. She obviously resented the interference of a doctor and took no trouble to hide her distrust. It was clear that only the influence of her legal adviser, who was present, induced her to tell the following story, one which set me a problem to be referred to later. Neither in her manner nor by any kind of expression of emotion did she betray the slightest shame or shyness, although some such state of mind would naturally arise on such an occasion in the presence of a stranger. She was completely under the spell of the apprehension that her experience had induced in her.

For many years she had been on the staff of a big institution, where she held a responsible post. Her work had given her satisfaction and had been appreciated by her employers. She had never sought any love-affairs with men, but had lived quietly with her old mother whose only support she was. She had no brothers or slsters; her father had died many years before. Recently an official in the same institution, a cultured and attractive man, had paid her attentions and she had inevitably been drawn towards him. For external reasons, marriage was out of the question, but the man would not hear of giving up their relationship on that account. He had pleaded that it was senseless to sacrifice to social convention all that they longed for, that they had an indisputable right to enjoy and that could enrich their life as nothing else could. As he had promised not to expose her to any risk, she had at least consented to go to his bachelor rooms in the daytime. There they kissed and embraced as they lay side by side, and he began to admire the charms which were now partly revealed. In the midst of their love-making she was suddenly frightened by a noise, a kind of knock or tick. It came from the direction of the writing-desk, which was standing sideways in front of the window; the space between desk and window was partly filled up by a heavy curtain. She had at once asked her friend what this noise meant, and was told, so she said, that it probably came from the small clock on the writing-desk. I shall take the liberty, however, of commenting below on this part of her narrative.

As she left the house she had met two men on the staircase who whispered to each other as she passed. One of the strangers was carrying something which was wrapped up and looked rather like a box. She was much exercised over this meeting, and even on the way home her thoughts had already taken the following shape: the box could easily have been a camera, and the man a photographer who had been hidden behind the curtain while she was in the room; the tick had been the noise of the shutter; the photograph had been taken as soon as he saw her in a particularly compromising position of which he had wished to obtain pictorial evidence. From that moment nothing could abate her suspicion. She pursued her lover with reproaches and pestered him for explanations and reassurances, not only when they met but also by letter. In vain did he try to convince her that his feelings were sincere and that her suspicions were entirely without foundation. At last she called on the lawyer, told him of her experience and handed over the letters which the accused had written to her about the incident. Later I had an opportunity of seeing some of these letters. They made a very favourable impression on me, and contained mainly expressions of regret that such an unspoilt and tender understanding should have been destroyed by this "unfortunate morbid idea."

I need hardly justify my agreement with this view. But the case had a special interest for me other than a merely diagnostic one. The view had already been put forward in psychoanalytical literature that patients suffering from paranoia are struggling against an intensification of their homosexual trends, this pointing back to a narcissistic object-choice. And a further interpretation had been made: that the persecutor is in reality the loved person, past or present. A synthesis of the two propositions would lead us to expect that the persecutor must be of the same sex as the persecuted. We had not, it is true, asserted that paranoia is always without exception conditioned by homosexuality; but only because our observations were not sufficiently numerous. It was one of those conceptions which in view of certain connections become important only when universal application can be claimed for them. In psychiatric literature there is certainly no lack of cases in which the patient imagines himself persecuted by a person of the opposite sex. It is one thing, however, to read of such cases.

and quite a different thing to come into personal contact with one. The relation between paranoia and homosexuality had so far been easily confirmed by my own observations and analyses and by those of my friends. But the present case emphatically contradicted it. The girl seemed to defend herself against love for a man by transforming the lover straightaway into a persecutor: there was no sign of the influence of a woman, no trace of a struggle against a homosexual attachment.

In these circumstances the simplest thing to do would have been to abandon the theory that the delusion of persecution invariably depends on homosexuality, and with it everything based on this view. Either that theory must be given up or else, in view of this lack of conformation to rule, one must side with the lawyer and assume that this was no paranoiac combination but an actual experience which had been accurately interpreted. But I saw another way out, by which a final verdict could for the moment be postponed. I recollected how often wrong views were taken about psychotic patients simply because they had not been studied carefully enough and had not told enough about themselves. I therefore said that I could not form an immediate opinion, and asked the lady to call on me a second time, when she could relate her story again and add any details that had perhaps been omitted. Thanks to the lawyer's influence I secured this promise from the reluctant patient; while the former aided me in another way by saying that at our second meeting his presence would be superfluous.

The story told on this second occasion did not conflict with the previous narrative, but the additional details supplied resolved all doubts and difficulties. To begin with, she had visited the young man not once but twice. It was on the second occasion that she had been disturbed by the suspicious noise: she had suppressed, or omitted to mention, the first visit because it had no longer seemed of importance to her. On the first day nothing had happened, but something did happen on the day following. Her department in the business concern was under the direction of an elderly lady whom she described as follows: "She has white hair like my mother." This elderly superintendent had a great liking for her and treated her with affection, though sometimes she teased her;

the girl regarded herself as her particular favourite. On the day after her first visit to the young man's rooms he appeared in the office to discuss some business matter with this elderly woman. During their whispered conversation the patient suddenly felt convinced that he was telling her about their adventure of the previous day, and even concluded that there had been for some time a love-relationship between the two which she had overlooked. The white-haired motherly old lady now knew everything, and her speech and conduct throughout the rest of the day seemed to confirm the patient's suspicion. At the first opportunity she took her lover to task about his treachery. He naturally raised a vigorous protest against what he called a senseless accusation. This time he succeeded in freeing her from her delusion and she regained enough confidence to repeat her visit to his room a short time, I believe a few weeks, afterwards. The rest we know from her first narrative.

These new details remove first of all any doubts as to the pathological nature of her suspicion. It is easy to see that the white-haired elderly manageress is a mother-substitute, that in spite of his youth the lover has been put in the place of the father, and that the strength of the mother-complex has driven the patient to suspect a love-relationship between these ill-matched partners, however unlikely such a relation might be. Moreover, this fresh information resolves the apparent contradiction with the view maintained by psychoanalysis, that the development of a delusion of persecution is conditioned by an over-powerful homosexual bond. The *original* persecutor—the agency whose influence the patient wishes to escape—is here again not a man but a woman. The manageress knows about the girl's love-affairs, disapproves of them, and shows her disapproval by mysterious allusions. The woman's attachment to her own sex hinders her attempts to adopt a person of the other sex as a love-object. Love for the mother becomes the protagonist of all those tendencies which, acting as her "conscience," would arrest the girl's first step along the new road to normal sexual satisfaction, in many respects a dangerous one; and indeed it succeeds in destroying her relation with the man.

When the mother hinders or arrests a daughter's sexual activity she fulfils a normal function. This function is outlined in the early relationship between mother and infant; it is based on powerful, unconscious motivations, and has the sanction of society. It is the daughter's business to emancipate herself from this influence and to decide for herself on broad and rational grounds what her share of enjoyment or denial of sexual pleasure shall be. If in the attempt to emancipate herself she falls a victim to a neurosis there is present a mother-complex, which is as a rule over-powerful, and is certainly unmastered. This conflicts with the new direction taken by the libido, and the conflict is disposed of in the form of this or that neurosis, according to the disposition present. The manifestations of the neurotic reaction will always be determined, however, not by the actual relation to the actual mother, but by the infantile relation to the original mother-imago.

We know that our patient had been fatherless for many years: we may also assume that she would not have kept away from men up to the age of thirty if she had not been sustained by a powerful emotional attachment to her mother. This supporting tie becomes a burdensome obstacle when her libido begins to respond to the call of a man's insistent wooing. She tries to free herself, to throw off her homosexual bond; and her disposition, which need not be discussed here, enables her to achieve this by the formation of a paranoiac delusion. The mother thus becomes the hostile and jealous watcher and persecutor. As such she could be overcome, were it not that the mother-complex retained power enough to carry out its purpose of keeping her at a distance from men. At the end of the first phase of the conflict the patient has thus become estranged from the mother without having definitely gone over to the man. Indeed, both of them are plotting against her. Then with a vigorous effort the man draws her to himself. She conquers the mother's opposition in her mind and is willing to grant her lover a second meeting. In the later developments the mother does not reappear, but we may rightly assume that in this earlier phase the lover was not a persecutor directly; his character as such was acquired, as it were, through the mother and in virtue of his relationship to the mother, a factor which played the chief part in the formation of the first delusion.

One would think that the resistance was now definitely over-come, that the girl who had until now been bound to her mother had succeeded in coming to love a man. But after the second visit a new delusion appears, which by making ingenious use of acci-dental circumstances, destroys this love and thus successfully car-ries through the purpose of the mother-complex. It still seems strange that a woman should protect herself against the love of a man by means of a paranoiac delusion; but before examining this state of things more closely, let us glance at the accidental circum-stances that form the basis of this second delusion, the one aimed exclusively against the man.

Lying partly undressed on a sofa alongside her lover, she hears some noise, a tick, knock, or tap. She does not know its cause but she arrives at an interpretation of it after meeting on the stair-case two men, one of whom carries something that looks like a covered box. She is convinced that someone acting on instructions from her lover has watched and photographed her during their intimate tête-à-tête. We, of course, are far from thinking that had the fatal noise not occurred the delusion would not have been formed; on the contrary, we see behind this accidental circum-stance something compulsive, asserting itself again as inevitably as when the patient divined a love-relationship between her lover and the elderly manageress, her mother-substitute. Among the wealth of unconscious phantasies of neurotics, and probably of all human beings, there is one which is seldom absent and can be disclosed by analysis, concerning the watching of sexual inter-course between the parents. I call these phantasies, together with those of seduction, castration, and others, *primal phantasies;* and I shall discuss more fully elsewhere their origin and the relation of them to individual experience. The accidental noise is merely a stimulus which activates the typical phantasy of eavesdropping, itself a component of the parental complex. Indeed, it is doubtful whether we can rightly call it "accidental." As O. Rank has re-marked to me, it is an essential part of the phantasy of listening, and it reproduces either the sounds which betray parental inter-course or those by which the listening child fears to betray itself. But now we know at once where we stand. The lover is still the father, but the patient herself has taken the mother's place. The part of the listener must then be allotted to a third person. We can see by what means the girl has freed herself from her homosexual dependence on the mother. A partial regression has taken place; instead of choosing her mother as a love-object, she has identified herself with her, she herself has become the mother. The possibility of this regression points to the narcissistic origin of her homosexual object-choice and with that to the paranoiac disposition in her. One might sketch a train of thought which would bring about a similar result: "If mother does it, I can do it too; I've just as good a right as she."

One can go a step further in disproving the accidental nature of the noise. We do not, however, ask our readers to follow us, since the absence of thorough analytic investigation makes it impossible in this case to go beyond a certain probability. The patient mentioned in her first interview with me that she had immediately demanded an explanation of the noise, and had been told that it was probably the ticking of the little clock on the table. I take the liberty of assuming that this piece of information was a mistaken memory. It seems to me much more likely that at first she did not react to the noise at all, and that it became significant only after she met the two men on the staircase. Her friend, who had probably not even heard the noise, ventured the explanation, perhaps on some later occasion when she assailed him with her suspicions, "I don't know what noise you can have heard. Perhaps it was the little clock; it sometimes ticks like that." A subsequent use of impressions and displacement of recollections such as this occurs frequently in paranoia and is characteristic of it. But as I never met the man and did not continue the analysis of the woman, my hypothesis cannot be proved.

I might go still further in the analysis of this apparently real "accident." I do not believe that the clock ever ticked or that any noise was to be heard at all. The woman's situation justified a sensation of throbbing in the clitoris. This was what she subsequently projected as a perception of an external object. Similar things occur in dreams. An hysterical patient of mine once related to me a short "awakening" dream to which she could bring no spontaneous associations. She dreamt simply that someone knocked and then she awoke. Nobody had knocked, but during the previous nights she had been awakened by unpleasant sensations of pollutions: she had thus a motive for awakening as soon as she felt the first sign of genital excitation. There had been a "knocking" of the clitoris. In the case of our paranoiac patient, I should substitute for the accidental noise a similar process of projection. I certainly cannot guarantee that during our short acquaintance the patient, who was reluctantly yielding to necessity, gave me a truthful account of all that had taken place during the two meetings. But an isolated clitoris-contraction would be in keeping with her statement that no contact of the genitals had taken place. In her subsequent rejection of the man, lack of satisfaction undoubtedly played a part as well as "conscience."

Let us consider again the outstanding fact that the patient protects herself against her love for a man by means of a paranoiac delusion. The key to the understanding of this is to be found in the evolution of the delusion. As we might have expected, the latter was at first aimed against the woman; *the subsequent progression from a female to a male object* was, however, made on a *paranoiac basis*. Such a progression is unusual in paranoia; as a rule we find that the victim of persecution remains fixated to the same persons and therefore to the same sex as before the paranoiac transformation set in. But neurotic disorder does not preclude a progression of this kind, and our observation may be the prototype of many others. There are many similar processes beside that in paranoia which have never yet been classified under this heading, amongst them some which are very familiar. The so-called neurasthenic, for example, is prevented by his unconscious incestuous fixation from choosing a strange woman as a love-object; his sexual activity must remain within the limits of phantasy. But within the limits of this phantasy he achieves the progress denied him in reality and he succeeds in replacing mother and sister by new objects. Since the veto of the censorship does not then come into action, he can become conscious of his choice of these substitute-figures.

Alongside the phenomena of attempted progression from a position recently achieved, as a rule by regression, we may group the efforts made in some neuroses to regain a libido-position once held and subsequently lost. Indeed we can hardly draw any abstract distinction between these two categories. We are too apt to think that the conflict underlying a neurosis is removed when the symptom has been formed. In reality the struggle often goes on after this. Fresh instinctual components arise on both sides, and these continue it. The symptom itself becomes an object of this struggle; certain trends anxious to preserve it conflict with others which strive to remove it and to re-establish the *status quo*. In the attempt to render the symptom nugatory the expedient is often adopted of trying to regain through new channels what has been lost and is now frustrated by the symptom. These facts throw much light on a statement made by C. G. Jung to the effect that a peculiar psychic inertia, hostile to change and progress, is the fundamental condition of neurosis. This inertia is in fact most peculiar; it is not a general one, but is highly specialized; it is not even all-powerful within its own scope, but fights against tendencies towards progress and reconstruction which remain active even after the formation of neurotic symptoms. If we search for the starting-point of this specialized inertia, we discover that it is the expression of a conjunction of instincts with impressions and with the objects connected with these impressions. This conjunction has been effected very early, is very hard to resolve, and has the effect of bringing the development of the instincts concerned to a standstill. Or in other words, this specialized "psychic inertia" is only a different term, though hardly a better one, for what in psychoanalysis we are accustomed to call a *fixation*.

VII

"A Child Is Being Beaten"[1] (1919)

A Contribution to the Study of the Origin of Sexual Perversions

I

It is surprising how frequently people who come to be analysed for hysteria or an obsessional neurosis confess to having indulged in the phantasy: "A child is being beaten." Very probably it occurs even more often with other people who have not been obliged to come to this decision by manifest illness.

The phantasy has feelings of pleasure attached to it, and on their account it has been reproduced on innumerable occasions in the past or is even being reproduced still. At the climax of the imaginary situation there is almost invariably an onanistic gratification, that is to say, a gratification in the genitals. At first this takes place in accordance with the will of the person in question, but later on it does so in spite of his efforts, and with the characteristics of an obsession.

It is only with hesitation that this phantasy is confessed to. Its first appearance is recollected with uncertainty. The analytic treatment of the subject is met by unmistakable resistance. Shame and a sense of guilt are perhaps more strongly excited in this connection than when similar accounts are given of memories of the beginnings of sexual life.

---

[1]First published in *Zeitschrift*, Bd. V., 1919; reprinted in *Sammlung*, Fünfte Folge. [Translated by Alix and James Strachey.]

Eventually it becomes possible to establish that the first phantasies of the kind were entertained very early in life: certainly before school age, and not later than in the fifth or sixth year. When the child was at school and saw other children being beaten by the teacher, then, if the phantasies had become dormant, this experience called them up again, or, if they were still present, it reinforced them, and noticeably modified their content. From that time forward it was "an indefinite number" of children that were being beaten. The influence of the school was so clear that the patients concerned were at first tempted to trace back their beating-phantasies exclusively to these impressions of school life, which dated from later than their sixth year. But it was never possible for them to maintain this position; the phantasies had already been in existence before.

Though the children were no longer beaten in the higher forms at school, the influence of such occasions was replaced and more than replaced by the effects of reading, of which the importance was soon to be felt. In my patient's *milieu* it was almost always the same books whose contents gave a new stimulus to the beating-phantasies: those accessible to young people, such as the so-called *"Bibliothèque rose," Uncle Tom's Cabin*, etc. The child began to compete with these works of fiction by producing its own phantasies and by constructing a wealth of situations, and even whole institutions, in which children were beaten or were punished and disciplined in some other way because of their naughtiness and bad behaviour.

This phantasy—"a child is being beaten"—was invariably charged with a high degree of pleasure and had its issue in an act of pleasurable, auto-erotic gratification; it might therefore be expected that the sight of another child being beaten at school would also be a source of similar enjoyment. But as a matter of fact this was never so. The experience of real scenes of beating at school produced in the child who witnessed them a peculiarly excited feeling which was probably of a mixed character and in which repugnance had a large share. In a few cases the real experience of the scenes of beating was felt to be intolerable. Moreover, it was always a condition even of the elaborated phantasies of later years that the punishment should do the children no serious injury.

The question was bound to arise of what relation there might be between the importance of the beating-phantasies and the part that real corporal punishment might have played in the education of the child at home. It was impossible, on account of the one-sidedness of the material, to confirm the first suspicion that the relation was an inverse one. The individuals from whom the data for these analyses were derived were very seldom beaten in their childhood, or were at all events not brought up by the help of the rod. Naturally, however, each of these children was bound to have become aware at one time or another of the superior physical strength of its parents or educators; the fact that in every nursery the children themselves at time come to blows requires no special emphasis.

As regards the early and simple phantasies which could not obviously be traced to the influence of school impressions or of scenes taken from books, further information would have been welcome. Who was the child that was being beaten? The one who was himself producing the phantasy or another? Was it always the same child or as often as not a different one? Who was it beating the child? A grown-up person? And if so, who? Or did the child imagine that he himself was beating another one? Nothing could be ascertained that threw any light upon all these questions—only the one timid reply: "I know nothing more about it: a child is being beaten."

Inquiries as to the sex of the child that was being beaten met with more success, but none the less brought no enlightenment. Sometimes the answer was: "Always boys," or "Only girls;" more often it was: "I don't know," or "It doesn't matter which." But the point to which the questions were directed, the discovery of some constant relation between the sex of the child producing the phantasy and that of the child that was being beaten, was never established. Now and again another characteristic detail of the content of the phantasy came to light: "A little child is being beaten on its naked bottom."

In these circumstances it was impossible at first even to decide whether the pleasure attaching to the beating-phantasy was to be described as sadistic or masochistic.

II

A phantasy of this kind, arising, perhaps from some accidental cause, in early childhood and retained for the purpose of auto-erotic gratification, can, in the light of our present knowledge, only be regarded as a primary trait of perversion. One of the components of the sexual function has, it seems, developed in advance of the rest, has made itself prematurely independent, has undergone fixation and in consequence been withdrawn from the later processes of development, and has in this way given evidence of a peculiar and anomalous constitution in the individual. We know that an infantile perversion of this sort need not persist for a whole life-time; later on it can be subjected to repression, be replaced by a reaction-formation, or be transformed by sublima-tion. (It is possible, however, that sublimation arises out of some special process which would be kept in the background by repres-sion.) But if these events do not take place, then the perversion persists to maturity; and whenever we find a sexual aberration in adults—perversion, fetishism, inversion—we are justified in ex-pecting that anamnestic investigation will reveal some experience in the nature of a fixation in childhood. Indeed, long before the days of psychoanalysis, observers like Binet were able to trace the strange sexual aberrations of maturity back to similar impressions and to precisely the same period of childhood, namely, the fifth or sixth year. But at this point the inquiry was brought up against the limitations of our knowledge; for the impressions that brought about the fixation were without any traumatic force. They were for the most part commonplace and unexciting to other people. It was impossible to say why the sexual impulse had undergone fixa-tion particularly upon them. It was possible, however, to look for their significance in the fact that they provided an opportunity of fixation (even though it was an accidental one) for precisely that sexual component which was prematurely developed and was ready to spring forward. We had in any case to be prepared to find a provisional end somewhere or other to the chain of causal connection; and the congenital constitution seemed exactly to correspond with what was required for a stopping-place of that kind.

If the sexual component which has broken loose prematurely is the sadistic one, then we may expect, on the basis of knowledge derived from other sources, that a disposition to an obsessional neurosis will result from its subsequent repression. This expectation cannot be said to be contradicted by the results of inquiry. The present short paper is based upon the exhaustive study of six cases (four female and two male). Of these, two were cases of obsessional neurosis; one extremely severe and incapacitating, the other of moderate severity and quite well accessible to influence. There was also a third case which at all events exhibited clearly marked individual traits of obsessional neurosis. The fourth case, it must be admitted, was one of straightforward hysteria, with pains and inhibitions; and the fifth patient, who had come to be analysed merely on account of lack of decision in life, would not have been classified at all by coarse clinical diagnosis, or would have been dismissed as "psychasthenic." There is no need for feeling disappointed over these statistics. In the first place, we know that not every disposition is necessarily developed into a disorder; in the second place, we ought to be content to explain the facts before us, and ought as a rule to avoid the additional task of making it clear why something has *not* taken place.

The present state of our knowledge would allow us to make our way so far and no farther towards the comprehension of beating-phantasies. But in the mind of the analytical physician there remains an uneasy suspicion that this is not a final solution of the problem. He is obliged to admit to himself that to a great extent these phantasies subsist apart from the rest of the content of the neurosis, and find no proper place in its structure. But impressions of this kind, as I know from my own experience, are only too easily put on one side.

III

Strictly considered—and why should this question not be considered with all possible strictness?—analytic work deserves to be recognized as genuine psychoanalysis only when it has succeeded in removing the amnesia which conceals from the adult his knowledge of his childhood from its beginning (that is, from about the second to the fifth year). This cannot be said among analysts too emphatically or repeated too often. The motives for disregarding this reminder are, indeed, intelligible. It would be desirable to obtain practical results in a shorter time and with less trouble. But at the present time theoretical knowledge is still far more important to all of us than therapeutic success, and anyone who neglects childhood analysis is bound to fall into the most disastrous errors. The emphasis which is laid here upon the importance of the earliest experiences does not imply any underestimation of the influence of later ones. But the later impressions of life speak loudly enough through the mouth of the patient, while it is the physician who has to raise his voice on behalf of the claims of childhood.

It is in the years of childhood between the ages of two and four or five that the congenital libidinal factors are first awakened by actual experiences and become attached to certain complexes. The beating-phantasies which are now under discussion show themselves only towards the end of this period or after its termination. So it may quite well be that they have an earlier history, that they go through a process of development, that they represent an end-product and not an initial manifestation.

This suspicion is confirmed by analysis. A systematic application of it shows that beating-phantasies have an historical development which is by no means simple, and in the course of which they are changed in most respects more than once—as regards their relation to the author of the phantasy, and as regards their object, their content, and their significance.

In order to make it easier to follow these transformations in beating-phantasies I shall venture to confine my descriptions to the female cases, who, since they are four as against two, in any case constitute the greater part of my material. Moreover, beating-phantasies among men are connected with another subject, which I shall leave on one side of this paper. In my description I shall be careful to avoid being more schematic than is inevitable in presenting an average case. If then upon further observation a greater complexity of circumstances should come to light, I shall nevertheless be sure of having secured a typical occurrence and not one of an uncommon kind.

The first phase of beating-phantasies among girls must therefore belong to a very early period of childhood. Some features remain curiously indefinite, as though they were a matter of indifference. The scanty information given by the patients in their first statement, "a child is being beaten," seems to be justified in respect to this phase. But another of their features can be established with certainty, and to the same effect in every case. The child being beaten is never the one producing the phantasy, but is invariably another child, most often a brother or a sister if there is any. Since this other child may be a boy or a girl, there is no constant relation between the sex of the child producing the phantasy and that of the child being beaten. The phantasy, then, is certainly not masochistic. It would be tempting to call it sadistic, but one cannot neglect the fact that the child producing the phantasy is never doing the beating himself. The actual identity of the person beating remains obscure at first. Only this much can be established: it is not a child but an adult. Later on this indeterminate grown-up person becomes recognizable clearly and unambiguously as the (girl's) *father*.

This first phase of the beating-phantasy is therefore completely represented by the phrase: *"My father is beating the child."* I am betraying a great deal of what is to be brought forward later when instead of this I say: "My father is beating the child *whom I hate.*" Moreover, one may hesitate to say whether the characteristics of a "phantasy" can yet be ascribed to this first step towards the later beating-phantasy. It is perhaps rather a question of recollections of events which have been witnessed, or of desires which have arisen on various occasions. But these doubts are of no importance.

Profound transformations have taken place between this first phase and the next. It is true that the person beating remains the same (that is, the father); but the child who is beaten has been changed into another one and is now invariably the child producing the phantasy. The phantasy is accompanied by a high degree of pleasure, and has now acquired a significant content, with the origin of which we shall be concerned later. Now, therefore, the wording runs: *"I am being beaten by my father."* It is of an unmistakably masochistic character.

This second phase is the most important and the most momentous of all. But we may say of it in a certain sense that it has never had a real existence. It is never remembered, it has never succeeded in becoming conscious. It is a construction of analysis, but it is no less a necessity on that account.

The third phase once more resembles the first. It has the wording which is familiar to us from the patient's statement. The person beating is never the father, but is either left undetermined just as in the first phase, or turns in a characteristic way into a representative of the father, such as a teacher. The figure of the child who is producing the beating-phantasy no longer itself appears in it. In reply to pressing inquiries the patients only declare: "I am probably looking on." Instead of the one child that is being beaten, there are now a number of children present as a rule. Most frequently it is boys who are being beaten (in girls' phantasies), but none of them is personally known to the subject. The situation of being beaten, which was originally simple and monotonous, may go through the most complicated alterations and elaborations; and punishments and humiliations of another kind may be substituted for the beating itself. But the essential characteristic which distinguishes even the simplest phantasies of this phase from those of the first, and which establishes the connection with the intermediate phase, is this: the phantasy now has strong and unambiguous sexual excitement attached to it, and so provides a means for onanistic gratification. But this is precisely what is puzzling. By what path has the phantasy of strange and unknown boys being beaten (a phantasy which has by this time become sadistic) found its way into the permanent possession of the little girl's libidinal tendencies?

Nor can we conceal from ourselves that the interrelations and sequence of the three phases of the beating-phantasy, as well as all its other peculiarities, have so far remained quite unintelligible.

IV

If the analysis is traced through the early period to which the beating-phantasies are referred and from which they are recollected, it shows us the child involved in the agitations of its parental complex.

The affections of the little girl are fixed upon her father, who has probably done all he could to win her love, and in this way has sown the seeds of an attitude of hatred and rivalry towards her mother. This attitude exists side by side with a current of affectionate dependence upon her, and as years go on it may be destined to come into consciousness more and more clearly and forcibly, or to give an impetus to an excessive reaction of devotion to her. But it is not with the girl's relation to her mother that the beating-phantasy is connected. There are other children in the nursery, only a few years older or younger, who are disliked on all sorts of other grounds, but chiefly because the parents' love has to be shared with them, and for this reason they are repulsed with all the wild energy characteristic of the emotional life of those years. If it is a younger brother or sister (as in three of my four cases) it is despised as well as hated; yet it attracts to itself the share of affection which the blinded parents are always ready to give to the youngest child, and this is a spectacle the sight of which cannot be avoided. One soon learns that being beaten, even if it does not hurt very much, signifies a deprivation of love and a humiliation. And many children who believed themselves securely enthroned in the unshakable affection of their parents have by a single blow been cast down from all the heavens of their imaginary omnipotence. The idea of the father beating this hateful child is therefore an agreeable one, quite apart from whether he has actually been seen doing it. It means: "My father does not love this other child, *he loves only me.*"

This then is the content and meaning of the beating-phantasy in its first phase. The phantasy obviously gratifies the child's jealousy and is dependent upon the erotic side of its life, but it is also powerfully reinforced by its egoistic interests. It remains doubtful, therefore, whether it ought to be described as purely "sexual," nor can one venture to call it "sadistic." As is well known, all the signs upon which we are accustomed to base our distinctions tend to melt as we come nearer to the source. So perhaps we may say in words like those of the promise given by the three Witches to Banquo: "Not clearly sexual, not in itself sadistic, but yet the stuff from which both will later come." In any case, however, there is no ground for suspecting that in this first phase the phantasy is already at the service of an excitement which involves the genitals and finds its outlet in an onanistic act.

It is clear that the sexual life of the child has reached the stage of genital organization, now that its incestuous love has achieved this premature object-choice. This can be demonstrated more easily in the case of boys, but is also indisputable in the case of girls. Something like a premonition of what are later to be the final and normal sexual aims governs the libidinal tendencies of a child; we may justly wonder why this should be so, but we may regard it as a proof of the fact that the genitals have already taken on their share in the process of excitation. With boys the wish to beget a child from their mother is never absent, with girls the wish to have a child by their father is equally constant; and this in spite of their being completely incapable of forming any clear idea of the means of fulfilling these wishes. The child seems to be convinced that the genitals have something to do with the matter, even though in its constant brooding it may look for the essence of the presumed intimacy between its parents in relations of another sort, such as in their sleeping together, micturating in each other's presence, etc.; and material of the latter kind can be more easily apprehended in verbal images than the mystery that is connected with the genitals.

But the time comes when this early blossoming is nipped by the frost. None of these incestuous loves can avoid the fate of repression. They may succumb to it on the occasion of some discoverable external event which leads to disillusionment—such as unexpected slights, the unwelcome birth of a new brother or sister (which is felt as faithlessness), etc.; or the same thing may happen owing to internal conditions apart from any such events, perhaps simply because their yearning remains unsatisfied too long. It is unquestionably true that the events are not the effective causes, but that these love-affairs are bound to be wrecked sooner or later, though we cannot say upon what. Most probably they pass because their time is over, because the children have entered upon a new phase of development in which they are compelled to recapitulate from the history of mankind the repression of an incestuous object-choice, just as at an earlier stage they were obliged to effect an object-choice of that very sort.[2] Nothing that is unconsciously present as a mental product of the incestuous love-impulses is taken over by consciousness in the new phase; and whatever has already come into consciousness is expelled from it. At the same time as this process of repression takes place, a sense of guilt appears. This is also of unknown origin, but there is no doubt whatever that it is connected with the incestuous wishes, and that it is justified by the persistence of those wishes in the unconscious.

The phantasy of the period of incestuous love had said: "He (my father) loves only me, and not the other child, for he is beating it." The sense of guilt can discover no punishment more severe than the reversal of this triumph: "No, he does not love you, for he is beating you." In this way the phantasy of the second phase, that of being beaten by the father, is a direct expression of the sense of guilt, to which the love for the father is now subordinated. The phantasy, therefore, has become masochistic. So far as I know, this is always so; a sense of guilt is invariably the factor that transforms sadism into masochism. But this is certainly not the whole content of masochism. The sense of guilt cannot have won the field alone; a share must also fall to the love-impulse. We must remember that we are dealing with children in whom the sadistic component was able for constitutional reasons to develop prematurely and in isolation. We need not abandon this point of view. It is precisely such children who find it particularly easy to hark back to the pregenital, sadistic-anal organization of their sexual life. If the genital organization, when it has scarcely been effected, is met by repression, it not only follows that every mental counterpart of the incestuous love becomes unconscious, or remains so, but there is another result as well: a regressive debasement of the genital organization itself to a lower level. "My father loves me" was meant in a genital sense; owing to the regression it is turned into "My father is beating me (I am being beaten

---

[2]Cf. the part played by Fate in the myth of Oedipus.

by my father).'' This being beaten is now a meeting-place between the sense of guilt and sexual love. *It is not only the punishment for the forbidden genital relation, but also the regressive substitute for it,* and from this latter source it derives the libidinal excitation which is from this time forward attached to it, and which finds its outlet in onanistic acts. Here for the first time we have the essence of masochism.

This second phase—the child's phantasy of being itself beaten by its father—remains as a rule unconscious, probably in consequence of the intensity of the repression. I cannot explain why nevertheless in one of my six cases, that of a male, it was consciously remembered. This man, now grown up, had preserved the fact clearly in his memory that he used to employ the idea of being beaten by his mother for the purpose of onanism, though to be sure he soon substituted for his own mother the mothers of his school-fellows or other women who in some way resembled her. It must not be forgotten that when a boy's incestuous phantasy is transformed into the corresponding masochistic one, one more reversal has to take place than in the case of a girl, namely the substitution of passivity for activity; and this additional degree of distortion may save the phantasy from having to remain unconscious as a result of repression. In this way the sense of guilt would be satisfied by regression instead of by repression. In the female cases the sense of guilt, in itself perhaps more exacting, could be appeased only by a combination of the two.

In two of my four female cases an artistic superstructure of daydreams, which was of great significance for the life of the person concerned, had grown up over the masochistic beating-phantasy. The function of this superstructure was to make possible a feeling of gratified excitation, even though the onanistic act was abstained from. In one of these cases the content—being beaten by the father—was allowed to venture again into consciousness, so long as the subject's own ego was made unrecognizable by a thin disguise. The hero of these stories was invariably beaten (or later only punished, humiliated, etc.) by his father.

I repeat, however, that as a rule the phantasy remains unconscious, and can only be reconstructed in the course of the analysis.

This fact perhaps vindicates patients who say they remember that with them onanism made its appearance before the third phase of the beating-phantasy (shortly to be discussed), and that this phase was only a later addition, made perhaps under the impression of scenes at school. Every time we have given credit to these statements we have felt inclined to assume that the onanism was at first under the dominion of unconscious phantasies and that conscious ones were substituted for them later.

We look upon the beating-phantasy in its familiar third phase, which is its final form, as a substitute of this sort. Here the child who produces the phantasy appears at most as a spectator, while the father persists in the shape of a teacher or some other person in authority. The phantasy, which now resembles that of the first phase, seems to have become sadistic once more. It appears as though in the phrase, "My father is beating the other child, he loves only me," the stress has been shifted back on to the first part after the second part has undergone repression. But only the form of this phantasy is sadistic; the gratification which is derived from it is masochistic. Its significance lies in the fact that it has taken over the libidinal cathexis of the repressed portion and at the same time the sense of guilt which is attached to its content. All of the many indeterminate children who are being beaten by the teacher are, after all, nothing more than substitutes for the child itself.

We find here for the first time too something like a constant relation of sex among the persons who play a part in the phantasy. The children who are being beaten are almost invariably boys, in the phantasies of boys just as much as in those of girls. This characteristic is naturally not to be explained by any rivalry between the sexes, as otherwise of course in the phantasies of boys it would be girls who were being beaten; and it has nothing to do with the sex of the child who was hated in the first place; but it points to a complication in the case of girls. When they turn away from their incestuous love for their father, with its genital significance, they easily abandon their feminine rôle. They spur their "masculinity complex" (v. Ophuijsen) into activity, and from that time forward only want to be boys. For that reason the whipping-boys who represent them are boys too. In both the cases of day-dreaming—one of which almost rose to the level of a work of art—the heroes were always young men; indeed women used not to come into these creations at all, and only made their first appearance after many years, and then in minor parts.

V

I hope I have brought forward my analytic observations in sufficient detail, and I should only like to add that the six cases I have mentioned so often do not exhaust my material. Like other analysts, I have at my disposal a far larger number of cases which have been investigated less thoroughly. These observations can be made use of along various lines: for elucidating the genesis of the perversions in general and of masochism in particular, and for estimating the part played by difference of sex in the dynamics of neurosis.

The most obvious result of such a discussion is its application to the origin of the perversions. The view which brought into the foreground in this connection the constitutional reinforcement or premature growth of a single sexual component is not shaken, indeed; but it is seen not to comprise the whole truth. The perversion is no longer an isolated fact in the child's sexual life, but falls into its place among the typical, not to say normal, processes of development which are familiar to us. It is brought into relation with the child's incestuous object-love, with its Oedipus-complex. It first comes into prominence in the sphere of this complex, and after the complex has broken down it remains over, often quite by itself, the inheritor of its charge of libido, and weighed down by the sense of guilt that was attached to it. The abnormal sexual constitution, finally, has shown its strength by forcing the Oedipus-complex into a particular direction, and by compelling it to leave an unusual residue behind.

A perversion in childhood, as is well known, can become the basis for the construction of a perversion having a similar sense and persisting throughout life, one which consumes the subject's whole sexual life. On the other hand the perversion can be broken off and remain in the background of a normal sexual development, from which, however, it continues to withdraw a certain amount of energy. The former case is the one which was already known before the days of analysis, but the gulf between the two is almost filled up by the analytic investigation of fully developed perversions of this sort. For we find often enough with these perverts that they too made an attempt at developing normal sexual activity, usually at the age of puberty. But their attempt had not enough force in it and was abandoned in the face of the first obstacles which inevitably arise, whereupon they fell back upon their infantile fixation once and for all.

It would naturally be important to know whether the origin of infantile perversions from the Oedipus-complex can be asserted as a general principle. While this cannot be decided without further investigation, it does not seem impossible. When we recall the anamneses which have been obtained in adult cases of perversion we cannot fail to notice that the decisive impression, the "first experience," of all these perverts, fetishists, etc., is scarcely ever referred back to a time earlier than the sixth year. At this time, however, the supremacy of the Oedipus-complex is already over; the experience which is recalled, and which has been effective in such a puzzling way, may very well have represented the legacy of that complex. The connections between the experience and the complex which is by this time repressed are bound to remain obscure so long as analysis has not thrown any light on the time before the first "pathogenic" impression. So it may be imagined how littie value is to be attached, for instance, to an assertion that a case of homosexuality is congenital, when the ground given for this belief is that ever since his eighth or sixth year the person in question has felt inclinations only towards his own sex.

If, however, the derivation of perversions from the Oedipus-complex can be generally established, our estimate of its importance will have gained added strength. For in our opinion the Oedipus-complex is the actual nucleus of neuroses, and the infantile sexuality which culminates in this complex is the true determinant of neuroses. What remains of the complex in the unconscious represents the disposition to the later development of neuroses in the adult. In this way the beating-phantasy and other analogous perverse fixations would also only be precipitates of the Oedipus-complex, scars, so to say, after the process is completed, just as the notorious "sense of inferiority" corresponds to a narcissistic scar of the same sort. In taking this view of the matter I must express my unreserved agreement with Marcinowski, who has recently put it forward most happily.[3] As is well known, this neurotic delusion of inferiority is only a partial one, and is completely compatible with the existence of a self-overestimation derived from other sources. The origin of the Oedipus-complex itself, and the destiny which compels man, probably alone among all animals, to begin his sexual life twice over, first like all other creatures in his early childhood, and then after a long interruption once more at the age of puberty—all the problems that are connected with man's "archiac inheritance"—have been discussed by me elsewhere, and I have no intention of going into them in this place.

Little light is thrown upon the genesis of masochism by our discussion of the beating-phantasy. To begin with, there seems to be a confirmation of the view that masochism is not the manifestation of a primary instinct, but originates from sadism which has been turned round and directed upon the self, that is to say, by means of regression from an object to the ego.[4] Instincts with a passive aim must be taken for granted as existing, especially among women. But passivity is not the whole of masochism. The characteristic of "pains" [Unlust] belongs to it as well,—a bewildering accompaniment to the gratification of an instinct. The transformation of sadism into masochism appears to be due to the influence of the sense of guilt concerned in the act of repression. Repression, therefore, is operative here in three ways: it renders the consequences of the genital organization unconscious, it compels that organization itself to regress to the earlier sadistic-anal stage, and it transforms the sadism of this stage into masochism, which is passive and again in a certain sense narcissistic. The second of these three effects is made possible by the weakness of

---

[3]Die erotischen *Quellen der Minderwertigkeitsgefühle*, 1918.

[4]Cf. "Instincts and their Vicissitudes," *General Psychological Theory*, Collier Books edition AS 582V.

the genital organization, which must be presupposed in these cases. The third becomes necessary because the sense of guilt takes as much objection to sadism as to incestuous object-choice genitally conceived. Again, the analyses do not tell us the origin of the sense of guilt itself. It seems to be brought along by the new phase upon which the child is entering, and if it afterwards persists it seems to correspond to a scar-like formation similar to the sense of inferiority. According to our present orientation in the structure of the ego, which is as yet uncertain, we should assign it to that institution in the mind which sets itself up as a critical conscience over against the rest of the ego, which produces Silberer's functional phenomenon in dreams, and which cuts itself loose from the ego in delusions of observation.

We may note too in passing that the analysis of the infantile perversion dealt with here is also of help in solving an old riddle— one which, it is true, has always troubled those who have not accepted psychoanalysis more than analysts themselves. Yet quite recently even E. Bleuler regarded it as a remarkable and inexplicable fact that neurotics make onanism the central point of their sense of guilt. We have long assumed that this sense of guilt relates to the onanism of early childhood and not to that of puberty, and that in the main it is to be connected not with the act of onanism but with the phantasy which, although unconscious, lies at its root—that is to say, with the Oedipus-complex.

As regards the third and apparently sadistic phase of the beating-phantasy, I have already discussed the significance that it gains from carrying with it an excitation impelling towards onanism; and I have shown how it arouses activities of phantasy which on the one hand continue the phantasy along the same line, and on the other hand neutralize it by way of compensation. Nevertheless the second phase, the unconscious and masochistic one, in which the child itself is being beaten by its father, is incomparably the more important. Not only because it continues to operate through the agency of the phase that takes its place; but we can also detect effects upon the character which are directly derived from its unconscious setting. People who harbour phantasies of this kind develop a special sensitiveness and irritability towards anyone whom they can put among the class of fathers. They allow themselves to be easily offended by a person of this kind, and in that way (to their own sorrow and cost) bring about the realization of the imagined situation of being beaten by their father. I should not be surprised if it were one day possible to prove that the same phantasy is the basis of the delusional litigiousness of paranoia.

VI

It would have been quite impossible to give a clear survey of infantile beating-phantasies if I had not limited it, except in one or two connections, to the state of things in women. I will briefly recapitulate the conclusions. The little girl's beating-phantasy goes through three phases, of which the first and third are consciously remembered, the middle one remaining unconscious. The two conscious phases appear to be sadistic, whereas the middle and unconscious one is undoubtedly of a masochistic nature; its content consists in being beaten by the father, and it carries with it the libidinal cathexis and the sense of guilt. In the first and third phantasies the child who is being beaten is always someone else; in the middle phase it is only the child itself; in the third phase it is almost invariably only boys who are being beaten. The person beating is from the first the father, but is later on a substitute taken from the class of fathers. The unconscious phantasy of the middle phase had primarily a genital significance and developed by means of repression and regression out of an incestuous wish to be loved by the father. Another fact, though its connection with the rest does not appear to be close, is that between the second and third phases the girls change their sex, for in the phantasies of the latter phase they turn into boys.

I have not been able to get so far in my knowledge of beating-phantasies among boys, perhaps because my material was unfavourable. I naturally expected to find a complete analogy between the state of things in the case of boys and in that of girls, the mother taking the father's place in the phantasy. This expectation seemed to be fulfilled; for the content of the boy's phantasy which was taken to be the corresponding one was actually his being beaten by his mother (or later on by a substitute for her). But this phantasy, in which the boy's own self was retained as the object, differed from the second phase in girls in that it was able to become conscious. If on this account, however, an attempt was made to draw a parallel between it and the third phase of the girl's phantasy, a new difference was found, for the boy's own person was not replaced by many, unknown, and undetermined children, least of all by many girls. Therefore the expectation of a complete parallelism was mistaken.

My male cases with an infantile beating-phantasy comprised only a few who did not exhibit some other gross injury to their sexual activities, but on the other hand they included a fairly large number of persons who would have to be described as true masochists in the sense of being sexual perverts. They were either people who obtained their sexual satisfaction exclusively from onanism accompanied by masochistic phantasies; or they were people who had succeeded in combining masochism with their genital activity in such a way as to bring about erection and emission, or to carry out normal coitus with the help of masochistic contrivances and under similar conditions. In addition to this there was the rarer case in which a masochist is interfered with in his perverse activities by the appearance of obsessional ideas of unbearable intensity. Now perverts who can obtain satisfaction rarely have occasion to come in search of analysis. But as regards the three classes of masochists that have been mentioned there may be strong motives to induce them to go to an analyst. The masochistic onanist finds that he is absolutely impotent if after all he does attempt coitus with a woman; and the man who has hitherto effected coitus with the help of a masochistic idea or contrivance may suddenly make the discovery that the alliance which was so convenient for him has broken down, his genital organs no longer reacting to the masochistic stimulus. We are accustomed confidently to promise recovery to psychically impotent patients who come to us for treatment; but we ought to be more guarded in making this prognosis so long as the dynamics of the disturbance are unknown to us. It comes as a disagreeable surprise if the analysis reveals the cause of the "merely psychical" impotence to be a typically masochistic attitude, perhaps deeply embedded since infancy.

As regards these masochistic men, however, a discovery is

made at this point which warns us not to pursue the analogy between their case and that of women any further at present but to judge the matter independently. For the fact emerges that in their masochistic phantasies, as well as in the contrivances they adopt for their realization, they invariably transfer themselves into the part of a woman; that is to say, their masochistic attitude coincides with a *feminine* one. This can easily be demonstrated from details of the phantasies: but many patients are even aware of it themselves, and give expression to it as a subjective conviction. It makes no difference if in a fanciful embellishment of the masochistic scene they keep up the fiction that a mischievous boy, or page, or apprentice is going to be punished. On the other hand the persons who administer chastisement are always women, both in the phantasies and in the contrivances. This is confusing enough; and the further question must be asked whether this feminine attitude already forms the basis of the masochistic element in the infantile beating-phantasy.

Let us therefore leave aside consideration of the state of things in cases of adult masochism, which it is so hard to clear up, and turn to the infantile beating-phantasy in the male sex. Analysis of the earliest years of childhood once more allows us to make a surprising discovery in this field. The phantasy which has as its content being beaten by the mother, and which is conscious or can become so, is not a primary one. It possesses a preceding stage which is invariably unconscious and has as its content: *"I am being beaten by my father."* This preliminary stage, then, really corresponds to the second phase of the phantasy in the girl. The familiar and conscious phantasy: "I am being beaten by my mother," takes the place of the third phase in the girl, in which, as has been mentioned already, unknown boys are the objects that are being beaten. I was not able to demonstrate among boys a preliminary stage of a sadistic nature that could be set beside the first phase of the phantasy in girls, but I will not now express any final disbelief in its existence, for I can readily see the possibility of meeting with more complicated types.

In the male phantasy—as I shall call it briefly, and, I hope, without any risk of being misunderstood—the being beaten also stands for being loved (in a genital sense), though this has been debased to a lower level owing to regression. So the original form of the unconscious male phantasy was not the provisional one that we have hitherto given: "I am being beaten by my father," but rather: *"I am loved by my father."* The phantasy has been transformed by the processes with which we are familiar into the conscious phantasy: *"I am being beaten by my mother."* The boy's beating-phantasy is therefore passive from the very beginning, and is derived from a feminine attitude towards his father. It corresponds with the Oedipus-complex just as the feminine one (that of the girl) does; only the parallel relation which we expected to find between the two must be given up in favour of a common character of another kind. *In both cases the beating-phantasy has its origin in an incestuous attachment to the father.*

It will help to make matters clearer if at this point I enumerate the other similarities and differences between beating-phantasies in the two sexes. In the case of the girl the unconscious masochistic phantasy starts from the normal Oedipus attitude; in that of the boy it starts from the inverted attitude, in which the father is taken as the object of love. In the case of the girl there is a first step towards the phantasy (the first phase), in which the beating bears no special significance and is performed upon a person who is viewed with jealous hatred. Both of these features are absent in the case of the boy, but this is precisely a difference which might be removed by more fortunate observation. In her transition to the conscious phantasy which takes the place of the unconscious one the girl retains the figure of her father, and in that way keeps unchanged the sex of the person beating; but she changes the figure and sex of the person being beaten, so that eventually a man is beating male children. The boy, on the contrary, changes the figure and sex of the person beating, by putting his mother in the place of his father; but he retains his own figure, with the result that the person beating and the person being beaten are of opposite sexes. In the case of the girl the situation, which was originally masochistic (passive), is transformed into a sadistic one by means of repression, and its sexual quality is effaced. In the case of the boy the situation remains masochistic, and shows a greater resemblance to the original phantasy with its genital significance, since there is a difference of sex between the person beating and the person being beaten. The boy evades his homosexuality by repressing and re-modeling his unconscious phantasy; and the remarkable thing about his later conscious phantasy is that it has for its content a feminine attitude without a homosexual object-choice. By the same process, on the other hand, the girl escapes from the demands of the erotic side of her life altogether. She turns herself in phantasy into a man, without herself becoming active in a masculine way, and is no longer anything but a spectator of the event which takes the place of a sexual act.

We are justified in assuming that no great change is effected by the *repression* of the original unconscious phantasy. Whatever is repressed from consciousness or replaced in it by something else remains intact and potentially operative in the unconscious. The effect of *regression* to an earlier stage of the sexual organization is quite another matter. As regards this we are led to believe that the state of things changes in the unconscious as well: so that in both sexes the masochistic phantasy of being beaten by the father, though not the passive phantasy of being loved by him, lives on in the unconscious after repression has taken place. There are, besides, plenty of indications that the repression has only very incompletely attained its object. The boy, who has tried to escape from a homosexual object-choice, and who has not changed his sex, nevertheless feels like a woman in his conscious phantasies, and endows the women who are beating him with masculine attri-butes and characteristics. The girl, who has even renounced her sex, and who has upon the whole accomplished a more thorough-going work of repression, nevertheless does not become freed from her father; she does not venture to do the beating herself; and since she has herself become a boy, it is principally boys whom she causes to be beaten.

I am aware that the differences that I have here described be-tween the two sexes in regard to the nature of the beating-phantasy have not been cleared up sufficiently. But I shall not make the attempt to unravel these complications by tracing out their depen-dence upon other factors, as I do not consider that the material for observation is exhaustive. So far as it goes, however, I should like to make use of it as a test for two theories. These theories stand in opposition to each other, though both of them deal with the relation between repression and sexual character, and each, according to its own view, represents the relation as a very intimate one. I may say at once that I have always regarded both theories as incorrect and misleading.

The first of these theories is anonymous. It was brought to my notice many years ago by a colleague with whom I was at that time on friendly terms. The theory is so attractive on account of its simplicity and comprehensiveness that the only wonder is that it should not hitherto have found its way into the literature of the subject except in a few scattered allusions. It is based upon the fact of the bisexual constitution of human beings, and asserts that the motive force of repression in each individual is a struggle between the two sexual characters. The dominant sex of the person, that which is the more strongly developed, has repressed the mental representation of the subordinated sex into the unconscious. Therefore the nucleus of the unconscious (that is to say, the repressed) is in each human being that side of him which belongs to the opposite sex. Such a theory as this can only have an intelligible meaning if we assume that a person's sex is to be determined by the formation of his genitals; for otherwise it would not be certain which is the stronger sex of a person, and we should run the risk of reaching from the results of our inquiry the very fact which has to serve as its point of departure. To put the theory briefly: with men, what is unconscious and repressed can be reduced to feminine instinctual impulses; and conversely with women.

The second theory is of more recent origin. It is in agreement with the first one in so far as it too represents the struggle between the two sexes as being the decisive cause of repression. In other respects it comes into conflict with the former theory; moreover, it looks for support to sociological rather than biological sources. According to this theory of the "masculine protest," formulated by Alfred Adler, every individual makes efforts not to remain on the inferior "feminine line of development" and struggles towards the masculine line of development, from which gratification can alone be derived. Adler makes the masculine protest responsible for the whole formation both of character and of neuroses. Unfortunately he makes so little distinction between the two processes, which certainly have to be kept separate, and sets altogether so little store in general by the fact of repression, that to attempt to apply the doctrine of the masculine protest to repression brings with it the risk of being misunderstood. In my opinion such an attempt could only lead us to infer that the masculine protest, the desire to break away from the feminine line of development, was in every case the motive force of repression. The repressing agency, therefore, would always be a masculine instinctual impulse, and the repressed would be a feminine one. But symptoms would also be the result of a feminine impulse, for we cannot discard the characteristic feature of symptoms—that they are substitutes for the repressed, substitutes that have made their way out in spite of repression.

Now let us take these two theories, which may be said to have in common a sexualization of the process of repression, and test them by applying them to the example of the beating-phantasies which we have been studying. The original phantasy, "I am being beaten by my father," corresponds, in the case of the boy, to a feminine attitude, and is therefore an expression of that part of his disposition which belongs to the opposite sex. If this part of him undergoes repression, the first theory seems shown to be correct; for this theory set it up as a rule that what belongs to the opposite sex is identical with the repressed. It scarcely answers to our expectations, it is true, when we find that the conscious phantasy, which arises after repression has been accomplished, nevertheless exhibits the feminine attitude once more, though this time directed towards the mother. But we will not go into these doubtful points, when the whole question can be so quickly decided. There can be no doubt that the original phantasy in the case of the girl, "I am being beaten (*i.e.* I am loved) by my father," represents a feminine attitude, and corresponds to her dominant and manifest sex; according to the theory, therefore, it ought to escape repression, and there would be no need for its becoming unconscious. But as a matter of fact it does become unconscious, and is replaced by a conscious phantasy which disavows the girl's manifest sexual character. The theory is therefore useless as an explanation of beating-phantasies, and is contradicted by the facts. It might objected that it is precisely in unmanly boys and unwoman'' that these beating-phantasies appeared and went throug' cissitudes; or that it was a trait of femininity in the masculinity in the girl which must be made responsib   is, for the production of a passive phantasy in the boy, and its repression in the girl. We should be inclined to agree with this view, but it would be none the less impossible to defend the supposed relation between manifest sexual character and the choice of what is destined for repression. In the last resort we can only see that both in male and female individuals masculine as well as feminine instinctual impulses are found, and that each can equally well undergo repression and so become unconscious.

The theory of the masculine protest seems to maintain its ground very much better on being tested in regard to the beating-phantasies. In the case of both boys and girls the beating-phantasy corresponds with a feminine attitude—one, that is, in which the individual is lingering upon the feminine line of development—and both sexes hasten to get free from this attitude by repressing the phantasy. Nevertheless, it seems to be only with the girl that the masculine protest is attended with complete success, and in that instance, indeed, an ideal example is to be found of the operation of the masculine protest. With the boy the result is not entirely satisfactory; the feminine line of development is not given up, and the boy is certainly not "on the top" in his conscious masochistic phantasy. It would therefore agree with the expectations derived from the theory if we were to recognize that this phantasy was a symptom which had come into existence through the failure of the masculine protest. It is a disturbing fact, to be sure, that the girl's phantasy, which owes its origin to the forces of repression, should also have the value and meaning of a symptom. In this instance, where the masculine protest has completely achieved its object, surely the determining condition for the formation of a symptom must be absent.

Before we are led by this difficulty to a suspicion that the whole conception of the masculine protest is inadequate to meet the problem of neuroses and perversions, and that its application to them is unfruitful, we will for a moment leave the passive beating-phantasies and turn our attention to other instinctual manifestations of infantile sexual life—manifestations which have equally undergone repression. No one can doubt that there are also wishes and phantasies which keep to the masculine line of development from their very nature, and which are the expression of masculine instinctual impulses—sadistic tendencies, for instance, or a boy's lustful feelings towards his mother arising out of the normal Oedipus-complex. It is no less certain that these impulses are also overtaken by repression. If the masculine protest is to be taken as having satisfactorily explained the repression of passive phantasies (which later become masochistic), then it becomes for that very reason totally inapplicable to the opposite case of active phantasies. That is to say, the doctrine of the masculine protest is altogether incompatible with the fact of repression. Unless we are prepared to throw away all that has been acquired in psychology since Breuer's first cathartic treatment and through its agency, we cannot expect that the principle of the masculine protest will acquire any significance in the elucidation of the neuroses and perversions.

The theory of psychoanalysis (a theory based upon observation) holds firmly to the view that the motive forces of repression must not be sexualized. Man's archaic inheritance forms the nucleus of the unconscious mind; and whatever part of that inheritance has to be left behind in the advance to later phases of development, because it is useless or incompatible with what is new and harmful to it, falls a victim to the process of repression. This selection is made more successfully with one group of instincts than with the other. In virtue of special circumstances which have often been pointed out already, the latter group, that of the sexual instincts, are able to defeat the intentions of repression, and to enforce their representation by substitute-formations of a disturbing kind. For this reason infantile sexuality, which is held under repression, acts as the chief motive force in the formation of symptoms; and the essential part of its content, the Oedipus-complex, is the nuclear complex of the neurosis. I hope that in this paper I have raised an expectation that the sexual aberrations of childhood, as well as those of mature life, are ramifications of the same complex.

VIII

The Psychogenesis of a Case of Homosexuality in a Woman[1] (1920)

I

Homosexuality in women, which is certainly not less common than in men, although much less glaring, has not only been ignored by the law, but has also been neglected by psychoanalytic research. The narration of a single case, not too pronounced in type, in which it was possible to trace its origin and development in the mind with complete certainty and almost without a gap may, therefore, have a certain claim to attention. If this presentation of it furnishes only the most general outlines of the various events concerned and of the conclusions reached from a study of the case, while suppressing all the characteristic details on which the interpretation is founded, this limitation is easily to be explained by the medical discretion necessary in discussing a recent case.

A beautiful and clever girl of eighteen, belonging to a family of good standing, had aroused displeasure and concern in her parents by the devoted adoration with which she pursued a certain lady "in society" who was about ten years older than herself. The parents asserted that, in spite of her distinguished name, this lady was nothing but a *cocotte*. It was said to be well known that she lived with a married woman as her friend, having intimate relations with her, while at the same time she carried on promiscuous affairs with a number of men. The girl did not contradict these evil re-

---

[1]First published in *Zeitschrift*, Bd. VI., 1920; reprinted in *Sammlung*, Fünfte Folge. [Translated by Barbara Low and R. Gabler.]

ports, but neither did she allow them to interfere with her worship of the lady, although she herself was by no means lacking in a sense of decency and propriety. No prohibitions and no supervision hindered the girl from seizing every one of her rare opportunities of being together with her beloved, of ascertaining all her habits, of waiting for her for hours outside her door or at a tram-halt, of sending her gifts of flowers, and so on. It was evident that this one interest had swallowed up all others in the girl's mind. She did not trouble herself any further with educational studies, thought nothing of social functions or girlish pleasures, and kept up relations only with a few girl friends who could help her in the matter or serve as confidantes. The parents could not say to what lengths their daughter had gone in her relations with the questionable lady, whether the limits of devoted admiration had already been exceeded or not. They had never remarked in their daughter any interest in young men, nor pleasure in their attentions, while, on the other hand, they were sure that her present attachment to a woman was only a continuation, in a more marked degree, of a feeling she had displayed of recent years for other members of her own sex which had already aroused her father's suspicion and anger.

There were two details of her behaviour, in apparent contrast with each other, that most especially vexed her parents. On the one hand, she did not scruple to appear in the most frequented streets in the company of her questionable friend, being thus quite neglectful of her own reputation; while, on the other hand, she disdained no means of deception, no excuses and no lies that would make meetings with her possible and cover them. She thus showed herself too brazen in one respect and full of deceitfulness in the other. One day it happened, indeed, as was sooner or later inevitable in the circumstances, that the father met his daughter in the company of the lady. He passed them by with an angry glance which boded no good. Immediately after, the girl rushed off and flung herself over a wall down the side of a cutting on to a railway line. She paid for this undoubtedly serious attempt at suicide with a considerable time on her back in bed, though fortunately little permanent damage was done. After her recovery she found it easier to get her own way than before. The parents did not dare to oppose her with so much determination, and the lady, who up till then had received her advances coldly, was moved by such an unmistakable proof of serious passion and began to treat her in a more friendly manner.

About six months after this episode the parents sought medical advice and entrusted the physician with the task of bringing their daughter back to a normal state of mind. The girl's attempted suicide had evidently shown them that the instruments of domestic discipline were powerless to overcome the existing disorder. Before going further it will be desirable, however, to deal separately with the attitude of her father and of her mother to the matter. The father was an earnest, worthy man, at bottom very tender-hearted, but he had to some extent estranged his children by the sternness he had adopted towards them. His treatment of his only daughter was too much influenced by consideration for his wife. When he first came to know of his daughter's homosexual tendencies he flared up in rage and tried to suppress them by threatening her; at that time perhaps he hesitated between different, though equally painful, views—regarding her either as vicious, as degenerate, or as mentally afflicted. Even after the attempted suicide he did not achieve the lofty resignation shown by one of our medical colleagues who remarked of a similar irregularity in his own family, "It is just a misfortune like any other." There was something about his daughter's homosexuality that aroused the deepest bitterness in him, and he was determined to combat it with all the means in his power; the low estimation in which psychoanalysis is so generally held in Vienna did not prevent him from turning to it for help. If this way failed he still had in reserve his strongest counter-measure; a speedy marriage was to awaken the natural instincts of the girl and stifle her unnatural tendencies.

The mother's attitude towards the girl was not so easy to grasp. She was still a youngish woman, who was evidently unwilling to relinquish her own claim to find favour by means of her beauty. All that was clear was that she did not take her daughter's passion so tragically as did the father, nor was she so incensed at it. She had even for a long time enjoyed her daughter's confidence concerning the love-affair, and her opposition to it seemed to have been aroused mainly by the harmful publicity with which the girl displayed her feelings. She had herself suffered for some years from neurotic troubles and enjoyed a great deal of consideration from her husband; she was quite unfair in her treatment of her children, decidedly harsh towards her daughter and overindulgent to her three sons, the youngest of whom had been born after a long interval and was then not yet three years old. It was not easy to ascertain anything more definite about her character, for, owing to motives that will only later become intelligible, the patient was always reserved in what she said about her mother, whereas in regard to her father she showed no feeling of the kind.

To a physician who was to undertake psychoanalytic treatment of the girl there were many grounds for a feeling of discomfort. The situation he had to deal with was not the one that analysis demands, in which alone it can demonstrate its effectiveness. As is well known, the ideal situation for analysis is when someone who is otherwise master of himself is suffering from an inner conflict which he is unable to resolve alone, so that he brings his trouble to the analyst and begs for his help. The physician then works hand in hand with one part of the personality which is divided against itself, against the other partner in the conflict. Any situation but this is more or less unfavourable for psychoanalysis and adds fresh difficulties to those already present. Situations like that of a proprietor who orders an architect to build him a villa according to his own tastes and desires, or of a pious donor who commissions an artist to paint a picture of saints, in the corner of which is to be a portrait of himself worshipping, are fundamentally incompatible with the conditions of psychoanalysis. It constantly happens, to be sure, that a husband informs the physician as follows, "My wife suffers from nerves, so that she gets on badly with me; please cure her, so that we may lead a happy married life again." But often enough it turns out that such a request is impossible to fulfil, *i.e.* that the physician cannot bring about the result for which the husband sought the treatment. As soon as the wife is freed from her neurotic inhibitions she sets about dissolving the marriage, for her neurosis was the sole condition under which maintenance of the marriage was possible. Or else parents expect one to cure their nervous and unruly child. By a healthy child they mean one who never places his parents in difficulties, but only gives them pleasure. The physician may succeed in curing the child, but after that it goes its own way all the more decidedly, and the parents are now far more dissatisfied than before. In short, it is not a matter of indifference whether someone comes to analysis of his own accord or because he is brought to it, whether he himself desires to be changed, or only his relatives, who love him (or who might be expected to love him), desire this for him.

Further unfavourable features in the present case were the facts that the girl was not in any way ill—she did not suffer from anything in herself, nor did she complain of her condition—and that the task to be carried out did not consist in resolving a neurotic conflict but in converting one variety of the genital organization of sexuality into the other. The removal of genital inversion or homosexuality is in my experience never an easy matter. On the contrary, I have found success possible only under specially favourable circumstances, and even then the success essentially consisted in being able to open to those who are restricted homosexually the way to the opposite sex, which had been till then barred, thus restoring to them full bisexual functions. After that it lay with themselves to choose whether they wished to abandon the other way that is banned by society, and in individual cases they have done so. One must remember that normal sexuality also depends upon a restriction in the choice of object; in general, to undertake to convert a fully developed homosexual into a heterosexual is not much more promising than to do the reverse, only that for good practical reasons the latter is never attempted.

In actual numbers the successes achieved by psychoanalytic treatment of the various forms of homosexuality, which, to be sure, are manifold, are not very striking. As a rule the homosexual is not able to give up the object of his pleasure, and one cannot convince him that if he changed to the other object he would find again the pleasure that he has renounced. If he comes to be treated at all, it is mostly through the pressure of external motives, such as the social disadvantages and dangers attaching to his choice of object, and such components of the instinct of self-preservation prove themselves too weak in the struggle against the sexual impulses. One then soon discovers his secret plan, namely, to obtain from the striking failure of his attempt the feeling of satisfaction that he has done everything possible against his abnormality, to which he can now resign himself with an easy conscience. The case is somewhat different when consideration for beloved parents and relatives has been the motive for his attempt to be cured. Then there really are libidinal tendencies present which may put forth energies opposed to the homosexual choice of object, though their strength is rarely sufficient. It is only where the homosexual fixation has not yet become strong enough, or where there are considerable rudiments and vestiges of a heterosexual choice of object, *i.e.* in a still oscillating or in a definitely bisexual organization, that one may make a more favourable prognosis for psychoanalytic therapy.

For these reasons I declined altogether holding out to the parents any prospect of their wish being fulfilled. I merely said I was prepared to study the girl carefully for a few weeks or months, so as then to be able to pronounce how far a continuation of the analysis might influence her. In quite a number of cases, indeed, the analysis divides itself into two clearly distinguishable stages: in the first, the physician procures from the patient the necessary information, makes him familiar with the premises and postulates of psychoanalysis, and unfolds to him the reconstruction of the genesis of his disorder as deduced from the material brought up in the analysis. In the second stage the patient himself lays hold of the material put before him, works on it, recollects what he can of the apparently repressed memories, and behaves as if he were living the rest over again. In this way he can confirm, supplement, and correct the inferences made by the physician. It is only during this work that he experiences, through overcoming resistances, the inner change aimed at, and acquires for himself the convictions that make him independent of the physician's authority. These two stages in the course of the analytic treatment are not always sharply divided from each other; this can only happen when the resistance maintains certain conditions. But when this is so, one may institute a comparison with two stages of a journey. The first comprises all the necessary preparations, to-day so complicated and hard to effect, before, ticket in hand, one can at last go on to the platform and secure a seat in the train. One then has the right, and the possibility, of travelling into a distant country, but after all these preliminary exertions one is not yet there—indeed, one is not a single mile nearer to one's goal. For this to happen one has to make the journey itself from one station to the other, and this part of the performance may well be compared with the second stage in the analysis.

The analysis of the patient I am discussing took this course of two stages, but it was not continued beyond the beginning of the second stage. A special constellation of the resistance made it possible, nevertheless, to gain full confirmation of my inferences, and to obtain an adequate insight on broad lines into the way in which her inversion had developed. But before relating the findings of the analysis I must deal with a few points which have either been touched upon already by myself or which will have roused special interest in the reader.

I had made the prognosis partly dependent on how far the girl had succeeded in satisfying her passion. The information I gleaned during the analysis seemed favourable in this respect. With none of the objects of her adoration had the patient enjoyed anything beyond a few kisses and embraces; her genital chastity, if one may use such a phrase, had remained intact. As for the lady who led a double life, and who had roused the girl's most recent and by far her strongest emotions, she had always treated her coldly and had never allowed any greater favour than kissing her hand. Probably the girl was making a virtue of necessity when she kept insisting on the purity of her love and her physical repulsion against the idea of any sexual intercourse. But perhaps she was not altogether wrong when she vaunted of her wonderful beloved that, aristocrat as she was, forced into her present position only by adverse family circumstances, she had preserved, in spite of her situation, a great deal of nobility. For the lady used to recommend the girl every time they met to withdraw her affection from herself and from women in general, and she had persistently rejected the girl's advances up to the time of the attempted suicide.

A second point, which I at once tried to investigate, concerned any possible motives in the girl herself which might serve to support a psychoanalytic treatment. She did not try to deceive me by saying that she felt any urgent need to be freed from her homosexuality. On the contrary, she said she could not conceive of any other way of being in love, but she added that for her parents' sake she would honestly help in the therapeutic endeavour, for it pained her very much to be the cause of so much grief to them. I had to take this as a propitious sign to begin with; I could not divine the unconscious affective attitude that lay behind it. What came to light later in this connection decisively influenced the course taken by the analysis and determined its premature conclusion.

Readers unversed in psychoanalysis will long have been awaiting an answer to two other questions. Did this homosexual girl show physical characteristics plainly belonging to the opposite sex, and did the case prove to be one of congenital or acquired (later developed) homosexuality?

I am aware of the importance attaching to the first of these questions. Only one should not exaggerate it and obscure in its favour the fact that sporadic secondary characteristics of the opposite sex are very often present in normal individuals, and that well-marked physical characteristics of the opposite sex may be found in persons whose choice of object has undergone no change in the direction of inversion; in other words, that in both sexes *the degree of physical hermaphroditism is to a great extent independent of the psychical hermaphroditism*. In modification of this statement it must be added that this independence is more evident in men than women, where bodily and mental traits belonging to the opposite sex are apt to coincide in their incidence. Still I am not in a position to give a satisfactory answer to the first of our questions about my patient; the psychoanalyst customarily forgoes thorough bodily examination of his patients in certain cases. Certainly there was no obvious deviation from the feminine physical type, nor any menstrual disturbance. The beautiful and well-developed girl had, it is true, her father's tall figure, and her facial features were sharp rather than soft and girlish, traits which might be regarded as indicating a physical masculinity. Some of her intellectual attributes also could be connected with masculinity: for instance, her acuteness of comprehension and her lucid objectivity, in so far as she was not dominated by her passion; though these distinctions are conventional rather than scientific. What is certainly of greater importance is that in her behaviour towards her love-object she had throughout assumed the masculine part: that is to say, she displayed the humility and the sublime over-estimation of the sexual object so characteristic of the male lover, the renunciation of all narcissistic satisfaction, and the preference for being lover rather than beloved. She had thus not only chosen a feminine love-object, but had also developed a masculine attitude towards this object.

The second question, whether this was a case of inherited or acquired homosexuality, will be answered by the whole history of the patient's abnormality and its development. The study of this will show how fruitless and inappropriate this question is.

II

After an introduction which digresses in so many directions, the sexual history of the case under consideration can be presented quite concisely. In childhood the girl had passed through the normal attitude characteristic of the feminine Oedipus-complex[2] in a way that was not at all remarkable, and had later also begun to substitute for her father a brother slightly older than herself. She did not remember any sexual traumata in early life, nor were any discovered by the analysis. Comparison of her brother's genital organs and her own, which took place about the beginning of the latency period (at five years old or perhaps a little earlier), left a strong impression on her and had far-reaching aftereffects. There were only slight hints pointing to infantile onanism, or else the analysis did not go deep enough to throw light on this point. The birth of a second brother when she was between five and six years old left no special influence upon her development. During the prepubertal years at school she gradually became acquainted with the facts of sex, and she received this knowledge with mixed feelings of fascination and frightened aversion, in a way which may be called

---

[2] I do not see any progress or advantage in the introduction of the term "Electra-complex," and do not advocate its use.

normal and was not exaggerated in degree. This amount of information about her seems meagre enough, nor can I guarantee that it is complete. It may be that the history of her youth was much richer in experiences; I do not know. As I have already said, the analysis was broken off after a short time, and therefore yielded an anamnesis not much more reliable than the other anamneses of homosexuals, which there is good cause to question. Further, the girl had never been neurotic, and came to the analysis without even one hysterical symptom, so that opportunities for investigating the history of her childhood did not present themselves so readily as usual.

At the age of thirteen to fourteen she displayed a tender and, according to general opinion, exaggeratedly strong affection for a small boy, not quite three years old, whom she used to see regularly in a playground in one of the parks. She took to the child so warmly that in consequence a permanent friendship grew up between herself and his parents. One may infer from this episode that at that time she was possessed of a strong desire to be a mother herself and to have a child. However, after a short time she grew indifferent to the boy, and began to take an interest in mature, but still youthful, women; the manifestations of this in her soon led her father to administer a mortifying chastisement to her.

It was established beyond all doubt that this change occurred simultaneously with a certain event in the family, and one may therefore look to this for some explanation of the change. Before it happened, her libido was focussed on motherhood, while afterwards she became a homosexual attracted to mature women, and has remained so ever since. The event which is so significant for our understanding of the case was a new pregnancy of her mother's, and the birth of a third brother when she was about sixteen.

The network of causes and effects that I shall now proceed to lay bare is not a product of my gift for combination; it is based on such trustworthy analytic evidence that I can claim objective validity for it; it was in particular a series of inter-related dreams, easy of interpretation, that proved decisive in this respect.

The analysis revealed beyond all shadow of doubt that the beloved lady was a substitute for—the mother. It is true that she herself was not a mother, but then she was not the girl's first love.

The first objects of her affection after the birth of her youngest brother were really mothers, women between thirty and thirty-five whom she had met with their children during summer holidays or in the family circle of acquaintances in town. Motherhood as a "condition of love" was later on given up, because it was difficult to combine in real life with another one, which grew more and more important. The specially intensive bond with her latest love, the "Lady," had still another basis which the girl discovered quite easily one day. On account of her slender figure, regular beauty, and off-hand manner, the lady reminded her of her own brother, a little older than herself. Her latest choice corresponded, therefore, not only with her feminine but also with her masculine ideal; it combined gratification of the homosexual tendency with that of the heterosexual one. It is well known that analysis of male homosexuals has in numerous cases revealed the same combination, which should warn us not to form too simple a conception of the nature and genesis of inversion, and to keep in mind the extensive influence of the bisexuality of mankind.[3]

But how are we to understand the fact that it was just the birth of a child who came late in the family, at a time when the girl herself was already mature and had strong wishes of her own, that moved her to bestow her passionate tenderness upon her who gave birth to this child, *i.e.* her own mother, and to express that feeling towards a substitute for her mother? From all that we know we should have expected just the opposite. In such circumstances mothers with daughters of about a marriageable age usually feel embarrassed in regard to them, while the daughters are apt to feel for their mothers a mixture of compassion, contempt and envy which does nothing to increase their tenderness for them. The girl we are considering, however, had altogether little cause to feel affection for her mother. The latter, still youthful herself, saw in her rapidly developing daughter an inconvenient competitor; she favoured the sons at her expense, limited her independence as much as possible, and kept an especially strict watch against any close relation between the girl and her father. A yearning from the

---

[3] Cf. J. Sadger, *Jahresbericht über sexuelle Perversionen.*

beginning for a kinder mother would, therefore, have been quite intelligible, but why it should have flamed up just then, and in the form of a consuming passion, is not comprehensible.

The explanation is as follows: The girl was just experiencing the revival of the infantile Oedipus-complex at puberty when she suffered a great disappointment. She became keenly conscious of the wish to have a child, and a male one; that it was her father's child and his image that she desired, her consciousness was not allowed to know. And then—it was not she who bore the child, but the unconsciously hated rival, her mother. Furiously resentful and embittered, she turned away from her father, and from men altogether. After this first great reverse she forswore her womanhood and sought another goal for her libido.

In doing so she behaved just as many men do who after a first painful experience turn their backs for ever upon the faithless female sex and become woman-haters. It is related of one of the most attractive and unfortunate princes of our time that he became a homosexual because the lady he was engaged to marry betrayed him with a stranger. I do not know whether this is true historically, but much psychological truth lies behind the rumour. In all of us, throughout life, the libido normally oscillates between male and female objects; the bachelor gives up his men friends when he marries, and returns to club-life when married life has lost its savour. Naturally, when the swing-over is fundamental and final, we suspect some special factor which has definitely favoured one side or the other, and which perhaps only waited for the appropriate moment in order to turn the choice of object finally in its direction.

After her disappointment, therefore, this girl had entirely repudiated her wish for a child, the love of a man, and womanhood altogether. Now it is evident that at this point the developments open to her were very manifold; what actually happened was the most extreme one possible. She changed into a man, and took her mother in place of her father as her love-object.[4] Her relation to her mother

---

[4] It is by no means rare for a love-relation to be broken off by means of a process of identification on the part of the lover with the loved object, a process equivalent to a kind of regression to narcissism. After this has been accomplished, it is easy in making a fresh choice of object to direct the libido to a member of the sex opposite to that of the earlier choice.

had certainly been ambivalent from the beginning, and it proved easy to revive her earlier love for her mother and with its help to bring about an over-compensation for her current hostility towards her. Since there was little to be done with the real mother, there arose from the conversion of feeling described the search for a mother-substitute to whom she could become passionately attached.[5]

In her actual relations with her mother there was a practical motive furthering the change of feeling which might be called an "advantage through illness." The mother herself still attached great value to the attentions and the admiration of men. If, then, the girl became homosexual and left men to her mother (in other words, "retired in favour of" the mother), she removed something which had hitherto been partly responsible for her mother's disfavour.[6]

The attitude of the libido thus adopted was greatly reinforced

---

[5] The displacements of the libido here described are doubtless familiar to every analyst from investigation of the anamneses of neurotics. With the latter, however, they occur in early childhood, at the beginning of the love-life; with our patient, who was in no way neurotic, they took place in the first years following puberty, though, by the way, they were just as completely unconscious. Perhaps one day this temporal factor may turn out to be of great importance.

[6] As "retiring in favour of someone else" has not previously been mentioned among the causes of homosexuality, or in the mechanism of libido-fixation in general, I will adduce here another analytical observation of the same kind which has a special feature of interest. I once knew two twin brothers, both of whom were endowed with strong libidinal impulses. One of them was very successful with women, and had innumerable affairs with women and girls. The other went the same way at first, but it became unpleasant for him to be trespassing on his brother's beat, and, owing to the likeness between them, to be mistaken for him on intimate occasions, so he got out of the difficulty by becoming homosexual. He left the women to his brother, and thus "retired" in his favour. Another time I treated a young man, an artist, unmistakably bisexual in disposition, in whom the homosexual trend had come to the fore simultaneously with a disturbance in his work. He fled from both women and work together. The analysis, which was able to bring him back to both, showed that the fear of the father was the most powerful psychic motive for both the disturbances, which were really renunciations. In his imagination all women belonged to the father, and he sought refuge in men out of submission, so as to "retire from" the conflict in favour of the father. Such a motivation of the homosexual object-choice must be by no means uncommon; in the primeval ages of the human race all women presumably belonged to the father and head of the primal horde.

Among brothers and sisters who are not twins this "retirement" plays a great part in other spheres as well as in that of the love-choice. For example, an elder brother studies music and is admired for it; the younger, far more gifted musically, soon gives up his own musical studies, in spite of his longing, and cannot be persuaded to touch an instrument again. This is one example of a very frequent occurrence, and investigation of the motives leading to this "retirement" rather than to open rivalry discloses very complicated conditions in the mind.

as soon as the girl perceived how much it displeased her father. Once she had been punished for an over-affectionate overture made to a woman she realized how she could wound her father and take revenge on him. Henceforth she remained homosexual out of defiance against her father. Nor did she scruple to lie to him and to deceive him in every way. Towards her mother, indeed, she was only so far deceitful as was necessary to prevent her father from knowing things. I had the impression that her behaviour followed the principle of the talion: "Since you have betrayed me, you must put up with my betraying you." Nor can I come to any other conclusion about the striking lack of caution displayed by this otherwise ingenious and clever girl. She *wanted* her father to know occasionally of her intercourse with the lady, otherwise she would be deprived of satisfaction of her keenest desire—namely, revenge. So she saw to this by showing herself openly in the company of her adored one, by walking with her in the streets near her father's place of business, and the like. This maladroitness was by no means unintentional. It was remarkable, by the way, that both parents behaved as though they understood the secret psychology of their daughter. The mother was tolerant, as though she appreciated the favour of her daughter's "retirement" from the arena; the father was furious, as though he realized the deliberate revenge directed against himself.

The girl's inversion, however, received its final reinforcement when she found in her "Lady" an object which promised to satisfy not only her homosexual tendency, but also that part of her heterosexual libido still attached to her brother.

III

Consecutive presentation is not a very adequate means of describing complicated mental processes going on in different layers of the mind. I am therefore obliged to pause in the discussion of the case and treat more fully and deeply some of the points brought forward above.

I mentioned the fact that in her behaviour to her adored lady the girl had adopted the characteristic masculine type of love. Her humility and her tender lack of pretensions, *"che poco spera e nulla chiede,"* her bliss when she was allowed to accompany the lady a little way and to kiss her hand on parting, her joy when she heard her praised as beautiful—while any recognition of her own beauty by another person meant nothing at all to her—her pilgrimages to places once visited by the loved one, the oblivion of all more sensual wishes: all these little traits in her resembled the first passionate adoration of a youth for a celebrated actress whom he regards as far above him, to whom he scarcely dares lift his bashful eyes. The correspondence with the "type of object-choice in men" that I have described elsewhere, whose special features I traced to the attachment to the mother[7] held good even to the smallest details. It may seem remarkable that she was not in the least repelled by the evil reputation of her beloved, although her own observations sufficiently confirmed the truth of such rumours. She was after all a well-brought-up and modest girl, who had avoided sexual adventures for herself, and who regarded coarsely sensual gratification as unaesthetic. But already her first passions had been for women who were not celebrated for specially strict propriety. The first protest her father made against her love-choice had been evoked by the pertinacity with which she sought the company of a cinematograph actress at a summer resort. Moreover, in all these affairs it had never been a question of women who had any reputation for homosexuality, and who might, therefore, have offered her some prospect of homosexual gratification; on the contrary, she illogically courted women who were coquettes in the ordinary sense of the word, and she rejected without hesitation the willing advances made by a homosexual friend of her own age. The bad reputation of her "Lady," however, was positively a "condition of love" for her, and all that is enigmatical in this attitude vanishes when we remember that in the case of the masculine type of object-choice derived from the mother it is also an essential condition that the loved object should be in some way or other "of bad repute" sexually, one who really may be called a "light woman." When the girl learnt later on how far her adored lady deserved to be called by this title and that she lived simply by giving her bodily favours, her

[7]See *supra*, essay IV.

reaction took the form of great compassion and of phantasies and plans for "rescuing" her beloved from these ignoble circumstances. We have been struck by the same endeavours to "rescue" in the men of the type referred to above, and in my description of it I have tried to give the analytical derivation of this tendency.

We are led into quite another realm of explanation by the analysis of the attempt at suicide, which I must regard as seriously intended, and which, by the way, considerably improved her position both with her parents and with the lady she loved. She went for a walk with her one day in a part of the town and at an hour at which she was not unlikely to meet her father on his way from his office. So it turned out. Her father passed them in the street and cast a furious look at her and her companion, whom he had by that time come to know. A few moments later she flung herself on to the railway cutting. Now the explanation she gave of the immediate reasons determining her resolution sounded quite plausible. She had confessed to the lady that the man who had given them such an irate glance was her father, and that he had absolutely forbidden their friendship. The lady became incensed at this and ordered the girl to leave her then and there, and never again to wait for her or to address her—the affair must now come to an end. In her despair at having thus lost her loved one for ever, she wanted to put an end to herself. The analysis, however, was able to disclose another and deeper interpretation behind the one she gave, which was confirmed by the evidence of her own dreams. The attempted suicide was, as might have been expected, determined by two other motives besides the one she gave: it was a "punishment-fulfilment" (self-punishment), and a wish-fulfilment. As a wish-fulfilment it signified the attainment of the very wish which, when frustrated, had driven her into homosexuality—namely, the wish to have a child by her father, for now she "fell"[8] through her father's fault.[9] The fact that at this moment the lady

---

[8] [In the text there is a play on the word *niederkommen*, which means both "to fall" and "to be delivered of a child." There is also in English a colloquial use of the verb "to fall," meaning pregnancy or childbirth.—Trans.]

[9] That the various means of suicide can represent sexual wish-fulfilments has long been known to all analysts. (To poison oneself = to become pregnant; to drown = to bear a child; to throw oneself from a height = to be delivered of a child.)

had spoken to the same effect as the father, and had uttered the same prohibition, forms the connecting link between this deeper interpretation and the superficial one of which the girl herself was conscious. From the point of view of self-punishment the girl's action shows us that she had developed in her unconscious strong death-wishes against one or other of her parents: perhaps against her father, out of revenge for impeding her love, but, more likely, also against her mother when she was pregnant with the little brother. For analysis has explained the enigma of suicide in the following way: probably no one finds the mental energy required to kill himself unless, in the first place, he is in doing this at the same time killing an object with whom he has identified himself, and, in the second place, is turning against himself a death-wish which had been directed against someone else. Nor need the regular discovery of these unconscious death-wishes in those who have attempted suicide surprise us as strange (any more than it need make an impression as confirming our deductions), since the unconscious of all human beings is full enough of such death-wishes, even against those we love.[10] The girl's identification of herself with her mother, who ought to have died at the birth of the child denied to herself, makes this "punishment-fulfilment" itself again into a "wish-fulfilment." Lastly, a discovery that several quite different motives, all of great strength, must have co-operated to make such a deed possible is only in accord with what we should expect.

In the girl's account of her conscious motives the father did not figure at all; there was not even any mention of fear of his anger. In the motivation laid bare by the analysis he played the principal part. Her relation to her father had this same decisive importance for the course and outcome of the analytic treatment, or rather, analytic exploration. Behind her pretended consideration for her parents, for whose sake she had been willing to make the attempt to be transformed, lay concealed her attitude of defiance and revenge against her father which held her fast to her homosexuality. Secure under this cover, the resistance allowed a considerable de-

---

[10]Cf. "Reflections upon War and Death," *Character and Culture*, Collier Books edition BS 193V.

gree of freedom to the analytic investigation. The analysis went forward almost without any signs of resistance, the patient participating actively with her intellect, though absolutely tranquil emotionally. Once when I expounded to her a specially important part of the theory, one touching her nearly, she replied in an inimitable tone, "How very interesting," as though she were a *grande dame* being taken over a museum and glancing through her lorgnon at objects to which she was completely indifferent. The impression one had of her analysis was not unlike that of an hypnotic treatment, where the resistance has in the same way withdrawn to a certain limit, beyond which it then proves to be unconquerable. The resistance very often pursues similar tactics—Russian tactics, as they might be called[11]—in cases of the obsessional neurosis, which for this reason yield the clearest results for a time and permit of a penetrating inspection of the causation of the symptoms. One begins to wonder how it is that such marked progress in analytic understanding can be unaccompanied by even the slightest change in the patient's compulsions and inhibitions, until at last one perceives that everything accomplished had been admitted only under the mental reservation of doubt,[12] and behind this protective barrier the neurosis may feel secure. "It would be all very fine," thinks the patient, often quite consciously, "if I were obliged to believe what the man says, but there is no question of that, and so long as that is not so I need change nothing." Then, when one comes to close quarters with the motivation of this doubt, the fight with the resistances breaks forth in earnest.

In the case of our patient, it was not doubt, but the affective factor of revenge against her father that made her cool reserve possible, that divided the analysis into two distinct stages, and rendered the results of the first stage so complete and perspicuous. It seemed, further, as though nothing resembling a transference to the physician had been effected. That, however, is of course absurd, or, at least, is a loose way of expressing it; for some kind of relation to the analyst must come about, and this is usually

[11][A reference to the European War, 1914–18.—Trans.]

[12][i.e. believed on condition that it is regarded as not certain.—Trans.]

transferred from an infantile one. In reality she transferred to me the deep antipathy to men which had dominated her ever since the disappointment she had suffered from her father. Bitterness against men is as a rule easy to gratify upon the analyst; it need not evoke any violent emotional manifestations, it simply expresses itself in rendering futile all his endeavours and in clinging to the neurosis. I know from experience how difficult it is to make the patient understand just this mute kind of symptomatic behaviour and to make him aware of this latent, and often exceedingly strong, hostility without endangering the treatment. So as soon as I recognized the girl's attitude to her father, I broke off the treatment and gave the advice that, if it was thought worth while to continue the therapeutic efforts, it should be done by a woman. The girl had in the meanwhile promised her father that at any rate she would not communicate with the "Lady," and I do not know whether my advice, the motive for which is evident, will be followed.

Only once in the course of this analysis did anything appear which I could regard as a positive transference, a greatly weakened revival of the original passionate love for the father. Even this manifestation was not quite free from other motives, but I mention it because it brings up, in another direction, an interesting problem of analytic technique. At a certain period, not long after the treatment had begun, the girl brought a series of dreams which, distorted as is customary and couched in the usual dream-language, could nevertheless be easily translated with certainty. Their content, when interpreted, was, however, remarkable. They anticipated the cure of the inversion through the treatment, expressed her joy over the prospects in life then opened before her, confessed her longing for a man's love and for children, and so might have been welcomed as a gratifying preparation for the desired change. The contradiction between them and the girl's utterances in waking life at the time was very great. She did not conceal from me that she meant to marry, but only in order to escape from her father's tyranny and to follow her true inclinations undisturbed. As for the husband, she remarked rather contemptuously, she would easily deal with him, and besides, one could have sexual relations with a man and a woman at one and the same time, as the example of the adored lady showed. Warned through some slight impression or other, I told her one day that I did not believe these dreams, that I regarded them as false or hypocritical, and that she intended to deceive me just as she habitually deceived her father. I was right; after this exposition this kind of dream ceased. But I still believe that, beside the intention to mislead me, the dreams partly expressed the wish to win my favour; they were also an attempt to gain my interest and my good opinion—perhaps in order to disappoint me all the more thoroughly later on.

I can imagine that to point out the existence of lying dreams of this kind, destined to please the analyst, will arouse in some readers who call themselves analysts a real storm of helpless indignation. "What!" they will exclaim, "so the unconscious, the real centre of our mental life, the part of us that is so much nearer the divine than our poor consciousness, so that too can lie! Then how can we still build on the interpretations of analysis and the accuracy of our findings?" To which one must reply that the recognition of these lying dreams does not constitute an astounding novelty. I know, indeed, that the craving of mankind for mysticism is ineradicable, and that it makes ceaseless efforts to win back for mysticism the playground it has been deprived of by the *Traumdeutung*, but in the case under consideration surely everything is simple enough. A dream is not the "unconscious" itself; it is the form into which a thought from the preconscious, or even from waking conscious life, can, thanks to the favouring conditions of sleep, be recast. During sleep this thought has been reinforced by unconscious wish-excitations and thus has experienced distortion through the "dreamwork," which is determined by the mechanisms valid for the unconscious. With our dreamer, the intention to mislead me, just as she did her father, certainly emanated from the preconscious, or perhaps even from consciousness; it could come to expression by entering into connection with the unconscious wish-impulse to please the father (or father-substitute), and in this way it created a lying dream. The two intentions, to betray and to please the father, originate in the same complex; the former resulted from the repression of the latter, and the later one was reduced by the dream-work to the earlier one. There can therefore be no question of any devaluation of the unconscious, nor of a shaking of our confidence in the results of our analysis.

I will not miss this opportunity of expressing for once my astonishment that human beings can go through such great and momentous phases of their love-life without heeding them much, sometimes even, indeed, without having the faintest suspicion of them: or else that, when they do become aware of these phases, they deceive themselves so thoroughly in their judgement of them. This happens not only with neurotics, where we are familiar with the phenomenon, but seems also to be common enough in ordinary life. In the present case, for example, a girl develops a devotion for women, which her parents at first find merely vexatious and hardly take seriously; she herself knows quite well that her feelings are greatly engaged, but still she is only slightly aware of the sensations of intense love until a certain disappointment is followed by an absolutely excessive reaction, which shows everyone concerned that they have to do with a consuming passion of elemental strength. Even the girl herself had never perceived anything of the conditions necessary for the outbreak of such a mental upheaval. In other cases we come across girls or women in a state of severe depression, who on being asked for a possible cause of their condition tell us that they have, it is true, had a little feeling for a certain person, but that it was nothing deep and that they soon got over it when they had to give up hope. And yet it was this renunciation, apparently so easily borne, that became the cause of serious mental disturbance. Again, we have to do with men who have passed through casual love-affairs and then realize only from the subsequent effects that they had been passionately in love with someone whom they had apparently regarded lightly. One is also amazed at the unexpected results that may follow an artificial abortion which had been decided upon without remorse and without hesitation. One must agree that the poets are right who are so fond of portraying people in love without knowing it, or uncertain whether they do love, or who think that they hate when in reality they love. It would seem that the knowledge received by our consciousness of what is happening to our love-instincts is especially liable to be incomplete, full of gaps, or falsified. Needless to say, in this discussion I have not omitted to allow for the part played by subsequent failures of memory.

IV

I now come back, after this disgression, to the consideration of my patient's case. We have made a survey of the forces which led the girl's libido from the normal Oedipus attitude into that of homosexuality, and of the paths thus traversed by it in the mind. Most important in this respect was the impression made by the birth of her little brother, and we might from this be inclined to classify the case as one of late acquired inversion.

But at this point we become aware of a state of things which also confronts us in many other instances in which light has been thrown by psychoanalysis on a mental process. So long as we trace the development from its final stage backwards, the connection appears continuous, and we feel we have gained an insight which is completely satisfactory or even exhaustive. But if we proceed the reverse way, if we start from the premises inferred from the analysis and try to follow these up to the final result, then we no longer get the impression of an inevitable sequence of events which could not be otherwise determined. We notice at once that there might have been another result, and that we might have been just as well able to understand and explain the latter. The synthesis is thus not so satisfactory as the analysis; in other words, from a knowledge of the premises we could not have foretold the nature of the result.

It is very easy to account for this disturbing state of affairs. Even supposing that we thoroughly know the aetiological factors that decide a given result, still we know them only qualitatively, and not in their relative strength. Some of them are so weak as to become suppressed by others, and therefore do not affect the final result. But we never know beforehand which of the determining factors will prove the weaker or the stronger. We only say at the end that those which succeeded must have been the stronger. Hence it is always possible by analysis to recognize the causation with certainty, whereas a prediction of it by synthesis is impossible.

We do not, therefore, mean to maintain that every girl who experiences a disappointment of this kind, of the longing for love that springs from the Oedipus attitude during puberty, will necessarily on that account fall a victim to homosexuality. On the contrary, other kinds of reaction to this trauma are probably commoner. Then, however, there must have been present in this girl special factors that turned the scale, factors outside the trauma, probably of an internal nature. Nor is there any difficulty in pointing them out.

It is well known that even in the normal person it takes a certain time before a decision in regard to the sex of the love-object is finally achieved. Homosexual enthusiasms, unduly strong friendships tinged with sensuality, are common enough in both sexes during the first years after puberty. This was also so with our patient, but in her these tendencies undoubtedly showed themselves to be stronger, and lasted longer, than with others. In addition, these presages of later homosexuality had always occupied her conscious life, while the attitude arising from the Oedipus-complex had remained unconscious and had appeared only in such signs as her tender fondling of the little boy. As a school-girl she was for a long time in love with a strict and unapproachable mistress, obviously a mother-substitute. A long time before the birth of her brother and still longer before the first reprimand at the hands of her father, she had taken a specially keen interest in various young mothers. From very early years, therefore, her libido had flowed in two streams, the one on the surface being one that we may unhesitatingly designate homosexual. This latter was probably a direct and unchanged continuation of an infantile mother-fixation. Possibly the analysis described here actually revealed nothing more than the process by which, on an appropriate occasion, the deeper heterosexual libido-stream was also deflected into the manifest homosexual one.

The analysis showed, further, that the girl had suffered from childhood from a strongly marked "masculinity complex." A spirited girl, always ready to fight, she was not at all prepared to be second to her slightly older brother; after inspecting his genital organs she had developed a pronounced envy of the penis, and the thoughts derived from this envy still continued to fill her mind. She was in fact a feminist; she felt it to be unjust that girls should not enjoy the same freedom as boys, and rebelled against the lot of woman in general. At the time of the analysis the idea of pregnancy and child-birth was disagreeable to her, partly, I surmise, on account of the bodily disfigurement connected with them. Her girlish narcissism had betaken itself to this refuge,[13] and ceased to express itself as pride in her good looks. Various clues indicated that she must formerly have taken great pleasure in exhibitionism and scoptophilia. Anyone who is anxious that the claims of environment in aetiology should not come short, as opposed to those of heredity, will call attention to the fact that the girl's behaviour, as described above, was exactly what would follow from the combined effect in a person with a strong mother-fixation of the two influences of her mother's indifference and of her comparison of her genital organs with her brother's. It is possible here to trace back to the impression of an effective external influence in early life something which one would have been ready to regard as a constitutional peculiarity. But a part even of this acquired disposition, if it has really been acquired, has to be ascribed to the inborn constitution. So we see in practice a continual mingling and blending of what in theory we should try to separate into a pair of opposites—namely, inherited and acquired factors.

An earlier, more tentative conclusion of the analysis might have led to the view that this was a case of late-acquired homosexuality, but deeper consideration of the material undertaken later impels us to conclude that it is rather a case of inborn homosexuality which, as usual, became fixed and unmistakably manifest only in the period following puberty. Each of these classifications does justice only to one part of the state of affairs ascertainable by observation, but neglects the other. It would be best not to attach too much value to this way of stating the problem.

Publications on homosexuality usually do not distinguish clearly enough between the questions of the choice of object, on the one hand, and of the sexual characteristics and sexual attitude of the

---

[13]Cf. Kriemhilde's confession in the *Nibelungenlied*.

subject, on the other, as though the answer to the former necessarily involved the answers to the latter. Experience, however, proves the contrary: a man with predominantly male characteristics and also masculine in his lovelife may still be inverted in respect to his object, loving only men instead of women. A man in whose character feminine attributes evidently predominate, who may, indeed, behave in love like a woman, might be expected, from this feminine attitude, to choose a man for his love-object; but he may nevertheless be heterosexual, and show no more inversion in respect of his object than an average normal man. The same is true of women; here also mental sexual character and object-choice do not necessarily coincide. The mystery of homosexuality is therefore by no means so simple as it is commonly depicted in popular expositions, e.g. a feminine personality, which therefore has to love a man, is unhappily attached to a male body; or a masculine personality, irresistibly attracted by women, is unfortunately cemented to a female body. It is instead a question of three series of characteristics, namely—

Physical sexual characteristics—Mental sexual characteristics
(physical hermaphroditism)   (masculine, or feminine, attitude)
Kind of object-choice

which, up to a certain point, vary independently of one another, and are met with in different individuals in manifold permutations. Tendencious publications have obscured our view of this inter-relationship by putting into the foreground, for practical reasons, the third feature (the kind of object-choice), which is the only one that strikes the layman, and in addition by exaggerating the closeness of the association between this and the first feature. Moreover, they block the way leading to a deeper insight into all that is uniformly designated homosexuality by rejecting two fundamental facts which have been revealed by psychoanalytic investigation. The first of these is that homosexual men have experienced a specially strong fixation in regard to the mother; the second, that, in addition to their manifest heterosexuality, a very considerable measure of latent or unconscious homosexuality can be detected in all normal people. If these findings are taken into account, then, to be sure, the supposition that nature in a freakish mood created a "third sex" falls to the ground.

It is not for psychoanalysis to solve the problem of homosexuality. It must rest content with disclosing the psychical mechanisms that resulted in determination of the object-choice, and with tracing the paths leading from them to the instinctual basis of the disposition. There its work ends, and it leaves the rest to biological research, which has recently brought to light, through Steinach's[14] experiments, such very important results concerning the influence exerted by the first factor mentioned above on the second and third. Psychoanalysis has a common basis with biology, in that it presupposes an original bisexuality in human beings (as in animals). But psychoanalysis cannot elucidate the intrinsic nature of what in conventional or in biological phraseology is termed "masculine" and "feminine": it simply takes over the two concepts and makes them the foundation of its work. When we attempt to reduce them further, we find masculinity vanishing into activity and femininity into passivity, and that does not tell us enough. In what has gone before I have tried to explain how far we may reasonably expect, or how far experience has already proved, that the elucidations yielded by analysis furnish us with the means for altering inversion. When one compares the extent to which we can influence it with the remarkable transformations that Steinach has effected in some cases by his operations, it does not make a very imposing impression. Thus it would be premature, or a harmful exaggeration, if at this stage we were to indulge in hopes of a "therapy" of inversion that could be generally used. The cases of male homosexuality in which Steinach has been successful fulfilled the condition, which is not always present, of a very patent physical "hermaphroditism." Any analogous treatment of female homosexuality is at present quite obscure. If it were to consist in removing the probably hermaphroditic ovaries, and in implanting others, which would, it is hoped, be of a single

---

[14]Cf. A. Lipschütz, *Die Pubertäsdrüse und ihre Wirkungen.*

sex, there would be little prospect of its being applied in practice. A woman who has felt herself to be a man, and has loved in masculine fashion, will hardly let herself be forced into playing the part of a woman when she must pay for this transformation, which is not in every way advantageous, by renouncing all hope of motherhood.

IX

Certain Neurotic Mechanisms in Jealousy, Paranoia and Homosexuality[1] (1922)

A. Jealousy is one of those affective states, like grief, that may be described as normal. If anyone appears to be without it, the inference is justified that it has undergone severe repression and consequently plays all the greater part in his unconscious mental life. The instances of abnormally intense jealousy met with in analytic work reveal themselves as constructed of three layers. The three layers or stages of jealousy may be described as (1) *competitive* or normal, (2) *projected,* and (3) *delusional* jealousy.

There is not much to be said from the analytic point of view about normal jealousy. It is easy to see that essentially it is compounded of grief, the pain caused by the thought of losing the loved object, and of the narcissistic wound, in so far as this is distinguishable from the other wound; further, of feelings of enmity against the successful rival, and of a greater or lesser amount of self-criticism which tries to hold the person himself accountable for his loss. Although we may call it normal, this jealousy is by no means completely rational, that is, derived from the actual situation, proportionate to the real circumstances and under the complete control of the conscious ego; for it is rooted deep in the unconscious, it is a continuation of the earliest stirrings of the child's affective life, and it originates in the Oedipus or family complex of the first sexual period. Moreover, it is noteworthy that in many persons it is experienced bisexually; that is to say, in a

---

[1]First published in *Zeitschrift*, Bd. VIII., 1922. [Translated by Joan Riviere.]

man, beside the suffering in regard to the loved woman and the hatred against the male rival, grief in regard to the unconsciously loved man and hatred of the woman as a rival will add to its intensity. I even know of a man who suffered exceedingly during his attacks of jealousy and who, according to his own account, went through unendurable torments by consciously imagining himself in the position of the faithless woman. The sensation of helplessness which then came over him, the images he used to describe his condition—exposed to the vulture's beak like Prometheus, or cast fettered into a serpent's den—he himself referred to the impressions received during several homosexual aggressions to which he had been subjected as a boy.

The jealousy of the second layer, the *projected*, is derived in both men and women either from their own actual unfaithfulness in real life or from impulses towards it which have succumbed to repression. It is a matter of everyday experience that fidelity, especially that degree of it required in marriage, is only maintained in the face of continual temptation. Anyone who denies this in himself will nevertheless be impelled so strongly in the direction of infidelity that he will be glad enough to make use of an unconscious mechanism as an alleviation. This relief—more, absolution by his conscience—he achieves when he projects his own impulses to infidelity on to the partner to whom he owes faith. This weighty motive can then make use of the material at hand (perception-material) by which the unconscious impulses of the partner are likewise betrayed, and the person can justify himself with the reflection that the other is probably not much better than he is himself.[2]

Social conventions have taken this universal state of things into account very adroitly, by granting a certain amount of latitude to the married woman's thirst to find favour in men's eyes and the married man's thirst to capture and possess, in the expectation that this inevitable tendency to unfaithfulness will thus find a safety-

---

[2] Cf. Desdemona's song:
   "I called my love false love; but what said he then?
   If I court moe women, you'll couch with moe men."

valve and be rendered innocuous. Convention has laid down that neither partner is to hold the other accountable for these little excursions in the direction of unfaithfulness, and it achieves the result on the whole that the desire awakened by the new love-object is gratified by a kind of turning-back to the object already possessed. The jealous person, however, does not recognize this convention of tolerance; he does not believe in any such thing as a halt or a turning-back once the path has been trod, nor that a social "flirtation" may be a safeguard against actual infidelity. In the treatment of a jealous person like this one must refrain from disputing with him the material on which he bases his suspicions; one can only aim at bringing him to regard the matter in a different light.

The jealousy that arises from this projection has, it is true, an almost delusional character; it is, however, amenable to the analytic work of exposing the unconscious phantasies of personal infidelity. The jealousy of the third layer, the true *delusional* type, is worse. It also has its origin in repressed impulses towards unfaithfulness—the object, however, in these cases is of the same sex as the subject. Delusional jealousy represents an acidulated homosexuality, and rightly takes its position among the classical forms of paranoia. As an attempt at defence against an unduly strong homosexual impulse it may, in a man, be described in the formula: "Indeed I do not love him, *she* loves him!"[3] In a delusional case one will be prepared to find the jealousy arising in all three layers, never in the third alone.

B. Paranoia.—Cases of paranoia are for well-known reasons not usually amenable to analytic investigation. I have recently been able, nevertheless, by an intensive study of two paranoiacs, to discover something new to me.

The first case was that of a youngish man with a fully developed paranoia of jealousy, the object of which was his impeccably faithful wife. A stormy period in which the delusion had possessed him uninterruptedly already lay behind him. When I saw him he

---

[3]Cf. Freud, "Psychoanalytic Notes upon an Autobiographical Account of a Case of Paranoia," *Three Case Histories*, Collier Books edition BS 191V.

was still subject only to clearly defined attacks, which lasted for several days and, curiously enough, regularly appeared on the day following an act of intercourse, which was, incidentally, satisfying to both of them. The inference is justified that after every satiation of the heterosexual libido the homosexual component, likewise stimulated by the act, forced for itself an outlet in the attack of jealousy.

The jealousy of the attack drew its material from his observation of the smallest possible indications, in which the utterly unconscious coquetry of the wife, unnoticeable to any other person, had betrayed itself to him. She had unintentionally touched the man sitting next her with her hand; she had turned too much towards him, or she had smiled more pleasantly than when alone with her husband. To all these manifestations of her unconscious feelings he paid extraordinary attention, and always knew how to interpret them correctly, so that he really was always in the right about it, and could justify his jealousy still more by analytic interpretation. His abnormality really reduced itself to this, that he watched his wife's unconscious mind much more closely and then regarded it as far more important than anyone else would have thought of doing.

We are reminded that sufferers from persecutory paranoia act in just the same way. They, too, cannot regard anything in others as indifferent, and into their "delusions of reference" they, too, take up the smallest possible indications which these others, strangers, offer them. The meaning of their delusion of reference is that they expect from every stranger something like love; these "others" show them nothing of the kind, however—they laugh to themselves, fiddle with their sticks, even spit on the ground as they go by—and one really does not do these things while anyone in whom one takes a friendly interest is near. One does them only when one is quite indifferent to the passer-by, when one can treat him like air; and when we consider the fundamental kinship of the words "stranger" and "enemy," the paranoiac is not so far wrong in regarding this indifference as hate, in comparison with his claim for love.

We begin to see that we describe the behaviour of both jealous and persecuted paranoiacs very inadequately by saying that they project outwards on to others what they do not wish to recognize in themselves.

Certainly they do this; but they do not project it into the sky, so to speak, where there is nothing of the sort already. They let themselves be guided by their knowledge of the unconscious, and displace to the unconscious minds of others the attention which they have withdrawn from their own. Our jealous husband perceives his wife's unfaithfulness instead of his own; by becoming conscious of hers and magnifying it enormously he succeeds in keeping unconscious his own. If we accept his example as typical, we may infer that the enmity which the persecuted paranoiac sees in others is the reflection of his own hostile impulses against them. Since we know that with the paranoiac it is precisely the most loved person of his own sex that becomes his persecutor, the question arises where this reversal of affect takes its origin: the answer is not far to seek—the ever-present ambivalence of the feelings provides its source and the unfulfilment of his claim for love strengthens it. This ambivalence thus serves the same purpose for the persecuted paranoiac as jealousy serves for our patient—that of a defence against homosexuality.

The dreams of my jealous patient contained a great surprise for me. They were not simultaneous with the outbreaks of the attacks, though they occurred within the period influenced by the delusion; they were completely free from the delusion and showed themselves based on homosexual tendencies which were disguised no more strictly than usual. In view of my slight knowledge of the dreams of paranoiacs I was inclined to suppose at that time that the disease did not penetrate into dreams.

The homosexuality of this patient was easily surveyed. He had made no friendships and developed no social interests; one had the impression that the delusion had constituted the first actual development of his relations with men, as if it had taken over a piece of work that had been neglected. The fact that his father was of no great importance in the family life, combined with a humiliating homosexual trauma in early childhood, had forced his homosexuality into repression and barred the way to its sublimation.

The whole of his youth was governed by a strong attachment to his mother. Of all her many sons he was her declared favorite, and he developed marked jealousy of the normal type in regard to her. When later he made his choice of a wife—mainly prompted by the impulse to enrich his mother—his longing for a virgin mother expressed itself in obsessive doubts about his wife's virginity. The first years of his marriage were free from jealousy. Then he became unfaithful to his wife and entered upon an intimate relationship with another woman that lasted for a considerable time. Startled by a certain suspicion, he at length made an end of this love affair, and not until then did the jealousy of the second, projected type break out, by means of which he was able to assuage his self-reproaches about his own unfaithfulness. It was soon complicated by an accession of homosexual impulses, of which his father-in-law was the object, and became a fully formed jealousy paranoia.

My second case would probably not have been classified as persecutory paranoia without analysis; but I had to recognize the young man as a candidate for this diagnosis of the illness. In his attitude to his father there existed an ambivalence which in its range was quite extraordinary. On the one hand, he was the most pronounced rebel imaginable, and had developed manifestly in every direction in opposition to his father's wishes and ideals; on the other hand, at a deeper level he was still the most utterly abject son, in loving remorse after his father's death denying himself all enjoyment of women. His actual relations with men were clearly dominated by suspiciousness; his keen intellect easily rationalized this attitude; and he knew how to bring it about that both friends and acquaintances deceived and exploited him. The new thing I learned from studying him was that classical persecution-ideas may be present without finding belief or acceptance. They flashed up occasionally during the analysis, but he regarded them as unimportant and invariably scoffed at them. This may occur in many cases of paranoia; it may be that the delusions which we regard as new formations when the disease breaks out have already long been in existence.

It seems to me that this is an important recognition—namely, that the qualitative factor, the presence of certain neurotic formations, has less practical significance than the quantitative factor, the degree of attention, or more correctly, the measure of cathexis that these formations engage. Our consideration of the first case, the jealousy paranoia, led to a similar estimate of the importance of the quantitative factor, by showing that there also the abnormality essentially consisted in the hyper-cathexis of the interpretations of another's unconscious behaviour. We have long known of an analogous fact in the analysis of hysteria. The pathogenic phantasies, derivatives of repressed instinctual trends, are for a long time tolerated alongside the normal life of the mind, and have no pathogenic effect until by a revolution in the libido-economy they undergo hyper-cathexis; not till then does the conflict which leads to symptom-formation break out. Thus as our knowledge increases we are ever being impelled to bring the *economic* point of view into the foreground. I should also like to throw out the question whether this quantitative factor that I am now dwelling on does not suffice to cover the phenomena for which Bleuler and others have lately wished to introduce the term "switching." One need only assume that increased resistance in one direction of the psychical currents results in hyper-cathexis along some other path and thus causes the whole current to be switched into this path.

The dreams of my two cases of paranoia showed an instructive contrast. Whereas those of the first case were free from delusion, as has already been said, the other patient produced great numbers of persecution-dreams, which may be regarded as forerunners or substitutive formations of the delusional ideas. The pursuer, from whom he managed to escape only in terror, was usually a powerful bull or some other male symbol which even in the dream itself he sometimes recognized as representing his father. One day he produced a very characteristic paranoiac transference-dream. He saw me shaving in front of him, and from the scent of the soap he realized that I was using the same soap as his father had used. I was doing this in order to induce in him a father-transference on to myself. The choice of this incident out of which the dream was formed unmistakably betrays the patient's depreciatory attitude to his paranoiac phantasies and his disbelief in them; for his own eyes could tell him every day that I never require to avail myself of shaving-soap and that therefore there was in this respect nothing to which a father-transference could attach itself.

A comparison of the dreams of the two patients shows, however, that the question whether or not paranoia (or any other psychoneurosis) can penetrate into dreams is based on a false conception of dreams. Dreams are distinguishable from waking thought in that for their content they can draw from material (belonging to the region of the unconscious) which cannot emerge in waking thought. Apart from this, dreams are merely a *form of thinking*, a transformation of preconscious thought-material by the dream-work and its conditions. Our terminology of the neuroses is not applicable to repressed material; this cannot be called hysterical, nor obsessional, nor paranoiac. The other part of the material which is woven into the structure of a dream, the preconscious thoughts, may be normal or may bear the character of any neurosis; they may be the effects of all those pathogenic processes in which the essence of neurosis lies. It is not evident why any such morbid idea should not become woven into dreams. A dream may therefore quite simply represent an hysterical phantasy, an obsessional idea, or a delusion, that is, may reveal it upon interpretation. Observation of the two paranoiacs shows that the dreams of the one were quite normal while he was subject to his delusion, and that those of the other were paranoiac in content while he treated his delusional ideas with contempt. In both cases, therefore, the dream took up the material that was at the time being forced into the background in waking life. This too, however, need not necessarily be an invariable rule.

C. Homosexuality.—Recognition of the organic factor in homosexuality does not relieve us of the obligation of studying the psychical processes of its origin. The typical process, already established in innumerable cases, is that a few years after the termination of puberty the young man, who until this time has been strongly fixated to his mother, turns in his course, identifies himself with his mother, and looks about for love-objects in whom he can re-discover himself, and whom he wishes to love as his mother loved him. The characteristic mark of this process is that usually for several years one of the "conditions of love" is that the male object shall be of the same age as he himself was when the change took place. We know of various factors contributing to this result, probably in different degrees. First there is the fixation on the mother, which renders passing on to another woman difficult. The identification with the mother is an outcome of this attachment, and at the same time in a certain sense it enables the son to keep true to her, his first object. Then there is the inclination towards a narcissistic object-choice, which lies in every way nearer and is easier to put into effect than the move towards the other sex. Behind this factor there lies concealed another of quite exceptional strength, or perhaps it coincides with it: the high value set upon the male organ and the inability to tolerate its absence in a love-object. Depreciation of women, and aversion from them, even horror of them, are generally derived from the early discovery that women have no penis. We subsequently discovered, as another powerful motive urging towards the homosexual object-choice, regard for the father or fear of him; for the renunciation of women means that all rivalry with him (or with all men who may take his place) is avoided. The two last motives, the clinging to the condition of a penis in the object as well as the retiring in favour of the father, may be ascribed to the castration complex. Attachment to the mother, narcissism, fear of castration—these are the factors (which by the way have nothing specific about them) that we have hitherto found in the psychical aetiology of homosexuality; and on them is superimposed the effect of any seduction bringing about a premature fixation of the libido, as well as the influence of the organic factor favouring the passive rôle in love.

We have, however, never regarded this analysis of the origin of homosexuality as complete; and I can now point to a new mechanism leading to homosexual object-choice, although I cannot say how large a part it plays in the formation of the extreme, manifest and exclusive type of homosexuality. Observation has directed my attention to several cases in which during early childhood feelings of jealousy derived from the mother-complex and of very great intensity arose against rivals, usually older brothers. This jealousy led to an exceedingly hostile aggressive attitude against brothers (or sisters) which might culminate in actual death-wishes, but which could not survive further development. Under the influences of training—and certainly not uninfluenced also by their own constant powerlessness—these feelings yielded to repression and to a transformation, so that the rivals of the earlier period became the first homosexual love-objects. Such an outcome of the attachment to the mother shows various interesting relations with other processes known to us. First of all it is a complete contrast to the development of persecutory paranoia, in which the person who has before been loved becomes the hated persecutor, whereas here the hated rivals are transformed into love-objects. It represents, too, an exaggeration of the process which, according to my view, leads to the birth of social instincts in the individual.[4] In both processes there is first the presence of jealous and hostile feelings which cannot achieve gratification; and then both the personal affectionate and the social identification feelings arise as reaction-formations against the repressed aggressive impulses.

This new mechanism in the homosexual object-choice, its origin in rivalry which has been overcome and in aggressive impulses which have become repressed, is often combined with the typical conditions known to us. In the history of homosexuals one often hears that the change in them took place after the mother had praised another boy and set him up as a model. The tendency to a narcissistic object-choice was thus stimulated, and after a short phase of keen jealousy the rival became a love-object. Otherwise, however, the new mechanism is a separate one, in that the change takes place at a much earlier period, and the identification with the mother recedes into the background. Moreover, in the cases I have observed, it led only to homosexual attitudes, which did not exclude heterosexuality and did not involve a horror of women.

It is well known that a good number of homosexual persons are distinguished by a special development of the social instincts and by a devotion to the interests of the community. It would be tempting, as a theoretical explanation of this, to say that the behaviour towards men in general of a man who sees in other men potential

---

[4]Cf. Freud, *Group Psychology and the Analysis of the Ego.*

love-objects must be different from that of a man who looks upon other men first as rivals in regard to women. Against this there is only the objection that jealousy and rivalry play their part in homosexual love also, and that the community of men also includes these potential rivals. Apart from this speculative explanation, however, the fact that the homosexual object-choice not rarely proceeds from an early conquest of the rivalry in regard to men cannot be unimportant for the connection between homosexuality and social feeling.

In the light of psychoanalysis we are accustomed to regard social feeling as a sublimation of homosexual attitudes towards objects. In the homosexual person with marked social interests, the detachment of social feeling from object-choice has not been fully carried through.

X

The Infantile Genital Organization of the Libido (1923)

A Supplement to the Theory of Sexuality[1]

It is indicative of the difficulties which beset the work of psychoanalytic research that it is possible, in spite of unremitting observation extending over periods of years, to overlook quite broad general features and typical situations, until at last they confront one in a completely unmistakable guise. The remarks that follow are intended to retrieve a lapse of this sort in the field of infantile sexuality.

Readers of my *Drei Abhandlungen zur Sexualtheorie* (1905) will be aware that I have never undertaken any thorough alteration of this work for later editions, but have preserved the original arrangement and have fulfilled the claims of later advances in our knowledge by supplementing and correcting the text. Thus it may well be that the old and the new do not admit of fusion without indications of contradiction. In the beginning, for instance, the emphasis fell upon pointing out the fundamental difference between the sexual life of children and of adults; later on the pregenital organizations of the libido swung into the foreground, together with the remarkable and significant fact of the double thrust of sexual development, twice making a start at separate periods. Finally, the curiosity of the child engaged our interest; and from this proceeded the recognition of the far-reaching similarity between the last stages of infantile sexuality (about the fifth year) and the final form to which it develops in the adult.

---

[1] First published in *Zeitschrift*, Bd. IX., 1923. [Translated by Joan Riviere.]

In the last edition of the *Sexualtheorie* (1922) I left things at this point.

I stated there (on p. 63) that "often, or perhaps regularly, complete object-choice is established in early childhood, of the kind that we have inferred to be characteristic of the pubertal phase of development, namely, such as occurs when all the sexual trends become directed towards one single person, and in that person seek to reach their aims. This constitutes the most complete approximation possible in childhood to the definitive form taken by sexual life after puberty. The sole difference from the latter is that the coalescence of the component-impulses and their concentration under the primacy of the genital organs is not effected in childhood, or only very imperfectly. The institution of this primacy is, therefore, the last phase which the sexual organization undergoes."

I am to-day no longer satisfied with the statement that the primacy of the genitals is not effected in the early period of childhood, or only very imperfectly. The approximation of childhood-sexuality to that of the adult goes much farther and is not limited solely to the establishment of an object-attachment. Even if perfect concentration of the component-impulses under the primacy of the genitals is not attained, at any rate at the height of the development of childhood-sexuality the functioning of the genitals and the interest in them reaches predominant significance, which comes little short of that reached in maturity. The *difference* between the two— the "infantile genital organization" and the final genital organization of the adult—constitutes at the same time the main characteristic of the infantile form, namely, that for both sexes in childhood only one kind of genital organ comes into account—the male. The primacy reached is, therefore, not a primacy of the *genital*, but of the *phallus*.

Unfortunately we can describe this state of things only as it concerns the male child; the corresponding processes in the little girl are not sufficiently known to us. The little boy undoubtedly perceives the distinction between men and women, but to begin with he has no occasion to connect it with any difference in the genitals. It is natural for him to assume that all living beings, persons and animals, possess a genital organ like his own; indeed we know that he investigates inanimate objects with a view to discovering something like his member in them.[2] This part of the body, so easily excitable and changeable, and so rich in sensation, occupies the boy's interest to a high degree, and never ceases to provide new problems for his epistemophilic impulse. He wants to see the same thing in other people, so as to compare it with his own; he behaves as if he had a dim idea that this member might be and should be larger. The driving force which this male portion of his body will generate later at puberty expresses itself in childhood essentially as an impulsion to inquire into things—as sexual curiosity. Many of those deeds of exhibitionism and aggression which children commit, and which in later years would be judged without hesitation to be manifestations of sensual passion, prove on analysis to be experiments undertaken in the search for sexual knowledge.

In the course of these investigations the child makes the discovery that the penis is not one of the possessions common to all creatures who are like himself. The accidental sight of the genitals of a little sister or a little playmate is the occasion of this. In unusually intelligent children the sight of girls urinating arouses the suspicion even earlier that something is different here; for they will have noticed the different position adopted and the different sound heard, and have taken steps to repeat their observations in such a way as to find out the truth. We know how they react to their first perception of the absence of the penis. They deny its absence, and believe they do see a penis all the same; the discrepancy between what they see and what they imagine is glossed over by the idea that the penis is still small and will grow; gradually they come to the conclusion, so fraught with emotion, that at least it had been there and had at some time been taken away. The absence of the penis is thought to be the result of a castration, and then the child is faced with the task of dealing with the thought

---

[2] It is remarkable, by the way, what a small degree of interest the other part of the male genitals, the little sac with its contents, arouses in the child. From all one hears in analyses one could not guess that the male genitals consist of anything more than the penis.

of a castration in relation to himself. Subsequent developments are too well known for it to be necessary to recapitulate them here. It seems to me, however, that the significance of the castration complex can only be rightly appreciated when its origin in the phase of *primacy of the phallus* is also taken into account.[3]

We know, too, to what a degree depreciation of women, loathing of women, and a disposition to homosexuality are derived from a final conviction of women's lack of a penis. Ferenczi has recently, with complete justification, traced back the mythological symbol of loathing—the head of Medusa—to the impression made by the female genitals devoid of a penis.[4]

It should not be presumed, however, that the child instantly and readily makes a generalization of its perception that many women possess no penis; in the way of this there lies the assumption that the absence of the penis is due to a castration performed as a punishment. On the contrary, the child imagines that only unworthy female persons have thus sacrificed their genital organ, such persons as have probably been guilty of the same forbidden impulses as he himself. Women who are regarded with respect, such as the mother, retain the penis long after this date. Not yet is being a woman the same thing to the child as having no penis.[5] Not till later, when the child takes up the problems of the origin and birth of children, and divines that only women can bear children, does the mother, too, become deprived of a penis; and along with this quite complicated theories are constructed, so as to ac-

---

[3]It has quite correctly been pointed out that the child acquires the idea of a narcissistic wound or deprivation of a part of its body by the experience of the loss of the nipple after suckling and of the daily production of its faeces, and even by its separation from the womb of the mother at birth. Nevertheless, the castration complex should be a term reserved for the occasion when the idea of such deprivations comes to be associated with the loss of the male organ.

[4]*Zur Symbolik des Medusenhauptes.* I will merely add that in the myth it is the genital of the mother that is represented. Athene, who carries the head of Medusa on her armour, becomes by virtue of it the unapproachable, the woman at sight of whom all thought of sexual desire is stifled.

[5]From the analysis of a young woman I learnt that, having no father and several aunts, until quite late in the latency-period she clung to a belief that her mother and some of her aunts possessed a penis. One of the aunts, however, was weak-minded, and she was regarded by the child as castrated like herself.

count for the exchange of a penis in return for a child. At the same time the real female genitals never seem to be discovered. As we know, the baby is supposed to live in the mother's body (bowels) and to be born through the bowel passage. These last theories take us up to the end of the period of infantile sexuality or beyond.

It is well, further, to bear in mind the transformations which the familiar polarity of the sexes goes through in the course of the sexual development of childhood. A first contrast is introduced with object-choice, which of course presupposes a subject and an object. At the level of the pregenital sadistic-anal organization nothing is yet heard of any maleness and femaleness: the dominant antithesis is that between active and passive.[6] In the following stage of the infantile genital organization *maleness* has come to life, but no femaleness. The antithesis runs: a male genital organ or a castrated condition. Not until completion of development at the time of puberty does the polarity of sexuality coincide with *male* and *female*. In maleness is concentrated subject, activity, and the possession of a penis; femaleness carries on the object, and passivity. The vagina becomes valued henceforth as an asylum for the penis; it comes into the inheritance of the mother's womb.

---

[6]Cf. *Drei Abhandlungen zur Sexualtheorie*. Fünfte Auflage, S.62.

XI

The Passing of the Oedipus-Complex[1]
(1924)

The significance of the Oedipus-complex as the central phenomenon of the sexual period in early childhood reveals itself more and more. After this it disappears; it succumbs to repression, as we say, and is followed by the latency period. But it is not yet clear to us what occasions its decay; analyses seem to show that the painful disappointments experienced bring this about. The little girl who wants to believe herself her father's beloved and partner in love must one day endure a harsh punishment at his hands, and finds herself hurled to earth from her cloud-castles. The boy who regards his mother as his own property finds that her love and care for him are transferred to a new arrival. Reflection deepens the effect of these impressions by insisting that painful experiences of this kind, antagonistic to the content of the complex, are inevitable. Even when no special events such as those mentioned occur, the absence of the hoped-for gratification, the continual frustration of the wish for a child, causes the lovelorn little one to turn from its hopeless longing. According to this, the Oedipus-complex becomes extinguished by its lack of success, the result of its inherent impossibility.

Another view would put it that the Oedipus-complex must come to an end because the time has come for its dissolution, just as the milk-teeth fall out when the permanent ones begin to press forward. Although the majority of human children individually pass through the Oedipus-complex, yet after all it is a phenomenon

---

[1] First published in *Zeitschrift*, Bd. X., 1924. [Translated by Joan Riviere.]

determined and laid down for him by heredity, and must decline according to schedule when the next pre-ordained stage of development arrives. It is therefore not very important what the occasions are through which this happens, or whether any such occasions are discoverable at all.

One cannot dispute the justice of both these views. They are compatible with each other, moreover; there is room for the ontogenetic alongside the more far-reaching phylogenetic one. Even at birth, indeed, the whole organism is destined to die, and an indication of what will eventually cause its death may possibly already be contained in its organic disposition. Yet after all it is of interest to follow up the way in which the innate schedule is worked out, the way in which accidental noxiae exploit the disposition.

We have lately recognized more clearly than before that the sexual development of a child advances up to a certain point, and that when it reaches this point the genital organ has already taken over the leading part. The genital organ in question, however, is the male alone, or, more exactly, the penis; the female organ is still undiscovered. This phallic phase, which is contemporaneous with the Oedipus-complex, does not develop further into the final stage of genital organization, but becomes submerged, and is succeeded by the latency period. Its conclusion, however, is effected in a typical manner and in conjunction with happenings that recur regularly.

When the (male) child's interest turns to his genital organ, he betrays this by handling it frequently, and then he is bound to discover that grown-up people do not approve of this activity. More or less plainly and more or less brutally the threat is uttered that this highly valued part of him will be taken away. Usually it is from women that the threat emanates; very often they seek to strengthen their authority by referring to the father or the doctor, who, as they assure the child, will carry out the punishment. In a number of cases women will themselves modify the threat in a symbolic manner by warning the child that his actively sinning hand will be removed, instead of his genital, which is after all passive. It happens particularly often that the little boy is threatened in this way not because he plays with his penis with his hand, but because he wets his bed every night and is not to be induced to learn cleanliness. Children's attendants behave as if this nocturnal incontinence were a result and a proof of undue preoccupation with the penis, and are probably right in their inference. In any case long-continued bed-wetting is comparable to pollutions in adults—an expression of the same excitation in the genitals that impels the child to masturbate at this period.

Now the view we hold is that the phallic stage of the genital organization succumbs to this threat of castration. But not immediately, and not without the assistance of further influences. For to begin with the boy does not believe in the threat, nor obey it in the least. Psychoanalysis has recently laid fresh emphasis on two experiences which all children go through, by which it is thought that they become prepared for the loss of a valued part of the body—the withdrawal from them of the mother's breast, at first intermittently and later finally, and the daily demand made on them to give up the contents of the bowel. But if these experiences have an effect when the threat of castration takes place, one sees nothing of it. Not until yet another experience comes its way does the child begin to reckon with the possibility of being castrated, and then only hesitatingly, unwillingly, and not without efforts to depreciate the significance of what it has itself observed.

The observation that finally breaks down the child's unbelief is the sight of the female genitalia. Some day or other it happens that the child whose own penis is such a proud possession obtains a sight of the genital parts of a little girl: he must then become convinced of the absence of a penis in a creature so like himself. With this, however, the loss of his own penis becomes imaginable, and the threat of castration achieves its delayed effect.

We must not be so short-sighted as the child's attendant who threatens it with castration; we cannot overlook the fact that the child's sexual life at this time is by no means exhausted by masturbation. The child is demonstrably under the influence of the Oedipus-attitude to its parents; masturbation is only the discharge in the genital of the excitation belonging to the complex, and to this connection between the two masturbation will owe its significance to him for ever after. The Oedipus-complex offered the child two possibilities of satisfaction, an active and a passive one. It could have put itself in its father's place and had intercourse with the mother as he did, so that the father was soon felt to be an obstacle; or else it had wanted to supplant the mother and be loved by the father, whereupon the mother became superfluous. The child may have had only the vaguest notions of what constituted the love-intercourse which serves as a gratification, but that the penis played a part in it was certain, for the feelings in his own organ were evidence of that. So far there had been no occasion for doubt about a penis in women. But now the acceptance of the possibility of castration, the recognition that women are castrated, makes an end of both the possibilities of satisfaction in the Oedipus-complex. For both of them—the male as a consequence, a punishment, and the other, the female, as a prerequisite—would indeed be accompanied by a loss of the penis. If the gratification desired in consequence of the love is to cost the child his penis, a conflict must arise between the narcissistic interest in this part of the body and the libidinal cathexis of the parent-objects. Normally, in this conflict the first of these forces triumphs; the child's ego turns away from the Oedipus-complex.

I have described elsewhere the way by which this aversion is accomplished. The object-cathexes are given up and replaced by identification. The authority of the father or the parents is introjected into the ego and there forms the kernel of the superego, which takes its severity from the father, perpetuates his prohibition against incest, and so insures the ego against a recurrence of the libidinal object-cathexis. The libidinal trends belonging to the Oedipus-complex are in part desexualized and sublimated, which probably happens with every transformation into identification; in part they are inhibited in their aim and changed into affectionate feelings. The whole process, on the one hand, preserves the genital organ, wards off the danger of losing it; on the other hand, it paralyses it, takes away its function from it. This process introduces the latency period which now interrupts the child's sexual development.

I see no reason to deny the name of "repression" to the ego's turning from the Oedipus-complex, although later repressions are for the most part effected with the participation of the super-ego, which is only built up during this process. But the process described is more than a repression; when carried out in the ideal way it is equivalent to a destruction and abrogation of the complex. It is not a great step to assume that here we have come upon the borderland between normal and pathological which is never very sharply defined. If the ego has really not achieved much more than a repression of the complex, then this latter persists unconsciously in the *id*, and will express itself later on in some pathogenic effect.

Analytic observation enables us to perceive or to infer these connections between the phallic organization, the Oedipus-complex, the threat of castration, the formation of the superego and the latency period. They justify the statement that the Oedipus-complex succumbs to the threat of castration. But this does not dispose of the problem; there is room for a theoretical speculation which may overthrow the results obtained or set them in a new light. Before we traverse this path, however, we must attend to a question which was already roused during this discussion and has long been left on one side. The process described relates, as we expressly stated, only to the male child. How is the corresponding development effected in a little girl?

Here our material—for some reason we do not understand—becomes far more shadowy and incomplete. The female sex develops an Oedipus-complex, too, a super-ego and a latency period. May one ascribe to it also a phallic organization and a castration complex? The answer is in the affirmative, but it cannot be the same as in the boy. The feministic demand for equal rights between the sexes does not carry far here; the morphological difference must express itself in differences in the development of the mind. "Anatomy is Destiny," to vary a saying of Napoleon's. The little girl's clitoris behaves at first just like a penis, but by comparing herself with a boy playfellow the child perceives that she has "come off short," and takes this fact as ill-treatment and as a reason for feeling inferior. For a time she still consoles herself with the expectation that later, when she grows up, she will acquire just as big an appendage as a boy. Here the woman's "masculine complex" branches off. The female child does not understand her actual loss as a sex characteristic, but explains it by assuming that at some earlier date she had possessed a member which was just as big and which had later been lost by castration. She does not seem to extend this conclusion about herself to other grown women, but in complete accordance with the phallic phase she ascribes to them large and complete, that is, male, genitalia. The result is an essential difference between her and the boy, namely, that she accepts castration as an established fact, an operation already performed, whereas the boy dreads the possibility of its being performed.

The castration-dread being thus excluded in her case, there falls away a powerful motive towards forming the superego and breaking up the infantile genital organization. These changes seem to be due in the girl far more than in the boy to the results of educative influences, of external intimidation threatening the loss of love. The Oedipus-complex in the girl is far simpler, less equivocal, than that of the little possessor of a penis; in my experience it seldom goes beyond the wish to take the mother's place, the feminine attitude towards the father. Acceptance of the loss of a penis is not endured without some attempt at compensation. The girl passes over—by way of a symbolic analogy, one may say—from the penis to a child; her Oedipus-complex culminates in the desire, which is long cherished, to be given a child by her father as a present, to bear him a child. One has the impression that the Oedipus-complex is later gradually abandoned because this wish is never fulfilled. The two desires, to possess a penis and to bear a child, remain powerfully charged with libido in the unconscious and help to prepare the woman's nature for its subsequent sex rôle. The comparative weakness of the sadistic component of the sexual instinct, which may probably be related to the penis-deficiency, facilitates the transformation of directly sexual trends into those inhibited in aim, feelings of tenderness. It must be confessed, however, that on the whole our insight into these processes of development in the girl is unsatisfying, shadowy and incomplete.

I have no doubt that the temporal and causal relations described between Oedipus-complex, sexual intimidation (the threat of castration), formation of the super-ego and advent of the latency period are of a typical kind; but I do not maintain that this type is the only possible one. Variations in the sequence and the linking up of these processes must be very significant in the development of the individual.

Since the publication of Otto Rank's interesting study on the trauma of birth, the conclusion of the present modest communication—that the boy's Oedipus-complex succumbs to the dread of castration—cannot be accepted without further discussion. It seems to me premature, however, to enter upon this discussion at the present time, and perhaps also inadvisable to begin to criticize or to assess the value of Rank's view in the present connection.

XII

Some Psychological Consequences of the Anatomical Distinction Between the Sexes[1] (1925)

In my own writings and in those of my followers more and more stress is laid upon the necessity for carrying the analyses of neurotics back into the remotest period of their childhood, the time of the early efflorescence of sexual life. It is only by examining the first manifestations of the patient's innate instinctual constitution and the effects of his earliest experiences that we can accurately gauge the motive forces that have led to his neurosis and can be secure against the errors into which we might be tempted by the degree to which they have become remodelled and overlaid in adult life. This requirement is not only of theoretical but also of practical importance, for it distinguishes our efforts from the work of those physicians whose interests are focussed exclusively upon therapeutic results and who employ analytic methods, but only up to a certain point. An analysis of early childhood such as we are considering is tedious and laborious and makes demands both upon the physician and upon the patient which cannot always be met. Moreover it leads us into dark regions where there are as yet no sign-posts. Indeed, analysts may feel reassured, I think, that there is no risk of their work becoming mechanical, and so of losing its interest, during the next few decades.

---

[1] ["Einige psychische Folgen des anatomischen Geschlechtsunterschieds." First published *Int. Z. Psychoanal.*, 11 (1925), 401; reprinted *Ges. Schr.*, 11, 8; and *Ges. W.*, 14, 19. Translation, reprinted from *Int. J. Psychoanal.*, 8 (1927), 133; by James Strachey.]

In the following pages I bring forward some findings of analytical research which would be of great importance if they could be proved to apply universally. Why do I not postpone publication of them until further experience has given me the necessary proof, if such proof is obtainable? Because the conditions under which I work have undergone a change, with implications which I cannot disguise. Formerly, I was never one of those who are unable to hold back what seems to be a new discovery until it has been either confirmed or corrected. My *Interpretation of Dreams* [1900] and my "Fragment of an Analysis of a Case of Hysteria" [1905*c*] (the case of Dora) [Collier Books edition AS 581V] were suppressed by me— if not for the nine years enjoined by Horace—at all events for four or five years before I allowed them to be published. But in those days I had unlimited time before me and material poured in upon me in such quantities that fresh experiences were hardly to be escaped. Moreover, I was the only worker in a new field, so that my reticence involved no danger to myself and no risk of loss to others.

But now everything has changed. The time before me is limited. The whole of it is no longer spent in working, so that my opportunities for making fresh observations are not so numerous. If I think I see something new, I am uncertain whether I can wait for it to be confirmed. And further, everything that is to be seen upon the surface has already been exhausted; what remains has to be slowly and laboriously dragged up from the depths. Finally, I am no longer alone. An eager crowd of fellow-workers is ready to make use of what is unfinished or doubtful, and I can leave to them that part of the work which I should otherwise have done myself. On this occasion, therefore, I feel justified in publishing something which stands in urgent need of confirmation before its value or lack of value can be decided.

In examining the earliest mental shapes assumed by the sexual life of children we have been in the habit of taking as the subject of our investigations the male child, the little boy. With little girls, so we have supposed, things must be similar, though in some way or other they must nevertheless be different. The point in development at which this difference lay could not clearly be determined.

In boys the situation of the Oedipus complex is the first stage that can be recognized with certainty. It is easy to understand, because at that stage a child retains the same object which he previously cathected with his pregenital libido during the preceding period while he was being suckled and nursed. The further fact that in this situation he regards his father as a disturbing rival and would like to get rid of him and take his place is a straightforward consequence of the actual state of affairs. I have shown elsewhere (1924b) how the Oedipus attitude in little boys belongs to the phallic phase, and how it succumbs to the fear of castration, that is, to narcissistic interest in their own genitals. The matter is made more difficult to grasp by the complicating circumstance that even in boys the Oedipus complex has a double orientation, active and passive, in accordance with their bisexual constitution; a boy also wants to take his *mother's* place as the love-object of his *father*—a fact which we describe as the feminine attitude.

As regards the prehistory of the Oedipus complex in boys we are far from complete clarity. We know that that period includes an identification of an affectionate sort with the boy's father, an identification which is still free from any sense of rivalry in regard to his mother. Another element of that stage is invariably, I believe, a masturbatory stimulation of the genitals, the masturbation of early childhood, the more or less violent suppression of which by the persons in charge of the child sets the castration complex in action. It is to be assumed that this masturbation is attached to the Oedipus complex and serves as a discharge for the sexual excitation belonging to it. It is, however, uncertain whether the masturbation has this character from the first, or whether on the contrary it makes its first appearance spontaneously as an activity of a bodily organ and is only brought into relation with the Oedipus complex at some later date; this second possibility is by far the more probable. Another doubtful question is the part played by bed-wetting and by the breaking of that habit through the intervention of training measures. We are inclined to adopt the simple generalization that continued bed-wetting is a result of masturbation and that its suppression is regarded by boys as an inhibition of their genital activity, that is, as having the meaning of a threat of castration; but whether we are always right in supposing this remains to be seen. Finally, analysis shows us in a shadowy way how the fact of a child at a very early age listening to his parents copulating may set up his first sexual excitation, and how that event may, owing to its after-effects, act as a starting-point for the child's whole sexual development. Masturbation, as well as the two attitudes in the Oedipus complex, later on become attached to this early experience, the child having subsequently interpreted its meaning. It is impossible, however, to suppose that these observations of coitus are of universal occurrence, so that at this point we are faced with the problem of "primal phantasies." Thus the prehistory of the Oedipus complex, even in boys, raises all of these questions for sifting and explanation; and there is the further problem of whether we are to suppose that the process invariably follows the same course, or whether a great variety of different preliminary stages may not converge upon the same terminal situation.

In little girls the Oedipus complex raises one problem more than in boys. In both cases the mother is the original object; and there is no cause for surprise that boys retain that object in the Oedipus complex. But how does it happen that girls abandon it and instead take their father as an object? In pursuing this question I have been able to reach some conclusions which may throw light upon the prehistory of the Oedipus relation in girls.

Every analyst has come across certain women who cling with especial intensity and tenacity to the bond with their father and to the wish in which it culminates of having a child by him. We have good reason to suppose that the same wishful phantasy was also the motive force of their infantile masturbation, and it is easy to form an impression that at this point we have been brought up against an elementary and unanalysable fact of infantile sexual life. But a thorough analysis of these very cases brings something different to light, namely, that here the Oedipus complex has a long prehistory and is in some respects a secondary formation.

The old paediatrician Lindner [1879] once remarked that a child discovers the genital zones (the penis or the clitoris) as a source of pleasure while indulging in sensual sucking (thumb-sucking)[2]: I shall leave it an open question whether it is really true that the child takes the newly found source of pleasure in exchange for the

---

[2]Cf. *Three Essays on the Theory of Sexuality* (1905*b*). [English Translation, 1949, 58f.].

recent loss of the mother's nipple—a possibility to which later phantasies (fellatio) seem to point. Be that as it may, the genital zone is discovered at some time or other, and there seems no justification for attributing any psychical content to its first stimulations. But the first step in the phallic phase which begins in this way is not the linking-up of the masturbation with the object-cathexes of the Oedipus situation, but a momentous discovery which little girls are destined to make. They notice the penis of a brother or playmate, strikingly visible and of large proportions, at once recognize it as the superior counterpart of their own small and inconspicuous organ, and from that time forward fall a victim to envy for the penis.

There is an interesting contrast between the behaviour of the two sexes. In the analogous situation, when a little boy first catches sight of a girl's genital region, he begins by showing irresolution and lack of interest; he sees nothing or disowns what he has seen, he softens it down or looks about for expedients for bringing it into line with his expectations. It is not until later, when some threat of castration has obtained a hold upon him, that the observation becomes important to him: if he then recollects or repeats it, it arouses a terrible storm of emotion in him and forces him to believe in the reality of the threat which he has hitherto laughed at. This combination of circumstances leads to two reactions, which may become fixed and will in that case, whether separately or together or in conjunction with other factors, permanently determine the boy's relations to women: horror of the mutilated creature or triumphant contempt for her. These developments, however, belong to the future, though not to a very remote one.

A little girl behaves differently. She makes her judgement and her decision in a flash. She has seen it and knows that she is without it and wants to have it.[3]

From this point there branches off what has been named the

---

[3]This is an opportunity for correcting a statement which I made many years ago. (Freud, 1905*b* (English Translation, 1949, 72).] I believed that the sexual interest of children, unlike that of pubescents, was aroused, not by the differences between the sexes, but by the problem of where babies come from. We now see that, at all events with girls, this is certainly not the case. With boys it may no doubt happen sometimes one way and sometimes the other; or with both sexes chance experiences may determine the event.

masculinity complex of women, which may put great difficulties in the way of their regular development towards femininity, it cannot be got over soon enough. The hope of some day obtaining a penis in spite of everything and so of becoming like a man may persist to an incredibly late age and may become a motive for the strangest and otherwise unaccountable actions. Or again, a process may set in which might be described as a "denial," a process which in the mental life of children seems neither uncommon nor very dangerous but which in an adult would mean the beginning of a psychosis. Thus a girl may refuse to accept the fact of being castrated, may harden herself in the conviction that she *does* possess a penis and may subsequently be compelled to behave as though she were a man.

The psychical consequences of penis-envy, in so far as it does not become absorbed in the reaction-formation of the masculinity complex, are various and far-reaching. After a woman has become aware of the wound to her narcissism, she develops, like a scar, a sense of inferiority. When she has passed beyond her first attempt at explaining her lack of a penis as being a punishment personal to herself and has realized that that sexual character is a universal one, she begins to share the contempt felt by men for a sex which is the lesser in so important a respect, and, at least in the holding of that opinion, insists upon being like a man.[4]

Even after penis-envy has abandoned its true object, it continues to exist: by an easy displacement it persists in the character-trait of *jealousy*. Of course, jealousy is not limited to one sex and has a wider foundation than this, but I am of opinion that it plays a

---

[4]In my first critical account of the "History of the Psychoanalytic Movement," written in 1914 (Collier Books edition AS 580V), I recognized that this fact represents the core of truth contained in Adler's theory. That theory has no hesitation in explaining the whole world by this single point ("organ inferiority," "the masculine protest," breaking away from "the feminine line") and prides itself upon having in this way robbed sexuality of its importance and put the desire for power in its place. Thus the only organ which could claim to be called "inferior" without any ambiguity would be the clitoris. On the other hand, one hears of analysts who boast that, though they have worked for dozens of years, they have never found a sign of the existence of a castration complex. We must bow our heads in recognition of the greatness of this achievement, even though it is only a negative one, a piece of virtuosity in the art of overlooking and mistaking. The two theories form an interesting pair of opposites: in one of them not a trace of a castration complex, in the other nothing at all but its effects.

far larger part in the mental life of women than of men and that that is because it is enormously reinforced from the direction of displaced penis-envy. While I was still unaware of this source of jealousy and was considering the phantasy "A Child Is Being Beaten" (1919), which occurs so commonly in girls, I constructed a first phase for it in which its meaning was that another child, a rival of whom the subject was jealous, was to be beaten. This phantasy seems to be a relic of the phallic period in girls. The peculiar rigidity which struck me so much in the monotonous formula "a child is being beaten" can probably be interpreted in a special way. The child which is being beaten (or caressed) may at bottom be nothing more nor less than the clitoris itself, so that at its very lowest level the statement will contain a confession of masturbation, which has remained attached to the content of the formula from its beginning in the phallic phase up to the present time.

A third consequence of penis-envy seems to be a loosening of the girl's relation with her mother as a love-object. The situation as a whole is not very clear, but it can be seen that in the end the girl's mother, who sent her into the world so insufficiently equipped, is almost always held responsible for her lack of a penis. The way in which this comes about historically is often that soon after the girl has discovered that her genitals are unsatisfactory she begins to show jealousy of another child on the grounds that her mother is fonder of it than of her, which serves as a reason for her giving up her affectionate relation to her mother. It will fit in with this if the child which has been preferred by her mother is made into the first object of the beating-phantasy which ends in masturbation.

There is yet another surprising effect of penis-envy, or of the discovery of the inferiority of the clitoris, which is undoubtedly the most important of all. In the past I had often formed an impression that in general women tolerate masturbation worse than men, that they more frequently fight against it and that they are unable to make use of it in circumstances in which a man would seize upon it as a way of escape without any hesitation. Experience would no doubt elicit innumerable exceptions to this statement, if we attempted to turn it into a rule. The reactions of human individuals of both sexes are of course made up of masculine and feminine traits. But it appeared to me nevertheless as though masturbation were further removed from the nature of women than of men, and the solution of the problem could be assisted by the reflection that masturbation, at all events of the clitoris, is a masculine activity and that the elimination of clitoridal sexuality is a necessary pre-condition for the development of femininity. Analyses of the remote phallic period have now taught me that in girls, soon after the first signs of penis-envy, an intense current of feeling against masturbation makes its appearance, which cannot be attributed exclusively to the educational influence of those in charge of the child. This impulse is clearly a forerunner of the wave of repression which at puberty will do away with a large amount of the girl's masculine sexuality in order to make room for the development of her femininity. It may happen that this first opposition to auto-erotic stimulation fails to attain its end. And this was in fact the case in the instances which I analyzed. The conflict continued, and both then and later the girl did everything she could to free herself from the compulsion to masturbate. Many of the later manifestations of sexual life in women remain unintelligible unless this powerful motive is recognized.

I cannot explain the opposition which is raised in this way by little girls to phallic masturbation except by supposing that there is some concurrent factor which turns her violently against that pleasurable activity. Such a factor lies close at hand in the narcissistic sense of humiliation which is bound up with penis-envy, the girl's reflection that after all this is a point on which she cannot compete with boys and that it would therefore be best for her to give up the idea of doing so. Thus the little girl's recognition of the anatomical distinction between the sexes forces her away from masculinity and masculine masturbation on to new lines which lead to the development of femininity.

So far there has been no question of the Oedipus complex, nor has it up to this point played any part. But now the girl's libido slips into a new position by means—there is no other way of putting it—of the equation "penis = child." She gives up her wish for a penis and puts in place of it a wish for a child: and *with this purpose in view* she takes her father as a love-object. Her mother becomes the object of her jealousy. The girl has turned into a little woman. If I am to credit a single exaggerated analytic instance, this new situation can give rise to physical sensations which would have to be regarded as a premature awakening of the female genital apparatus. If the girl's attachment to her father comes to grief later on and has to be abandoned, it may give place to an identification with him and the girl may thus return to her masculinity complex and perhaps remain fixated in it.

I have now said the essence of what I had to say: I will stop, therefore, and cast an eye over our findings. We have gained some insight into the prehistory of the Oedipus complex in girls. The corresponding period in boys is more or less unknown. In girls the Oedipus complex is a secondary formation. The operations of the castration complex precede it and prepare for it. As regards the relation between the Oedipus and castration complexes there is a fundamental contrast between the two sexes. *Whereas in boys the Oedipus complex succumbs to the castration complex,*[5] *in girls it is made possible and led up to by the castration complex.* This contradiction is cleared up if we reflect that the castration complex always operates in the sense dictated by its subject-matter: it inhibits and limits masculinity and encourages femininity. The difference between the sexual development of males and females at the stage we have been considering is an intelligible consequence of the anatomical distinction between their genitals and of the psychical situation involved in it; it corresponds to the difference between a castration that has been carried out and one that has merely been threatened. In their essentials, therefore, our findings are self-evident and it should have been possible to foresee them.

The Oedipus complex, however, is such an important thing that the manner in which one enters and leaves it cannot be without its effects. In boys (as I have shown at length in the paper to which I have just referred and to which all of my present remarks are closely related) the complex is not simply repressed, it is liter-

---

[5]"The Passing of the Oedipus-Complex" (1924*b*).

ally smashed to pieces by the shock of threatened castration. Its libidinal cathexes are abandoned, desexualized and in part sublimated; its objects are incorporated into the ego, where they form the nucleus of the super-ego and give that new structure its characteristic qualities. In normal, or rather in ideal cases, the Oedipus complex exists no longer, even in the unconscious; the superego has become its heir. Since the penis (to follow Ferenczi) owes its extraordinarily high narcissistic cathexis to its organic significance for the propagation of the species, the catastrophe of the Oedipus complex (the abandonment of incest and the institution of conscience and morality) may be regarded as a victory of the race over the individual. This is an interesting point of view when one considers that neurosis is based upon a struggle of the ego against the demands of the sexual function. But to leave the standpoint of individual psychology is not likely to be of any immediate help in clarifying this complicated situation.

In girls the motive for the destruction of the Oedipus complex is lacking. Castration has already had its effect, which was to force the child into the situation of the Oedipus complex. Thus the Oedipus complex escapes the fate which it meets with in boys: it may either be slowly abandoned or got rid of by repression, or its effects may persist far into women's normal mental life. I cannot escape the notion (though I hesitate to give it expression) that for women the level of what is ethically normal is different from what it is in men. Their super-ego is never so inexorable, so impersonal, so independent of its emotional origins as we require it to be in men. Character traits which critics of every epoch have brought up against women—that they show less sense of justice than men, that they are less ready to submit to the great necessities of life, that they are more often influenced in their judgements by feelings of affection or hostility—all these would be amply accounted for by the modification in the formation of their super-ego which we have already inferred. We must not allow ourselves to be deflected from such conclusions by the denials of the feminists, who are anxious to force us to regard the two sexes as completely equal in position and worth; but we shall, of course, willingly agree that the majority of men are also far behind the masculine ideal and that all human individuals, as a result of their bisexual disposition and of cross inheritance, combine in themselves both masculine and feminine characteristics, so that pure masculinity and femininity remain theoretical constructions of uncertain content.

I am inclined to set some value on the considerations I have brought forward upon the psychological consequences of the anatomical distinction between the sexes. I am aware, however, that this opinion can only be maintained if my findings, which are based on a handful of cases, turn out to have general validity and to be typical. If not, they would remain no more than a contribution to our knowledge of the different paths along which sexual life develops.

In the valuable and comprehensive studies upon the masculinity and castration complex in women by Abraham (1921), Horney (1923) and Helene Deutsch (1925) there is much that touches closely upon what I have written but nothing that coincides with it completely, so that here again I feel justified in publishing this paper.[6]

---

[6]Freud returned to this subject in a later work, on ''Female Sexuality'' (1931). See *infra*, Essay XIII.

XIII

Female Sexuality[1] (1931)

I

In that phase of children's libidinal development which is characterized by the normal Oedipus complex we find that they are ten-
derly attached to the parent of the opposite sex, while their relation
to the other parent is predominantly hostile. In the case of boys
the explanation is simple. A boy's mother was his first love-object;
she remains so, and, as his feelings for her become more passionate and he understands more of the relation between father and
mother, the former inevitably appears as a rival. With little girls
it is otherwise. For them, too, the mother was the first love-object;
how then does a little girl find her way to her father? How, when
and why does she detach herself from her mother? We have long
realized that in women the development of sexuality is complicated
by the task of renouncing that genital zone which was originally
the principal one, namely, the clitoris, in favour of a new zone—
the vagina. But there is a second change which appears to us no
less characteristic and important for feminine development: the
original mother-object has to be exchanged for the father. We
cannot as yet see clearly how these two tasks are linked up.

We know that women with a strong father-attachment are numerous and need not by any means be neurotic. In studying this
type I have made some observations which I propose to communi-

---

[1] ["Über die weibliche Sexualität." First published *Int. Z. Psychoanal.*, 17 (1931)
317; reprinted *Ges. Schr.*, 12, 120; and Ges. W., 14, 517. Translation, reprinted fron·
Int. J. Psychoanal., 13 (1932), 281; by Joan Riviere.]

cate here and which have led me to a certain view of female sexuality. I have been struck, above all, by two facts. First, analysis has shown that where the attachment to the father was peculiarly strong it had been preceded by a phase of equally strong and passionate attachment exclusively to the mother. Except for the change in the object, the love-life had acquired hardly a single new feature in the second phase. The primary mother-relation had developed in a very rich and many-sided way.

Secondly, I learnt that the duration of this attachment to the mother had been greatly underestimated. In a number of cases it persisted well into the fourth and, in one, into the fifth year, so that it comprised by far the longer period of the early sexual efflorescence. Indeed, one had to give due weight to the possibility that many a woman may remain arrested at the original mother-attachment and never properly achieve the change-over to men.

These facts show that the pre-Oedipus phase in women is more important than we have hitherto supposed.

Since there is time during this phase for all the fixations and repressions which we regard as the source of the neuroses, it seems that we shall have to retract the universality of the dictum that the Oedipus complex is the nucleus of neurosis. But if anyone feels reluctant to adopt this correction, he need not do so. For, on the one hand, we can extend the content of the Oedipus complex to include all the child's relations to both parents or, on the other, we can give due recognition to our new findings by saying that women reach the normal, positive Oedipus situation only after surmounting a first phase dominated by the negative complex. Actually, during this phase, to a little girl, her father is not very different from a troublesome rival even though her hostility towards him never reaches such a pitch as does the boy's. We have, after all, long given up any expectation of a neat parallelism between male and female sexual development.

Our insight into this early, pre-Oedipus phase in the little girl's development comes to us as a surprise, comparable in another field with the effect of the discovery of the Minoan-Mycenaean civilization behind that of Greece.

Everything connected with this first mother-attachment has in analysis seemed to me so elusive, lost in a past so dim and shadowy, so hard to resuscitate, that it seemed as if it had undergone some specially inexorable repression. But possibly I have received this impression because, when I have analysed women, they have been able to cling on to that very father-attachment in which they took refuge from the early phase of which I am speaking. It would in fact appear that women-analysts—for instance, Jeanne Lampl-de Groot and Helene Deutsch—had been able to apprehend the facts with greater ease and clearness because they had the advantage of being suitable mother-substitutes in the transference-situation with the patients whom they were studying. I have not indeed succeeded in completely unravelling any of the cases in point and will therefore confine myself to communicating my most general conclusions and giving only a few examples of the new ideas which have suggested themselves to me. Amongst these is my conjecture that this phase of mother-attachment is especially closely connected with the aetiology of hysteria (this is indeed by no means surprising when we reflect that both the phase and the neurosis in question are characteristically feminine); further, that in this dependence on the mother we have the germ of later paranoia in women.[2] For it appears that this germ is the surprising, yet regular, dread of being killed (? devoured) by the mother. It would seem plausible to conjecture that this anxiety corresponds to the hostility which the child develops towards her mother because of the manifold restrictions imposed by the latter in the process of training and physical care, and that the immaturity of the child's psychical organization favours the mechanism of projection.

II

I have begun by stating the two facts which have struck me as new: first, that the great dependence on the father in women merely takes over the heritage of an equally great attachment to the mother

---

[2] In the well-known case [of delusional jealousy] reported by Ruth Mack Brunswick (1928a) the direct source of the disorder was the patient's pre-Oedipus fixation (to her sister).—"The Analysis of a Case of Paranoia," *J. Nerv. Ment. Dis.*, 70 (1929), 177.

and, secondly, that this earlier phase lasts longer than we should have anticipated. I must now go back a little in order to insert these new conclusions in their proper place in the picture of female sexual development with which we are already familiar. A certain amount of repetition is here inevitable. It will help our exposition if, as we go along, we compare the course of female development with that of the male.

First of all, there can be no doubt that the bisexual disposition which we maintain to be characteristic of human beings manifests itself much more plainly in the female than in the male. The latter has only one principal sexual zone—only one sexual organ—whereas the former has two: the vagina, the true female organ, and the clitoris, which is analogous to the male organ. We believe that we may justly assume that for many years the vagina is virtually non-existent and possibly remains without sensation until puberty. It is true, however, that recently an increasing number of observers have been inclined to think that vaginal stirrings are present even in those early years. In any case female genitality must, in childhood, centre principally in the clitoris. The sexual life of the woman is regularly split up into two phases, the first of which is of a masculine character, whilst only the second is specifically feminine. Thus in female development there is a process of transition from the one phase to the other, to which there is nothing analogous in males. A further complication arises from the fact that the clitoris, with its masculine character, continues to function in later female sexual life in a very variable manner, which we certainly do not as yet fully understand. Of course, we do not know what are the biological roots of these specific characteristics of the woman, and we are still less able to assign to them any teleological purpose.

Parallel with this first great difference there is another, which concerns the love-object. The first love-object of the male is the mother, because it is she who feeds and tends him, and she remains his principal love-object until she is replaced by another which resembles her or is derived from her. With the female too the mother must be the first object, for the primary conditions of object-choice are the same for all children. But at the end of the girl's development it is the man—the father—who must come to be the new love-object; *i.e.* as she changes in sex, so must the sex of her love-object change. What we now have to discover is how this transformation takes place, how radical or how incomplete it is, and all the different things that may happen in this process of development.

We have already observed that there is yet another difference between the sexes in their relation to the Oedipus complex. We have the impression that what we have said about that complex applies in all strictness only to male children, and that we are right in rejecting the term "Electra complex" which seeks to insist that the situation of the two sexes is analogous. It is only in male children that there occurs the fateful simultaneous conjunction of love for the one parent and hatred of the other as rival. It is thereupon the discovery of the possibility of castration, as evidenced by the sight of the female genital, which necessitates the transformation of the boy's Oedipus complex, leads to the creation of the super-ego and thus initiates all the processes that culminate in enrolling the individual in civilized society. After the paternal function has been internalized so as to form the super-ego, the next task is to detach the latter from those persons of whom it was originally the psychical representative. In this remarkable course of development the agent employed to restrain infantile sexuality is precisely that narcissistic genital interest which centres in the preservation of the penis.

One residue of the castration complex in the man is a measure of disparagement in his attitude towards women, whom he regards as having been castrated. In extreme cases this inhibits his object-choice, and, if reinforced by organic factors, it may result in exclusive homosexuality. Very different is the effect of the castration complex on the girl. She acknowledges the fact of her castration, the consequent superiority of the male and her own inferiority, but she also rebels against these unpleasant facts. So divided in her mind, she may follow one of three lines of development. The first leads to her turning her back on sexuality altogether. The budding woman, frightened by the comparison of herself with boys, becomes dissatisfied with her clitoris and gives up her phallic activity and therewith her sexuality in general and a considerable part of her masculine proclivities in other fields. If she pursues the second line, she clings in obstinate self-assertion to her threatened masculinity; the hope of getting a penis sometime is cherished to an incredibly late age and becomes the aim of her life, whilst the phantasy of really being a man, in spite of everything, often dominates long periods of her life. This "masculinity complex" may also result in a manifestly homosexual object-choice. Only if her development follows the third, very circuitous path does she arrive at the ultimate normal feminine attitude in which she takes her father as love-object, and thus arrives at the Oedipus complex in its feminine form. Thus, in women, that complex represents the final result of a lengthy process of development; castration does not destroy but rather creates it, and it escapes the strong hostile influences which, in men, tend to its destruction—in fact, only too often a woman never surmounts it at all. Hence too the cultural effects of the break-up of this complex are slighter and less important in women than in men. We should probably not err in saying that it is this difference in the inter-relation of the Oedipus and the castration-complexes which gives its special stamp to the character of woman as a member of society.[3]

We see then that the phase of exclusive attachment to the mother, which may be called the *pre-Oedipus* phase, is far more important in women than it can claim to be in men. Many phenomena of feminine sexual life which were difficult to understand before can be fully explained by reference to this phase. For example, we had noted long ago that many a woman who takes her father as the model for her choice of a husband, or assigns her father's place to him, yet in her married life repeats with her

---

[3]It is to be anticipated that male analysts with feminist sympathies, and our women analysts also, will disagree with what I have said here. They will hardly fail to object that such notions have their origin in the man's "masculinity complex," and are meant to justify theoretically his innate propensity to disparage and suppress women. But this sort of psychoanalytic argument reminds us here, as it so often does, of Dostoevsky's famous "knife that cuts both ways." The opponents of those who reason thus will for their part think it quite comprehensible that members of the female sex should refuse to accept a notion that appears to gainsay their eagerly coveted equality with men. The use of analysis as a weapon of controversy obviously leads to no decision.

husband her bad relations with her mother. He should have succeeded to her relation with her father, but in reality he takes over her relation to her mother. This is easily explained as an obvious case of regression. The mother-relation was the original one, upon which the father-relation was built up; in married life the original basis emerges from repression. For her development to womanhood consisted mainly in transferring affective ties from the mother to the father-object.

With many women we have the impression that the period of their maturity is entirely taken up with conflicts with their husbands, just as they spent their youth in conflicts with their mothers. In the light of what I have now said we shall conclude that the hostile attitude to the mother is not a consequence of the rivalry implicit in the Oedipus complex, but rather originates in the preceding phase and has simply found in the Oedipus situation reinforcement and an opportunity for asserting itself. Direct analytic investigation confirms this view. Our interest must be directed to the mechanisms at work in the turning away from the mother-object, originally so vehemently and exclusively loved. We are prepared to find not one solitary factor but a whole number of these contributing to the same end.

Amongst these factors are some which are conditioned by the circumstances of infantile sexuality in general and so hold good equally for the love-relations of boys. First and foremost we must mention jealousy of other persons—brothers and sisters and rivals, amongst whom is also the father. Childish love knows no bounds, it demands exclusive possession, is satisfied with nothing less than all. But it has a second characteristic: it has no real aim; it is incapable of complete satisfaction and this is the principal reason why it is doomed to end in disappointment and to give place to a hostile attitude. Later on in life, the lack of ultimate gratification may conduce to a different result. This very factor may ensure the undisturbed continuance of the libidinal cathexis, as is the case in love-relations inhibited in their aim. But in the stress of the processes of development it regularly happens that the libido abandons its unsatisfactory position in order to find a new one.

There is another, far more specific motive for the turning away from the mother, arising out of the effect of the castration-complex on the little creature without a penis. Some time or other the little girl makes the discovery of her organic inferiority, of course earlier and more easily if she has brothers or other boy companions. We have already noted the three paths which diverge from this point: (*a*) that which leads to the suspension of the whole sexual life, (*b*) that which leads to the defiant over-emphasis of her own masculinity, and (*c*) the first steps towards definitive femininity. It is not easy to say precisely when these processes occur or to lay down their typical course. Even the point of time when the discovery of castration is made varies and many other factors seem to be inconstant and to depend on chance. The condition of the girl's own phallic activity plays a part, as also whether it is discovered or not, and how far it is hindered after the discovery.

The little girl generally finds out spontaneously her mode of phallic activity—masturbation of the clitoris—and in the first instance it is no doubt unaccompanied by phantasies. The way in which the tending of the child's body influences the awakening of this activity is reflected in the very common phantasy of seduction by her mother, her wet-nurse or nurse-maid. Whether little girls practise masturbation more rarely and from the beginning less energetically than little boys is a point which we must leave undecided: quite possibly this is the case. Actual seduction is likewise common enough, either at the hands of other children or of nurses who want to soothe the child, send her to sleep or make her dependent on them. Where seduction intervenes, it invariably disturbs the natural course of development and often has profound and lasting consequences.

The prohibition of masturbation may, as we have seen, act as an incentive for giving the habit up, but it may also operate as a motive for rebellion against the person who forbids, *i.e.* the mother, or the mother-substitute who later regularly merges into the mother. The defiant persistence in masturbation would appear to open the way to masculinity. Even when the child does not succeed in mastering her habit, the effect of the apparently unavailing prohibition is seen in her later efforts to free herself at all costs from a gratification which has been made distasteful to her. When the girl reaches maturity her object-choice may still be influenced by this firmly maintained purpose. Resentment at being prevented from free sexual activity has much to do with her detachment from her mother. The same motive recurs after puberty when the mother takes up the duty of protecting her daughter's chastity. Of course, we must remember here that the mother opposes masturbation in the boy in the same way, thus providing him also with a powerful motive for rebellion.

When a little girl has sight of a male genital organ and so discovers her own deficiency, she does not accept the unwelcome knowledge without hesitation and reluctance. As we have seen, she clings obstinately to the expectation of acquiring a similar organ sometime, and the desire for it survives long after the hope is extinguished. Invariably the child regards castration in the first instance as a misfortune peculiar to herself; only later does she realize that it extends to certain other children and at length to certain adults. When the universality of this negative character of her sex dawns upon her, womanhood, and with it also her mother, suffers a heavy loss of credit in her eyes.

Very possibly this account of the little girl's reaction to her impression of castration and the prohibition of masturbation will strike the reader as confused and contradictory. That is not altogether the writer's fault. A description which fits every case is in fact almost impossible. In different individuals we find the most various reactions; even in the same individual contrary attitudes exist side by side. With the first intervention of the prohibition there begins a conflict which from that moment will accompany the development of the sexual function. It is particularly difficult to get a clear insight into what takes place because it is so hard to distinguish the mental processes of this first phase from the later ones by which they become overlaid and distorted in memory. For example, the fact of castration is sometimes construed later as a punishment for masturbation, and its infliction is ascribed to the father; of course, neither of these ideas can be the original one. With boys also it is regularly the father from whom castration is dreaded, although in their case, as in the little girl's, it is mostly the mother who utters the threat.

However this may be, at the end of this first phase of attachment to the mother there emerges, as the strongest motive for turning away from her, the child's reproach that her mother has not given her a proper genital, *i.e.* that she was born a woman. A second reproach, not going quite so far back, comes as rather a surprise: it is that the mother gave the child too little milk and did not suckle her long enough. Under the conditions of modern civilization this may very often be quite true, but certainly not so often as is maintained in analysis. It would seem rather that this complaint expresses the general dissatisfaction of children who under our monogamous civilization are weaned at the age of from six to nine months, whereas the primitive mother devotes herself exclusively to her child for two or three years. It is as if our children remained for ever unappeased, as if they had never been suckled long enough. But I am not sure whether, if one analysed children who had been suckled as long as those of primitive races, one would not encounter the same complaint. So great is the greed of the childish libido! If we survey the whole range of motives brought to light by analysis for turning away from the mother: that she neglected to provide the little girl with the only proper genital organ, that she did not feed her enough, compelled her to share her mother's love with others, never fulfilled all the expectations of the child's love and, finally, that she first excited and then forbade her daughter's own sexual activity—all these seem inadequate as a justification of the hostility finally felt. Some of these reproaches follow inevitably from the nature of infantile sexuality; others look like rationalizations devised later to explain the uncomprehended change in feeling. Perhaps the real fact is that the attachment to the mother must inevitably perish just because it is the first and most intense, similarly to what we so often find in the first marriages of young women, entered into when they were most passionately in love. In both cases the love-relation probably comes to grief by reason of the unavoidable disappointments and an accumulation of occasions for aggression. As a rule second marriages turn out much better.

We cannot go so far as to assert that the ambivalence of emotional cathexes is a universally valid psychological law, that it is quite impossible to feel great love for a person without the accompaniment of a hatred perhaps as great, and vice versa. Normal adults do, undoubtedly, succeed in separating these two attitudes, and do not find themselves compelled to hate their love-objects and love as well as hate their enemies. But this seems to be the result of later development. In the first phases of the love-life ambivalence is evidently the rule. Many people retain this archaic trait throughout life; it is characteristic of obsessional neurotics that in their object-relations love and hate counterbalance one another. In members of primitive races also we may say that ambivalence predominates. We shall conclude, then, that the little girl's vehement attachment to her mother is strongly ambivalent and that, reinforced as it is by the above other factors, it is precisely this ambivalence which determines the child's turning away from her. That is to say, it is the consequence once more of one of the universal characteristics of infantile sexuality.

An objection immediately presents itself to the explanation I have suggested: "How is it that boys succeed in keeping intact their attachment to the mother, which is certainly no less strong than the girl's?" An instant answer is: "Because boys are able to deal with their ambivalent feelings towards her by transferring all their hostility to the father." But, in the first place, we should be chary of asserting this until we have exhaustively studied the pre-Oedipus phase in boys and, secondly, it would probably be more prudent altogether to admit that we have not yet got to the bottom of processes which, after all, we have only just come to know of.

III

Another question is this: "What exactly is it that the little girl demands of her mother? What is the nature of her sexual aims during the period of exclusive attachment to her mother?" The answer which we gather from the analytic material is just what we should expect. The little girl's sexual aims in relation to her mother are both active and passive and are determined by the different libidinal phases through which the child passes. Here the relation of activity to passivity is specially interesting. It is easy to observe how, in every field of psychical experience and not merely in that of sexuality, an impression passively received evokes in children a tendency to an active response. They try to do to themselves what has just been done to them. This is part of their task of mastering the outside world, and may even lead to their endeavouring to repeat impressions which they would have good reason to avoid because of their disagreeable content. Children's play, too, is made to serve this purpose of completing and thus, as it were, annulling a passive experience by active behaviour. When, in spite of resistance, a physician has opened a child's mouth to examine his throat, the same child will, after he has gone, play at being "the doctor" and will repeat the same forcible procedure on a little brother or sister, as defenceless against him as he was against the physician. We cannot fail to recognize here a revolt against passivity and a preference for the active role. This swing-over from passivity to activity does not take place with the same regularity and vigour in all children: in some it may not occur at all. From their behaviour in this respect we can draw some conclusion as to the relative strength of the masculine and the feminine tendencies which will be revealed in their sexual life.

The first sexual or sexually tinged experiences of a child in its relation to the mother are naturally passive in character. It is she who suckles, feeds, cleans and dresses it, and instructs it in the performance of all its physical functions. Part of the child's libido goes on clinging to these experiences and enjoys the various gratifications associated with them, while another part strives to convert them into activity. First, the process of being suckled at the mother's breast gives place to active sucking. In its other relations with its mother the child either contents itself with independence (*i.e.* with successfully performing itself what was previously done to it) or with actively repeating in play its passive experience, or else it does really make the mother the object in relation to which it assumes the role of the active subject. This last reaction, which comes into play in the form of real activity, I long held to be incredible, until experience removed all my doubts on the subject.

We seldom hear of a little girl's wanting to wash or dress her mother or tell her to perform her bodily functions. Sometimes she says: "Now let's play that I am mother and you are child"; but generally she fulfils these active wishes indirectly in playing with her doll, she herself representing the mother and the doll the child. The fact that girls are fonder of playing with dolls than are boys is commonly interpreted as an early sign of awakened femininity. That is quite true, only we must not overlook the fact that it is the *active* side of femininity which finds expression here and that the little girl's preference for dolls probably testifies to the exclusiveness of her attachment to her mother, accompanied by total neglect of her father-object.

The very surprising sexual activity of the little girl in relation to her mother manifests itself in chronological succession in oral, sadistic and finally even phallic impulses directed upon her. It is difficult to give a detailed account of these, because often they are dim impulses which it was impossible for the child to grasp psychically at the time and which were only interpreted later, and express themselves in analysis in forms that are certainly not the original ones. Sometimes we find them transferred to the later father-object, where they do not belong and badly interfere with our understanding of the situation. We find aggressive oral and sadistic wishes in a form forced on them by early repression, *i.e.* in the dread of being killed by the mother—a dread which on its side justifies the death-wish against her, if this enters consciousness. It is impossible to say how often this dread of the mother draws countenance from an unconscious hostility on her part, which the child divines. (The dread of being *eaten* I have so far found only in men; it is referred to the father, but is probably the result of the transformation of oral aggressive tendencies directed upon the mother. The person the child wants to devour is the mother who nourished him: in the case of the father there is no such obvious occasion for the wish.)

The women patients characterized by a strong attachment to the mother, in whom I have been able to study the pre-Oedipus phase, have all told me that when their mother gave them enemas or rectal douches they used to offer the strongest possible resistance and react with fear and screams of rage. This is probably very usual or even universal with children. I only came to understand the reasons for this specially passionate struggle through a remark by Ruth Mack Brunswick, who was studying these problems at the same time as I was. She said that she would compare the outbreak of fury after an enema with the orgasm following on genital excitation. The accompanying anxiety should be construed as a transformation of the desire for aggression which had been stirred up. I believe that this is actually the case and that, on the anal-sadistic level, the intense passive excitation of the intestinal zone evokes an outbreak of desire for aggression, manifesting itself either directly in the form of rage or, as a consequence of suppression, as anxiety. In later years this reaction seems to die away.

In considering the passive impulses of the phallic phase we are struck by the fact that girls regularly charge their mothers with seducing them, because their first or at any rate strongest genital sensations came to them when they were being cleansed and tended by their mothers (or the nurses representing them). Mothers have often told me that they have observed that their little daughters of two or three years old enjoy these sensations and try to get their mother to heighten them by repeated touching and rubbing of the parts. I believe that the fact that the mother so unavoidably initiates the child into the phallic phase is the reason why in the phantasies of later years the father so regularly appears as the sexual seducer. When the girl turns away from the mother she transfers to the father at the same time the responsibility for having introduced her to sexual life.

Finally in the phallic phase strong active wishes towards the mother also make their appearance. The sexual activity of this period culminates in clitoridal masturbation; probably the child accompanies this with images of her mother, but whether she really imagines a sexual aim and what that aim is my experience does not make clear. It is only when all her interests have received a fresh impetus through the arrival of a baby brother or sister that we can clearly recognize any such aim. The little girl, just like the boy, wants to believe that she has given her mother this new child, and her reaction to the event and her behaviour towards the child are the same as his. I know this sounds quite absurd, but perhaps only because the idea is such an unfamiliar one to us.

The turning-away from the mother is a most important step in the little girl's development: it is more than a mere change of object. We have already described what takes place and what a number of motives are alleged for it; we must now add that we observe, hand in hand with it, a marked diminution in the active and an augmentation of the passive sexual impulses. It is true that the active impulses have suffered more severely from frustration: they have proved totally impracticable and therefore the libido has more readily abandoned them. But the passive trends also have not escaped disappointment. Frequently, with the turning-away from the mother there is cessation of clitoridal masturbation, and very often when the little girl represses her previous masculinity a considerable part of her general sexual life is permanently injured. The transition to the father-object is accomplished with the assistance of the passive tendencies so far as these have escaped overthrow. The way to the development of femininity then lies open to the girl, except in so far as she is hampered by remains of the pre-Oedipus mother-attachment which she has passed through.

If we survey the phases of feminine sexual development I have described, there is a definite conclusion about femininity as a whole which we cannot resist: the same libidinal forces, we have found, are at work in female and in male children, and we have been able to convince ourselves that for a certain period these forces take the same course and produce the same results.

Subsequently, biological factors deflect them from their original aims and conduct even active and in every sense masculine strivings into feminine channels. Since we cannot dismiss the notion that sexual excitation is derived from the operation of certain chemical substances, it would at first seem natural to expect that some day biochemistry will reveal two distinct substances, the presence of which produces male and female sexual excitation respectively. But this hope is surely no less naïve than that other one which has happily been abandoned nowadays, namely, that it would be possible to isolate under the microscope the different causative factors of hysteria, obsessional neurosis, melancholia, etc.

In sexual chemistry, too, the processes must be rather more complicated. For psychology, however, it is a matter of indifference whether there is in the body a single sexually stimulating substance, or two, or an endless number. Psychoanalysis teaches us to manage with a single libido, though its aims, *i.e.* its modes of gratification, are both active and passive. In this antithesis, above all in the existence of libidinal impulses whose aims are passive, the rest of our problem is contained.

IV

A study of the analytical literature on this subject makes evident that it already contains everything that I have said here. This paper would be superfluous were it not that in so obscure a field of research every account of any worker's direct experience and the conclusions to which he personally is led may be of value. I have, moreover, I think, defined certain points more precisely and shown them in stricter isolation than has hitherto been done. Some of the other writings on the subject are confusing because they deal at the same time with the problems of the super-ego and the sense of guilt. This I have avoided, and also, in describing the various outcomes of this phase of development, I have refrained from touching on the complications which arise when a child, disappointed in her relation with her father, returns to the abandoned mother-attachment, or in the course of her life repeatedly shifts over from the one attitude to the other. But just because this article is only one contribution amongst others I may be dispensed from an exhaustive survey of the literature on the subject and will confine myself to indicating the more important points on which I agree with some or differ from other writers.[4]

Abraham's (1921) description of the manifestations of the female castration complex is still unsurpassed, but one would have liked it to include the factor of the original exclusive attachment to the mother. With the principal points in Jeanne Lampl-de Groot's[5] (1927) important work I am in agreement. She recognizes that the pre-Oedipus phase is completely identical in boys and in girls, and she affirms (and proves from her own observations) that the little girl's attitude towards the mother includes sexual (phallic)

---

[4][Freud does not mention his own earlier paper on the subject (1925b), page 145 of this volume.]

[5]In the *Zeitschrift* the author's name was given as "A. Lampl de Groot," and I make this correction at her request.

activity. The turning-away from the mother is traced by this writer to the influence of the child's perception of castration, which forces her to abandon her sexual object and often at the same time the practice of masturbation. The whole development is described in the following formula: the little girl has to pass through a phase of the "negative" Oedipus complex before arriving at the positive. There is one point in which I find her account inadequate: she represents the turning-away from the mother as merely a change of object and does not show that it is accompanied by the plainest manifestations of hostility. To this factor complete justice is done in Helene Deutsch's latest paper on the subject (1930), in which she also recognizes the little girl's phallic activity and the strength of her attachment to her mother. Helene Deutsch states, further, that in turning to the father the little girl follows her passive tendencies (already awakened in her relation with her mother). In her earlier book (1925) this author was still influenced by the endeavour to apply the Oedipus scheme to the pre-Oedipus phase and for this reason she interpreted the little girl's phallic activity as an identification with the father.

Fenichel (1930) rightly emphasizes the difficulty of recognizing in the material produced in analysis what represents the unchanged content of the pre-Oedipus phase and what has been distorted in the course of regression (or some other process). He does not accept Jeanne Lampl-de Groot's view of the little girl's phallic activity and he protests against Melanie Klein's (1928) "displacement backwards" of the Oedipus complex, whose beginnings she assigns to the commencement of the second year of life. This view of the date of origin of the complex, in addition to its necessitating a modification of our view of all the rest of the child's development, is in fact not in accordance with what we learn from the analyses of adults and is especially incompatible with my findings as to the long duration of the girl's pre-Oedipus attachment to her mother. This contradiction may be softened by the reflection that we are not as yet able to distinguish in this field between what is rigidly fixed by biological laws and what is subject to change or shifting under the influence of accidental experience. We have long recognized that seduction may have the effect of hastening and stimulating to maturity the sexual development of children, and it is quite possible that other factors operate in the same way; such, for instance, as the child's age when brothers or sisters are born or when it discovers the difference between the sexes, or, again, its direct observation of sexual intercourse, its parents' behaviour in evoking or repelling its love, and so forth.

Some authors are inclined to disparage the importance of the child's first, most primal libidinal impulses, laying stress rather on later developmental processes, so that—putting this view in its extreme form—all that the former can be said to do is to indicate certain trends, while the amounts of energy [*Intensitäten*] with which these trends are pursued are drawn from later regressions and reaction-formations. Thus, for example, K. Horney (1926) is of opinion that we greatly over-estimate the girl's primary penis-envy and that the strength of her subsequent striving towards masculinity is to be attributed to a *secondary* penis-envy, which is used to ward off her feminine impulses, especially those connected with her attachment to her father. This does not agree with the impressions that I myself have formed. Certain as it is that the earliest libidinal tendencies are reinforced later by regression and reaction-formation and difficult as it is to estimate the relative strength of the various confluent libidinal components, I still think that we must not overlook the fact that those first impulses have an intensity of their own which is greater than anything that comes later and may indeed be said to be incommensurable with any other force. It is certainly true that there is an antithesis between the attachment to the father and the masculinity-complex—this is the universal antithesis between activity and passivity, masculinity and femininity—but we have no right to assume that only the one is primary, while the other owes its strength merely to the process of defence. And if the defence against femininity is so vigorous, from what other source can it derive its strength than from that striving for masculinity which found its earliest expression in the child's penis-envy and might well take its name from this?

A similar objection applies to Jones's view (1927) that the phallic phase in girls represents a secondary, protective reaction rather than a genuine stage of development. This does not correspond to either the dynamic or the chronological conditions.

XIV

Medusa's Head[1] (1922)

We have not often attempted to interpret individual mythological themes, but an interpretation suggests itself easily in the case of the horrifying decapitated head of Medusa.

To decapitate = to castrate. The terror of Medusa is thus a terror of castration that is linked to the sight of something. Numerous analyses have made us familiar with the occasion for this: it occurs when a boy, who has hitherto been unwilling to believe the threat of castration, catches sight of the female genitals, probably those of an adult, surrounded by hair, and essentially those of his mother.

The hair upon Medusa's head is frequently represented in works of art in the form of snakes, and these once again are derived from the castration complex. It is a remarkable fact that, however frightening they may be in themselves, they nevertheless serve actually as a mitigation of the horror, for they replace the penis, the absence of which is the cause of the horror. This is a confirmation of the technical rule according to which a multiplication of penis symbols signifies castration.

The sight of Medusa's head makes the spectator stiff with terror, turns him to stone. Observe that we have here once again the same origin from the castration complex and the same transformation of affect! For becoming stiff means an erection. Thus in the original situation it offers consolation to the spectator: he is still in possession of a penis, and the stiffening reassures him of the fact.

---

[1]["Das Medusenhaupt." First published posthumously *Int. Z. Psychoanal, Imago*, 25 (1940), 105; reprinted *Ges. W.*, 17, 47. The manuscript is dated May 14, 1922, and appears to be a sketch for a more extensive work. Translation, reprinted from *Int. J. Psychoanal.*, 22 (1941), 69; by John Strachey.]

This symbol of horror is worn upon her dress by the virgin goddess Athena. And rightly so, for thus she becomes a woman who is unapproachable and repels all sexual desires—since she displays the terrifying genitals of the Mother. Since the Greeks were in the main strongly homosexual, it was inevitable that we should find among them a representation of woman as a being who frightens and repels because she is castrated.

If Medusa's head takes the place of a representation of the female genitals, or rather if it isolates their horrifying effects from the pleasure-giving ones, it may be recalled that displaying the genitals is familiar in other connections as an apotropaic act. What arouses horror in oneself will produce the same effect upon the enemy against whom one is seeking to defend oneself. We read in Rabelais of how the Devil took to flight when the woman showed him her vulva.

The erect male organ also has an apotropaic effect, but thanks to another mechanism. To display the penis (or any of its surrogates) is to say: "I am not afraid of you. I defy you. I have a penis." Here, then, is another way of intimidating the Evil Spirit.

In order seriously to substantiate this interpretation it would be necessary to investigate the origin of this isolated symbol of horror in Greek mythology as well as parallels to it in other mythologies.[2]

---

[2][The same topic was dealt with by Ferenczi (1923) in a very short paper which was itself briefly commented upon by Freud in his "Infantile Genital Organization of the Libido" (1923a), supra, Essay X. The whole subject has been treated at greater length by Flugel (1924).]

XV

Fetishism[1] (1927)

In the last few years I have had an opportunity of studying analyti-
cally a number of men whose object-choice was ruled by a fetish.
One need not suppose that these persons had sought analysis on
account of a fetish; the devotees of fetishes regard them as abnormalities, it is true, but only rarely as symptoms of illness; usually
they are quite content with them or even extol the advantages they
offer for erotic gratification. As a rule, therefore, the fetish made
its appearance in analysis as a subsidiary finding.

For obvious reasons I cannot go into the details of these cases
in a published paper; nor can I show how the selection of individual fetishes is in part conditioned by accidental circumstances. The
case of a young man who had exalted a certain kind of "shine on
the nose" into a fetishistic condition seemed most extraordinary.
The very surprising explanation of this was that the patient had
been first brought up in an English nursery and had later gone to
Germany, where he almost completely forgot his mother-tongue.
The fetish, which derived from his earliest childhood, had to be
deciphered into English, not German; the *Glanz auf der Nase*
[*shine* on the nose] was really "a *glance* at the nose;" the nose
was thus the fetish, which, by the way, he endowed when he
wished with the necessary special brilliance, which other people
could not perceive.

In all the cases the meaning and purpose of the fetish turned
out under analysis to be the same. It revealed itself so unequivo-

---

[1]["Fetischismus." First published *Int. Z. Psychoanal.*, 13 (1927), 373; reprinted
Ges. Schr., 11, 395; and *Ges. W.*, 14, 311. Translation, reprinted from *Int. J. Psychoanal.*, 9 (1928), 161; by Joan Riviere.]

cally and seemed to me so categorical that I should expect the same solution in all cases of fetishism. When I now disclose that the fetish is a penis-substitute I shall certainly arouse disappointment; so I hasten to add that it is not a substitute for any chance penis, but for a particular quite special penis that had been extremely important in early childhood but was afterwards lost. That is to say: it should normally have been given up, but the purpose of the fetish precisely is to preserve it from being lost. To put it plainly: the fetish is a substitute for the woman's (mother's) phallus which the little boy once believed in and does not wish to forego—we know why.[2]

What had happened, therefore, was that the boy had refused to take cognizance of the fact perceived by him that a woman has no penis. No, that cannot be true, for if a woman can be castrated then his own penis is in danger; and against that there rebels part of his narcissism which Nature has providentially attached to this particular organ. In later life grown men may experience a similar panic, perhaps when the cry goes up that throne and altar are in danger, and similar illogical consequences will also follow them. If I am not mistaken, Laforgue would say in this case that the boy "scotomizes" the perception of the woman's lack of a penis.[3] Now a new term is justified when it describes a new fact or brings it into prominence. There is nothing of that kind here; the oldest word in our psychoanalytical terminology, "repression," already refers to this pathological process. If we wish to differentiate between what happens to the *idea* as distinct from the *affect*, we can restrict "repression" to relate to the affect; the correct word for what happens to the idea is then "denial."[4] "Scotomization"

---

[2]This interpretation was mentioned in 1910, without any reasons being given for it, in my study on Leonardo da Vinci (1910).

[3]I correct myself here, however, by adding that I have the best reasons for knowing that Laforgue would not say this at all. It is clear from his own remarks that "scotomization" is a term deriving from a description of dementia praecox, not arising through the application of psychoanalytical conceptions to the psychoses, and cannot be applied to the processes of development and formation of neurosis. In the text I have been at pains to demonstrate this incompatibility. [Cf. Laforgue (1926).]

[4][Cf. Freud's paper on "Repression" (1915b), *General Psychological Theory*, Collier Books edition AS 582V.]

seems to me particularly unsuitable, for it suggests that the perception is promptly obliterated, so that the result is the same as when a visual impression falls on the blind spot on the retina. In the case we are discussing, on the contrary, we see that the perception has persisted and that a very energetic action has been exerted to keep up the denial of it. It is not true that the child emerges from his experience of seeing the female parts with an unchanged belief in the woman having a phallus. He retains this belief but he also gives it up; during the conflict between the deadweight of the unwelcome perception and the force of the opposite wish, a compromise is constructed such as is only possible in the realm of unconscious modes of thought—by the primary processes. In the world of psychical reality the woman still has a penis in spite of all, but this penis is no longer the same as it once was. Something else has taken its place, has been appointed its successor, so to speak, and now absorbs all the interest which formerly belonged to the penis. But this interest undergoes yet another very strong reinforcement, because the horror of castration sets up a sort of permanent memorial to itself by creating this substitute. Aversion from the real female genitals, which is never lacking in any fetishist, also remains as an indelible stigma of the repression that has taken place. One can now see what the fetish achieves and how it is enabled to persist. It remains a token of triumph over the threat of castration and a safeguard against it; it also saves the fetishist from being a homosexual by endowing women with the attribute which makes them acceptable as sexual objects. In later life the fetishist sees other advantages in his substitute for the genital. The significance of fetishes is not known to the world at large and therefore not prohibited; they are easily obtainable and sexual gratification by their means is thus very convenient. The fetishist has no trouble in getting what other men have to woo and exert themselves to obtain.

Probably no male human being is spared the terrifying shock of threatened castration at the sight of the female genitals. We cannot explain why it is that some of them become homosexual in consequence of this experience, others ward it off by creating a fetish, and the great majority overcome it. It is possible that we do not yet know, among all the many factors operating, those which determine the more rare pathological results; we must be satisfied when we can explain what has happened, and may for the present leave on one side the task of explaining why something has *not* happened.

One would expect that the organs or objects selected as substitutes for the penis whose presence is missed in the woman would be such as act as symbols for the penis in other respects. This may happen occasionally but is certainly not the determining factor. It seems rather that when the fetish comes to life, so to speak, some process has been suddenly interrupted—it reminds one of the abrupt halt made by memory in traumatic amnesias. In the case of the fetish, too, interest is held up at a certain point—what is possibly the last impression received before the uncanny traumatic one is preserved as a fetish. Thus the foot or shoe owes its attraction as a fetish, or part of it, to the circumstance that the inquisitive boy used to peer up the woman's legs towards her genitals. Velvet and fur reproduce—as has long been suspected—the sight of the pubic hair which ought to have revealed the longed-for penis; the underlinen so often adopted as a fetish reproduces the scene of undressing, the last moment in which the woman could still be regarded as phallic. But I do not maintain that it is always possible to ascertain the determination of every fetish.

Investigations into fetishism are to be recommended to all who still doubt the existence of the castration complex or who can still believe that the horror of the female genitals has some other foundation: for instance, that it derives from a supposed memory of the trauma of birth.

For me there was another point of interest in the explanation of fetishism. Not long ago in quite a speculative way I formulated the proposition that the essential difference between neurosis and psychosis consists in this: that in neurosis the ego suppresses part of the id out of allegiance to reality, whereas in psychosis it lets itself be carried away by the id and detached from a part of reality.[5] But soon after this I had cause to regret that I had been so daring. In the analyses of two young men I learnt that each of

---

[5] "Neurosis and Psychosis" (1924a) and "The Loss of Reality in Neurosis and Psychosis (1924c).

them—one in his second and the other in his tenth year—had refused to acknowledge the death of his father—had "scotomized" it—and yet neither of them had developed a psychosis. A very important piece of reality had thus been denied by the ego, in the same way as the fetishist denies the unwelcome fact of the woman's castrated condition. I also began to suspect that similar occurrences are by no means rare in childhood, and thought I had made a mistake in my differentiation between neurosis and psychosis. It is true, there was one way out of the difficulty: it might be that my formula held good only when a higher degree of differentiation existed in the mental apparatus; reactions might be possible in a child which would cause severe injury in an adult.

But further research led to another solution of the contradiction. It turned out, that is, as follows: the two young men had no more "scotomized" the death of their fathers than a fetishist scotomizes the castration of women. It was only one current of their mental processes that had not acknowledged the father's death; there was another which was fully aware of the fact; the one which was consistent with reality stood alongside the one which accorded with a wish. One of these two cases of mine had derived an obsessional neurosis of some severity from this dissociation; in every situation in life he oscillated between two assumptions—on the one his father was still alive and hindered him from action, on the other his father was dead and he had the right to regard himself as his successor. In a psychosis the true idea which accorded with reality would have been *really* absent.

To return to my description of fetishism, I have to add that there are numerous and very weighty proofs of the double attitude of fetishists to the question of the castration of women. In very subtle cases the fetish itself has become the vehicle both of denying and of asseverating the fact of castration. This was exemplified in the case of a man whose fetish was a suspensory belt which can also be worn as bathing drawers; this piece of clothing covers the genitals and altogether conceals the difference between them. The analysis showed that it could mean that a woman is castrated, or that she is not castrated, and it even allows of a supposition that a man may be castrated, for all these possibilities could be equally well hidden beneath the belt; its forerunner in childhood had been the fig-leaf seen on a statue. Naturally, a fetish of this kind constructed out of two opposing ideas is capable of great tenacity. Sometimes the double attitude shows itself in what the fetishist—either actually or in phantasy—does with the fetish. It is not the whole story to say that he worships it; very often he treats it in a way which is plainly equivalent to castrating it. This happens particularly when a strong father-identification has been developed, since the child ascribed the original castration of the woman to the father. Tender and hostile treatment of fetishes is mixed in unequal degrees—like the denial and the recognition of castration—in different cases, so that the one or the other is more evident. Here one gets a sort of glimpse of comprehension, as from a distance, of the behaviour of people who cut off women's plaits of hair; in them the impulse to execute the castration which they deny is what comes to the fore. The action contains within it two incompatible propositions: the woman has still got a penis and the father has castrated the woman. Another variety of this, which might be regarded as a race-psychological parallel to fetishism, is the Chinese custom of first mutilating a woman's foot and then revering it. The Chinese man seems to want to thank the woman for having submitted to castration.

The normal prototype of all fetishes is the penis of the man, just as the normal prototype of an organ felt to be inferior is the real little penis of the woman, the clitoris.[6]

---

[6][Freud reverted to the subject of fetishism later. Cf. 1938*a* (below, page 210) and 1938*b*, *An Outline of Psychoanalysis* (London, 1949), 73 ff.]

XVI

Splitting of the Ego in the Defensive Process[1] (1938)

I find myself for a moment in the interesting position of not knowing whether what I have to say should be regarded as something long familiar and obvious or as something entirely new and puzzling. But I am inclined to think the latter.

I have at last been struck by the fact that the ego of a person whom we know as a patient in analysis must, dozens of years earlier, when it was young, have behaved in a remarkable manner in certain particular situations of pressure. We can assign in general and somewhat vague terms the conditions under which this comes about by saying that it occurs under the influence of a psychical trauma. I prefer to select a single sharply defined special case, though it certainly does not cover all the possible modes of causation.

Let us suppose, then, that a child's ego is under the sway of a powerful instinctual demand which it is accustomed to satisfy and that it is suddenly frightened by an experience which teaches it that the continuance of this satisfaction will result in an almost intolerable danger. It must now decide either to recognize the real danger, give way to it and do without the instinctual satisfaction, or to repudiate reality and persuade itself that there is no reason for fear, so that it may be able to retain the satisfaction. Thus

---

[1] Unfinished fragment, "Die Ichspaltung im Abwehrvorgang." First published posthumously *Int. Z. Psychoanal. Imago*, 25 (1940), 241; reprinted *Ges. W.*, 17, 59. It takes up a subject already touched upon in Freud, 1927, page 172 above, and further dealt with in Freud, 1938*b*, 73 ff. The manuscript is dated January 2, 1938. Translation, reprinted from *Int. J. Psychoanal.*, 22 (1941), 65; by James Strachey.]

there is a conflict between the demand of the instinct and the command of reality. But in fact the child takes neither course, or rather he takes both simultaneously, which comes to the same thing. He replies to the conflict with two contrary reactions, both of which are valid and effective. On the one hand, with the help of certain mechanisms he rejects reality and refuses to accept any prohibition; on the other hand, in the same breath he recognizes the danger of reality, takes over the fear of that danger as a symptom and tries subsequently to divest himself of the fear. It must be confessed that this is a very ingenious solution of the difficulty. Both of the parties to the dispute obtain their share: the instinct is allowed to retain its satisfaction and proper respect is shown to reality. But everything has to be paid for in one way or another, and this success is achieved at the price of a rift in the ego which never heals but which increases as time goes on. The two contrary reactions to the conflict persist as the centre-point of a split in the ego. The whole process seems so strange to us because we take for granted the synthetic nature of the workings of the ego. But we are clearly at fault in this. The synthetic function of the ego, though it is of such extraordinary importance, is subject to particular conditions and is liable to a whole series of disturbances.

It will assist if I interpolate an individual case history into this schematic disquisition. A little boy, while he was between three and four years of age, had become acquainted with the female genitals through being seduced by an older girl. After these relations had been broken off, he carried on the sexual stimulation which had been set going in this way by zealously practising manual masturbation; but he was soon caught at it by his energetic nurse and was threatened with castration, the carrying out of which was, as usual, ascribed to his father. There were thus present in this case conditions calculated to produce a tremendous effect of fright. A threat of castration by itself need not produce a great impression. The child will refuse to believe in it, for he cannot easily imagine the possibility of losing such a highly prized part of his body. A sight of the female genitals, on the other hand, might convince him of that possibility. But he would draw no conclusion from this alone, since his disinclination to doing so would be too great and there would be no motive present which could compel him to. On the contrary, whatever uneasiness he might feel would be calmed by the reflection that what was missing would yet make its appearance: she would grow one (a penis) later. Anyone who has observed enough small boys will be able to recollect having come across some such remark at the sight of a baby sister's genitals. But it is different if both factors are present together. In that case the threat revives the memory of the perception which had hitherto been regarded as harmless and finds in that memory a dreaded confirmation. The little boy now thinks he understands why the girl's genitals showed no sign of a penis and no longer ventures to doubt that his own genitals may meet with the same fate. Thence-forward he cannot help believing in the reality of the danger of castration.

The usual result of the fright of castration, the result that passes as the normal one, is that, either immediately or after some considerable struggle, the boy gives way to the threat and obeys the prohibition either wholly or at least in part (that is, by no longer touching his genitals with his hand). In other words, he gives up, in whole or in part, the satisfaction of the instinct. We are prepared to hear, however, that our present patient found another way out. He created a substitute for the penis which he missed in women, that is to say, a fetish. In so doing, it is true that he had given the lie to reality, but he had saved his own penis. So long as he was not obliged to acknowledge that women have lost their penis, there was no need for him to believe the threat that had been made against him: he need have no fears for his own penis, so he could proceed with his masturbation undisturbed. This behaviour on the part of our patient strikes us forcibly as being a turning away from reality—a procedure which we should prefer to reserve for psychotics. And it is in fact not very different. Yet we must suspend our judgement, for upon closer inspection we shall discover a not unimportant distinction. The boy did not simply contradict his perceptions and hallucinate a penis where there is none to be seen; he effected no more than a displacement of value—he transferred the importance of the penis to another part of the body, a procedure in which he was assisted by the mechanism of regression (in a manner which need not be explained here). This displacement, it is true, related only to the female body; as regards his own penis nothing was changed.

This way of dealing with reality, which almost deserves to be described as artful, was decisive as regards the boy's practical behaviour. He continued with his masturbation as though it implied no danger to his penis; but at the same time, in complete contradiction to his apparent boldness or indifference, he developed a symptom which showed that he nevertheless did recognize the danger. He had been threatened with being castrated by his father, and immediately afterwards, simultaneously with the creation of his fetish, he developed an intense fear of his father punishing him, which it required the whole force of his masculinity to master and overcompensate. This fear of his father, too, was silent on the subject of castration; by the help of regression to an oral phase, it assumed the form of a fear of being eaten by his father. At this point it is impossible to forget a primitive fragment of Greek mythology which tells us how Kronos, the old Father God, swallowed his children and sought to swallow his youngest son Zeus like the rest, and how Zeus was saved by the craft of his mother and later on castrated his father. But we must return to our case history and add that the boy produced yet another symptom, though it was a slight one, which he has retained to this day. This was an anxious susceptibility against either of his little toes being touched, as though, in all the to and from between denial and acknowledgement, it was nevertheless castration that was finding the clearer expression. . . .